The Developmental Psychology of Personal Identity

Also available from Bloomsbury:

Ethics and Politics of the Self, by Daniele Lorenzini
The Evolution of Consciousness, by Paula Droege
The Moral Epistemology of Intuitionism, by Hossein Dabbagh
Wittgenstein and the Cognitive Science of Religion, edited by Robert Vinten

The Developmental Psychology of Personal Identity

A Philosophical Perspective

Massimo Marraffa and
Cristina Meini

BLOOMSBURY ACADEMIC
LONDON • NEW YORK • OXFORD • NEW DELHI • SYDNEY

BLOOMSBURY ACADEMIC
Bloomsbury Publishing Plc, 50 Bedford Square, London, WC1B 3DP, UK
Bloomsbury Publishing Inc, 1359 Broadway, 12th Floor, New York, NY 10018, USA
Bloomsbury Publishing Ireland, 29 Earlsfort Terrace, Dublin 2, D02 AY28, Ireland

BLOOMSBURY, BLOOMSBURY ACADEMIC and the Diana logo
are trademarks of Bloomsbury Publishing Plc

First published in Great Britain 2024
This paperback edition published in 2025

Copyright © Massimo Marraffa and Cristina Meini, 2024

Massimo Marraffa and Cristina Meini have asserted their right under the Copyright, Designs and Patents Act, 1988, to be identified as Authors of this work.

Series design by Charlotte Daniels
Cover image: Men's face sketch (© Jayesh / Getty Images)

All rights reserved. No part of this publication may be: i) reproduced or transmitted in any form, electronic or mechanical, including photocopying, recording or by means of any information storage or retrieval system without prior permission in writing from the publishers; or ii) used or reproduced in any way for the training, development or operation of artificial intelligence (AI) technologies, including generative AI technologies. The rights holders expressly reserve this publication from the text and data mining exception as per Article 4(3) of the Digital Single Market Directive (EU) 2019/790.

Bloomsbury Publishing Inc does not have any control over, or responsibility for, any third-party websites referred to or in this book. All internet addresses given in this book were correct at the time of going to press. The author and publisher regret any inconvenience caused if addresses have changed or sites have ceased to exist, but can accept no responsibility for any such changes.

A catalogue record for this book is available from the British Library.

ISBN: HB: 978-1-3503-6899-6
PB: 978-1-3503-6903-0
ePDF: 978-1-3503-6900-9
eBook: 978-1-3503-6901-6

Typeset by Deanta Global Publishing Services, Chennai, India

For product safety related questions contact productsafety@bloomsbury.com.

To find out more about our authors and books visit www.bloomsbury.com and sign up for our newsletters.

To Enrico Roberto, Giulio and Lucrezia

Contents

Preface		viii
1	Setting the philosophical stage	1
2	The psychological toolkit	13
3	From bodily awareness to bodily self-awareness	31
4	The origins of affective self-awareness and self-regulation	51
5	Naïve psychology	91
6	Expanding introspective space	119
7	Construction and defence of narrative identity	149
A brief overview		179
Notes		181
References		193
Index		223

Preface

Those who today, especially if they are psychologists, deal with the subject of personal identity, almost always build on what one of the founders of modern psychology, William James, wrote in 1890. For their part, philosophers who deal with this subject have as their historical referent one of the great English empiricists, John Locke. If we read these thinkers, we find that both of them offer us very clear pages that are extremely useful in clarifying our ideas about the current debate on personal identity.

Locke proposed a theory of person and personal identity in *Of Identity and Diversity*, Chapter XXVII of Book II of *An Essay Concerning Human Understanding*. The chapter was added to the second edition of the text, in 1694, on the advice of his friend William Molyneux. Such theory grounds the history of the concept of identity itself and provides its first modern definition.

According to Locke, the self is not determined by the identity of substance, but only by the identity of consciousness. Against substantialism, he relies on memory – the extension of consciousness to the past – as the most psychological and less metaphysical notion he can conceive to define the concepts of person and identity. On closer view, however, Locke's consciousness is a 'strong' stand-in for the soul; it is still a sort of secularized soul. Despite the philosopher's intentions, it is described as a sort of *essence*; for all that, the Lockean consciousness is still *given a priori*. It is not something that is constructed during life, which emerges from the multifarious qualities of the body and human existence.

Such a non-essentialist notion of consciousness is found instead in James' *Principles of Psychology*. His gaze is more analytical and less speculative than Locke's, and thus more concrete; it is a gaze turned to everyday life. James is above all a philosopher, but reading his writings, one perceives how psychology as an autonomous discipline, separate from philosophy, was emerging in those very years. Some philosophers, however, had paved the way for a *psychology without the soul*: 'It is to the imperishable glory of Hume and Herbart and their successors to have taken so much of the meaning of personal identity out of the clouds and made of the Self an empirical and verifiable thing' (James 1981, vol. 1, 319).

After James, the issue of personal identity disappears for a long time from the horizon of psychological research. Indeed, during the first half of the twentieth century, experimental psychology was almost exclusively concerned with basic problems concerning the structures of behaviour and perception, and not with issues of enormously greater complexity such as the identity of a person. As a result, for decades the issue of personal identity would be addressed with a sociological slant – even when sociologists who worked on it cross the line to psychology: think, for example, about the notion of *self-presentation* developed by Erving Goffman. And even when a philosopher and sociologist like George H. Mead uses James' ideas and terminology, it is to further emphasize the importance of sociocultural determinants for the definition of individual identity.

For its part, dynamic psychology, too, was late in approaching this subject. As Habermas and Kemper note, 'the concept of identity was initially only implicit in psychoanalytic theorising, foremost in Freud's synthetic function of the ego and Federn's cohesion of ego feeling' (2021, 193). The first explicit contribution of psychoanalysis to the concept of identity was Erik Erikson's, who introduced the concept of ego identity (also termed 'psychosocial identity') and made several fundamental remarks concerning the feeling of identity in adolescence, identity crises and changes in self-image. Other important developments will come from the revival of the theme of the self within the Neo-Freudian School (with Erich Fromm, Karen Horney, Harry S. Sullivan); from Heinz Kohut's theorization, with the birth of a psychology of Self; and finally, from Otto Kernberg's integration of Erikson's concept of identity with ego psychology and object relations theory.

Today, more than a century away from James's ground-breaking chapter *The Consciousness of Self*, 'one cannot make much progress through most areas of human psychology without encountering constructs that invoke the self' (Leary and Tangney 2012, vii). In the past sixty years, hundreds of thousands of scholarly articles and chapters have been published about the self. In this book, we focus on three factors that contribute to explaining why the topic of identity has played such a pivotal role in psychology.

The first factor concerns theoretical psychology, and consists of the idea of an inextricable link between identity self-description and self-consciousness, which is – we will argue – a fundamental aspect of James' theory of the self. There is no self-consciousness without there being some description of self, and thus without there being some description of identity. The theoretical advantage of stating that it is our identity that determines our consciousness rather than the reverse is that the idea of identity is more concrete than that of consciousness:

it does not concern a purported entity, or essence, but refers to the perceptible diversity of individual characteristics.

The second factor pertains to dynamic psychology and developmental psychology and consists of the fact that the construction of affectional life, in the course of infancy and, subsequently, throughout one's entire life, is closely linked to the construction of an identity that is well-defined and accepted as valid. The construction of a valid personal identity is inseparable from the construction and maintenance of self-esteem. In turn, the theme of self-esteem is inextricably linked to the theme of the solidity of ego (in the Freudian sense), or, if you like, the theme of the cohesion of self (in Kohut's sense).

Lastly, a third factor concerns social psychology and consists of the fact that each of us constantly negotiates the validity of our identity in exchanges with other people. Erving Goffman's aforementioned concept of *self-presentation* refers to the fact that each of us, without being aware of it, devotes a considerable amount of our energy to obtaining from others the continuous confirmation of the validity of our identity.

In the course of the book, we will immerse ourselves in this psychodynamic, socio-cognitive and developmental literature, to develop an inseparably socio-constructivist and cognitive-evolutionary perspective on the development of subjective identity aiming to unfold the potentialities of the Jamesian theory of personal identity. Within this framework, the self (the pair <I, Me>) will be defined as a psychobiological unifying process (the process of 'self-ing' or 'I-ing') incessantly building and updating self-representations, from bodily to narrative self-representation. The construction of subjective identity takes the form of an ongoing and inexhaustible search for a self-description; and the intertwining of cognitive and affective dimensions characterizing such process results in an identity that is not given once and for all: it is rather – following a tradition stretching from John Locke to Ernesto De Martino – something perpetually rebuilt and actively reconfirmed, something perennially precarious. Such precariousness makes the theme of self-identity construction inseparable from that of self-identity *defence*.

This theoretical and empirical path will lead us to take a stance on some crucial issues in the debate on personal identity. First, it allows us to distance ourselves from the non-naturalistic (sometimes anti-naturalistic) trends in the hermeneutic conception of narrative identity. Second, it enables us to reject the thesis according to which the socially and historically situated narrative self would constitute the foundational dimension of human selfhood. The bodily and autobiographical selves account for two different kinds of unity, corresponding to different aspects of human selfhood. Lastly, it allows us to claim that the process of self-representation originating in the dialectics between I and Me is not epiphenomenal but is rather a 'causal gravity centre' in the history of the agent. This is usually underestimated. Much data from the psychology of development, dynamic psychology, social psychology and psychology of personality supports the idea that the entire cycle of life takes shape in compliance with *a primary need to exist solidly as a unitary ego*. As a result, the incessant construction and reconstruction of an acceptable and adaptively functioning identity is the ongoing construction of a system of defences, the continuously renovated capacity to curb and cope with anxiety and disorder.

It is not a form of reciprocal courtesy that leads us to state that this is a book that was conceived together in all its parts and drafted by four hands, continuously intervening with new ideas and theoretical challenges in each other's writing. Nonetheless, for those interested in knowing who was mainly responsible for drafting the various chapters, we would like to point out that Massimo Marraffa was mainly responsible for Chapters 1, 3 and 7, and Cristina Meini for Chapters 4, 5 and 6. For Chapter 2, however, the authors are equally guilty.

Finally, we would like to express our gratitude to Michele Di Francesco and Alfredo Paternoster with whom, for several years now, we have been working on the topics addressed in this book. More recent, but fruitful and promising, is the collaboration with Emiliano Loria and Marco Viola. Thanks are also due to Chiara Testino for the linguistic revision of some parts of the text.

Rome-Turin, 9 October 2023

1

Setting the philosophical stage

1. Objective and subjective identity

A person's identity, in ordinary language, is in the first place that set of characteristics that are stable over time, both somatic (my physiognomy) and psychological (my personality, the constant style of my behaviour) and social (my age, marital status, cultural level and income bracket), by which every individual is well distinguishable compared to others. This is the identity *for others* or *objective* identity: all that characterizes each of us as a single and unmistakable individual, what prevents persons from mistaking us for someone else.

Just as each one has an identity for others, they also have an identity *for themselves*, a *subjective* identity. This is the set of my characteristics such as I perceive and I describe them in myself; it is the way an individual perceives oneself as a person, defines oneself as a person of a certain kind and tracks one's own continuous identity as a person through time and space. Every time we wake up it is as if we were saying '*I am the same self that I was yesterday*', writes James (1981, 316), who adds: 'Each of us when he awakens says, Here's the same old self again, just as he says, Here's the same old bed, the same old room, the same old world' (317).

The distinction between the objective and subjective dimensions of the identification of the person enables us to cope with an insidious feature of the English-speaking literature about personal identity. Both in philosophical tradition (from Locke to James), and in the psychodynamic one (from Sullivan to Jacobson, up to Kohut and modern Kohutians), as well as in sociological English literature, the theme of identity has been faced not as *personal identity*, but rather as *the self*. This is a non-technical, ordinary expression in the English language that means, inseparably, both 'identity' and 'the person'. Therefore, 'the self' displays an objective dimension by denoting the person both in her internal structure and in her facets of identity for others; but it displays a subjective dimension as well, by denoting the person in her concrete self-recognition, just as this latter is grasped through self-consciousness.

The self in its subjective or experiential dimension is what we find in the theories the entire philosophical and psychological reflections on identity continue to refer to, that is, those of John Locke and William James.[1]

2. Locke's anti-substantialist concept of personal identity

Locke begins his discussion of personal identity by distinguishing the concept of person from that of human being. If we consider, he suggests, a dull irrational man having no more reason than a cat or a parrot (1975, 333), and we compare him to a hypothetical philosophizing parrot, we realize that the former is a human being but not a person, while the rational parrot is, perhaps, a sort of person, but is not a human being.[2]

Thus, when we normally interact with our fellow human beings and we consider ourselves, it is not enough for us to know that we are all human beings; we need to know that we, and usually others too, are something more and something different: that is, Locke says, that we are *persons*.

'Person', the philosopher writes, is a normative ('forensic') term: it does not designate an essence, but a psychosocial attribute that is assigned to those subjects who possess a specific set of reflective capacities enabling them to govern their actions according to self-conscious mentation. The person is the subject who can form imaginary test scenarios to make a planning evaluation of what can happen as a consequence of her actions; but above all, she is someone who can grasp herself not only as a material agent in her present, past and future acts as *public* acts but also as an entity who has an 'interiority', that is, an inner virtual space in which thoughts and feelings can be situated as *private* events. Only someone with sufficient access to her interiority – to herself as objectified in the introspective consciousness of the self – can be a morally responsible agent that is capable of 'appropriating actions and their merit'.[3]

In Locke, therefore, individuals are persons only insofar as they can reflectively appropriate their actions and mentations, by understanding their meaning; a critical appropriation that originates from 'that consciousness, which is inseparable from thinking' (1975, 335). The identity of a person in time consists in the sameness of consciousness: 'as far as this consciousness can be extended backwards to any past Action or Thought, so far reaches the Identity of that *Person*' (1975, 335).

Thus, diachronic identity is no longer grounded on the old metaphysical and religious idea of the soul, understood as a unitary and indivisible substratum, which allows the permanence of our experiences; and is not even based on a corporeal substance. Rather, it rests on connections established by memory, the extension of consciousness to the past. Here, we find the idea of personal identity as a *conquest*, as *work* – an idea that is organic to Locke's political and economic philosophy (Bodei 2002, 41). Thus, a tradition is ushered in that proceeds with David Hume and continues to this day with Derek Parfit and Daniel C. Dennett, where identity is something risky that the individual must gamble with in time and that does not guarantee a continuous relation to oneself at all.

Personal identity develops over time, like a stream of consciousness whose continuity is guaranteed (with respect to the past) by memory and (with respect to the future) by concern, care, worry or planning. Once the substantiality of the soul has been denied, the stable foundation of the ego, the unity of its streams of consciousness that should have extended beyond the barriers of death, seems to be lost:

> Separated from the prospect of the eternal, the individual finds himself progressively immersed in an irredeemable time of frailty. The reduction of conscious life to transient grains on the Shakespearean 'bank and shoal of time', with the consequent contraction of expectations to purely physical existence, reveals to us our own intrinsic fragility, our exposure to the ever-present danger of disintegration and the forgetting of self. (Bodei 2011, 88)

Enormous is therefore the task Locke assigns to memory. In a passage with baroque tones, he points out the risk of our representations being deleted, as a sinister anticipation of each one's physical disappearance:

> Thus the *Ideas*, as well as Children, of our Youth, often die before us: And our Minds represent to us those Tombs, to which we are approaching; where, though the Brass and Marble remain, yet the inscriptions are effaced by time, and the imagery moulders away. *The Pictures drawn in our Minds are laid in fading Colours*; and if not sometimes refreshed, vanish and disappear. (1975, 151–2)

According to Locke, personal identity consists of such work of constant refreshing of all our ideas; if this work ceases,

> *Ideas* in the Mind quickly fade, and often vanish quite out of the Understanding, leaving no more footsteps or remaining Characters of themselves, than Shadows do flying over Fields of Corn; and the Mind is as void of them, as if they never had been there. (1975, 151)

The maintenance of personal identity is therefore not spontaneous: it costs effort, and it arises from the work of refreshing ideas and memories through the operations of the mind, the faint traces of which are in danger of vanishing like insubstantial dream images. In such a developmental and temporal conception of identity, 'only the commitment to renewal, which each person – implicitly or explicitly – assumes, consolidates a reconquest of self destined to remain always incomplete'.

3. A criticism of Kant's theory of self-consciousness

Three centuries later, and after endless debates on personal identity, Locke's uneasiness about the unstable nature of the construction of identity by the human subject will find its complete formulation in the concept of *presence* provided by the philosopher and ethnologist Ernesto De Martino. The questions of the *precarious* nature of the subject's self-construction and the resulting *defensive* character of self-consciousness lie at the core of his thought, thus forging a phenomenological psychology of identity hinged on the concepts of presence and the complementary *crisis of presence*.

In his 1948 ethnohistorical study *The Magic World*, De Martino (2022, 158) characterizes presence as 'the person's unitary being' or, in Kantian terms, 'the transcendental unity of self-consciousness'. There is, however, a fundamental difference between De Martino and Kant: the unity in question is not in itself guaranteed insofar as it is not an ahistorical datum, but is, rather, a precarious acquisition, continuously constructed by culture and constantly exposed to the risk of crisis, the crisis of presence.

To introduce the issue of the crisis of presence, De Martino examines a large body of ethnopsychiatric evidence that attests to the widespread presence of an altered state of consciousness called 'latah' by the Malays and 'olon' by the Tungus.[4] This state consists of access of echopraxia and echolalia[5] which causes a person to lose the boundaries of her ego:

> A *latah* person, when his attention is attracted by the oscillating movement of branches shaken by the wind, will imitate this movement passively. Two *latahs* surprised by an unexpected noise entered into a state of reciprocal mimetic automatism in which for about a half hour one continued to imitate the gestures of the other. (De Martino 2022, 70; English transl. in Guidorizzi 1997, 6)

Based on Shirokogoroff's (1935) study of Tungus shamanism, De Martino analyses the state of olon or latah as a loss of presence:

> Everything happens as if a presence that is fragile, non-guaranteed, labile, unable to withstand the shock caused by particular exciting content, cannot find enough energy to maintain itself present to such content, encompassing it, recognizing it and mastering it within a network of definite relationships. In this way, the content is lost as the content of present consciousness. Presence tends to remain focused on a certain content, *beyond* which it cannot go; as a consequence, it disappears and abdicates as presence. The distinction between presence and the world that makes itself present crumbles: the subject, instead of hearing or seeing the rustling of leaves in the wind, becomes the tree that has rustling leaves; instead of hearing a word, he becomes the word itself, etc. (De Martino 2022, 72; translation ours)

Most importantly, we find an intensive focus on this kind of experience today in the debate on the distortions in the subjective experience of one's self occasioned by psychedelic drugs (Letheby 2021; Letheby and Gerrans 2017).[6] This experience has been variously called 'ego-death', 'ego-loss', 'ego-disintegration' and 'ego-dissolution'; and it has been interpreted from a psychoanalytic perspective as a disruption of ego-boundaries, which results in 'a blurring of the distinction between self-representation and object-representation, and precludes the synthesis of self-representations into a coherent whole' (Nour et al. 2016, 2; these authors quote in this regard Federn 1952; Savage 1955, and Fischman 1983).

Indeed, this characterization is practically indistinguishable from De Martino's. The state of olon is an example of the abdication of the synthetic unity of apperception, which leads to the collapse of the distinction between presence and world. In this respect, De Martino speaks of an 'indiscriminate *koinonia*', namely a fusion (and thus mutual annihilation) of presence and world. Sinking into such a state means losing the 'function of discrimination', that is, the distinction between consciousness and its contents; as a result, presence devolves into absence, a simple mechanical echo of the surrounding world.

De Martino frames this negative moment from a dialectical perspective. He follows Kant in arguing that the act of the transcendental synthetic function grounds the distinction between the subjective unity of the I and the objective unity of the real – and thus the autonomy of the person. However, whereas Kant assumes the person's presence as 'a uniform historical given', De Martino argues that 'there does not exist any presence, any empirical "being there", that might be a datum, an original immediacy beyond all risk and incapable within its own sphere of any sort of drama and of any development – that is, of a history' (De Martino 2022, 159; Engl. transl. in Ginzburg 1991, 45).[7]

As a result, the principle of the transcendental unity of self-consciousness is seen as including within itself its opposite in the form of the risk of the disintegration of the person's unitary being:

> even the supreme principle of the transcendental unity of self-consciousness involves a supreme risk to the person, that is, the risk of losing the supreme principle that constitutes and grounds it. This risk arises when the person, instead of retaining her autonomy in her relationship to the contents, abdicates the task and allows the contents to assert themselves, outside the synthesis, as undominated elements, as given facts in an absolute sense. (De Martino 2022, 158–9; translation ours)

In other words, Kant does not consider the process of formation of the person, or the risks related to this self-making. As a result, the Kantian person is always given in its unity, as if the psychological level of analysis was always and, in all cases, guaranteed by the transcendental level. De Martino, in contrast, thinks that there is no such guarantee, that is, that empirical being there, far from always being given to itself, is exposed to the risk of not being there and that consequently, the loss of the original synthetic unity of apperception is a real existential risk.[8]

On the other hand, De Martino sees the ethnological and psychopathological literature on which he draws as showing precisely that the empirical being there is not given and guaranteed in its being but is rather characterized by structural lability, which causes it to struggle for its unity and autonomy. As a result, the self-conscious subject constitutes itself as a repertoire of activities that take pains to cope with its lack of ontological guarantee, constructing itself on the edge of its original 'non-being', as it were. We have seen it earlier with dissociative phenomena in shamanistic societies. But also in assimilating some aspects of Pierre Janet's dynamic psychiatry, De Martino built on concepts such as 'lability of the mental synthesis' and 'psychological misery' which led to a criticism of the 'metaphysical hypostasis of the self'.[9]

De Martino's philosophical and anthropological work anticipated the current centrality of identity in infant research, in social, personality and dynamic psychology and psychopathology. As we will see, hypotheses and evidence from such research fields confirm De Martino's idea of the human subject. The self as personal identity is a construction with no metaphysical guarantee; it is not something guaranteed once and for all, but is, rather, a precarious acquisition, continuously under construction by a human organism and constantly exposed to the risk of dissolution. This precariousness is the key to grasping the *defensive* nature of identity self-construction. The need to construct and protect an identity that is valid to the greatest extent possible is rooted in the primary need to subsist subjectively, and thus to exist solidly as a describable ego, as a unitary subject.

4. The Jamesian I as a process of selfing

In Chapter 10 of *Principles of Psychology* (1890), James provides the first conscious psychological formulation of the concept of *self* that, by drawing on the remarks made by Locke two centuries earlier, clarifies its experiential-reflective character.

The American philosopher starts by observing that our inner universe appears to us as a *self-referential* psychic field; that is, the subject (both the common man and the 'spiritualist' philosopher) is led to suppose that in one's own experiential space, there is an innermost centre, which is the starting point of will, 'the *active* element in all consciousness' (James 1981, 285). James defines '*this self of all the other selves*' (James 1981, 285) as 'pure Ego' and notes that its previously given interpretations lie along a spectrum that includes, at one end, the claim that it is 'a simple active substance, the soul' (286), which is the metaphysical guarantee of the presence of the self to the world, and at the other, an eliminativist perspective claiming that 'it is nothing but a fiction, the imaginary being denoted by the pronoun I' (James 1981).

Then James wonders: what does the pronoun 'I' denote? In the sentence 'I kick the ball', 'I' designates the *agent organism*, that is the individual taken as a whole and as opposed to an external object. Sometimes the 'I' is instead something much more intimate and limited. Indeed, I (as a global agent subject) can also consider an object that is not entirely external, such as my foot (that is part of my being but 'down there'), my hand, or even something else that is more 'here' (or 'less there') than my foot – for instance, my eyes or my head, which are almost part of the intimacy of the ego. In all these cases I keep detaching and differentiating my subjective ego, as a primary psychic subject, from all these other things, which are objects for the ego. Thus far, therefore, I am still rather certain of what my subjective ego is. But then I realize that I am also able to consider as objects things that are much more 'inner': the global image of my body, a sensation, a smell, a dream, a thought or a mood, such as anxiety or euphoria and also more abstract realities such as 'my level of self-esteem'. Then, facing this haemorrhage of my ego,

I wonder: if all these aspects of the mind are objects – insofar as they are objects of my introspective consciousness – what is the real subject, that is, the wellspring of consciousness? In other words, how can I capture the conscious subject who introspects, if any aspect of myself that I introspectively grasp is only an object of this supposed conscious subject? Ultimately, James states, the innermost ego, as the centre and driving force of any possible subjectivity, ends up being a pure grammatical trick, a sort of dimensionless point – or, more unsettlingly, the 'insubstantial phantom' evoked by Schopenhauer in a famous passage:

> as soon as we try for once to understand ourselves, and to do so by turning in on ourselves and directing our cognition inwardly, we lose ourselves in a bottomless void and find ourselves like hollow, transparent spheres from whose void a voice is speaking, while the cause of it is not to be found within, and in wanting to grasp ourselves we shudder as we catch nothing but an insubstantial phantom. (Schopenhauer 2010, 304)

This is, Jervis writes about the Jamesian remarks, 'the theory of evanescence of the ego' (2011, 162). The acting and observing self is an abstract and depthless subjectivity; ultimately, this subjectivity is a convention; it cannot be located anywhere. The subject, taken to its limit, does not exist.

Thus far, the Humean *pars destruens*,[10] but James does not stop here. Once the acting and observing self has melted into an abstract and depthless subjectivity, the subject regains the feeling of existence in experiencing itself as *Me*. The Me is for James the *empirical self*, that is, the way one presents oneself to oneself, thus objectifying oneself in the introspective consciousness of oneself. This self-presentation is a *description of identity*, which comes in three forms: the physical, material aspects of the self (material self) associated with the bodily subjectivity; the subject's social identity (social self); and lastly 'a man's inner or subjective being' (James 1981, 283) – the psychological identity grasped in one's interiority, that is, in the complexity of everyone's introspection – which James calls the 'spiritual self' (James 1981, 283).[11]

Within this framework, the I-self is not a something but 'is really more like a verb; it might be called "selfing" or "I-ing", the fundamental process of making a self out of experience' (McAdams 1996, 302). The Me-self is instead 'the primary product of the selfing process'; it is 'the self that selfing makes' (McAdams 1996, 302). The Me exists as an evolving collection of self-attributions (James' material, social and psychological selves) that result from the selfing process. It is 'the making of the Me that constitutes what the I fundamentally is' (McAdams and Cox 2010, 162).

So construed the Jamesian theory of *duplex self* presents an aspect that we will emphasize throughout our book: it allows self-consciousness to be understood in terms of identity. In contrast to an idealistic view of self-consciousness as a primary, elemental, simple awareness of the self, preceding any other form of knowing,[12] James views self-consciousness as the knowledge of being there *in a certain way*, a self-description, an identity-building. Such a process of selfing gives rise to different kinds of unity corresponding to the different forms of the Me.

Thus, there can be no consciousness of self without *knowledge* of self. One does not know *that* one is without knowing *who* one is; we only know that we are there insofar as we know that we are there in a certain way, that is, with particular features, as a *describable identity*: there is no consciousness of existence without there being a description of self, and therefore without there being a description of identity (Jervis 2019, 139).

It is important to note that again this contradicts Kant. As is well known, Kant agrees with Hume: the empirical apperception 'can give us no constant or enduring self in the flow of inner appearances' (Kant 1998, 232). Yet, Kant thinks that one may shift from the analysis level of psychological experience to that of transcendental arguing, and here posits a pure apperception: 'I am conscious of myself, not as I appear to myself, nor as I am in myself, but only that I am', he writes in the first *Critique* (B157); and in B158 he adds that '[t]he consciousness of self is [...] far from being a knowledge of the self' – that is, the consciousness of existing is distinguished from the consciousness of existing in a certain way. Thus, Kant's I think ('that accompanies all my representations') is something undetermined and void ('a something = X'), which, not unlike Descartes' cogito, lays a claim to being a *primum*.

5. Object consciousness versus self-consciousness

The considerations just made require clarification of some notions. To this end, some historical reminders of the cognitivist revolution may be extremely useful.

In the late 1940s, Edward Tolman's work indicated the impossibility of explaining the spatial orientation behaviour of rats in a maze based on the establishment of a mere association between certain stimuli and certain specific muscle responses. The experimental animal had to have constructed, within its nervous system, 'a functional adaptation' that operated as a 'cognitive map' (Tolman 1948). In the terminology that would later be that of cognitivism, the rats had constructed complex representational states in their nervous system that had enabled them to localize reinforcers.

With this construct, Tolman was beating a path of inquiry in tune with other pioneering attempts to address the problem of how animals perceive and experience their environment. In the field of ethology, Jakob von Uexküll argued for the necessity of assuming the presence of a subjective world (*Umwelt*) in relatively primitive animals (e.g. in an earthworm or molluscs such as limpets and scallops) (see Uexküll 2010). The animal lives in a space that is its world of life; the relationship to this world grounds an elementary subjectivity so that the object field is a subjective world (the *Umwelt* for that matter).

Also in complete consonance with the cognitive maps hypothesis is the text *The Nature of Explanation* (1943) by philosopher and psychologist Kenneth Craik. Here Craik argues that every animal organism develops relatively stable functional modifications of the nervous system, which are configured as *models of reality*.

The theorizing of Tolman, Uexküll and Craik pointed in the same *representationalist* direction. Certainly, it was no longer possible to accept the anthropomorphization of animal subjectivity typical of nineteenth-century scholars such as Darwin and Romanes; but neither was it possible to assume that animals were simple stimulus-response machines, as behaviourists proposed. Animals were now seen as capable of constructing, within their minds/brains, maps, models or representations of the world environment. In the idiom of the computational theory of mind, animals are systems whose cognitive states and processes are constituted by the occurrence, transformation and storage (in the mind/brain) of information-bearing structures (representations) of one kind or another. They are conscious precisely insofar as they are capable of taking in information about their environment, forming internal representations of it and manipulating these representations to select and execute actions. In what follows we will assume the soundness of this representational approach to consciousness.[13]

This *object* consciousness is distinct from self-consciousness. In ordinary linguistic usage, 'consciousness' coincides (in most cases) with 'self-consciousness' – or at least it is common to think of consciousness as a typically introspective state. However, one can be conscious of something without being self-conscious but not vice versa. Most animals are conscious without being self-conscious; the same is true of infants in the first year. On the other hand, it is impossible to develop self-consciousness without possessing object consciousness.

The clear distinction between object consciousness and self-consciousness can be drawn with the help of the theory of intentionality proposed by Franz Brentano (1874). For Brentano, consciousness is not a primary or essential quality or character of the mind, all internal to the latter; rather, it is a *relation* – which he calls 'intentionality' – between a subject and an object. More precisely, intentionality is 'the power of minds and mental states to be about, represent, or stand for, things, properties, and states of affairs. To say of an individual's mental states that they have intentionality is to say that they are mental representations or that they have contents' (Jacob 2019a).

Object consciousness necessarily goes together with intentionality. The conscious mind is a set of heterogeneous forms of active relationship (i.e. construction of representations) between a living organism (the subject) and its world environment (the object). Any organism endowed with perceptual and motor systems with a certain degree of complexity, that is, whose behaviour is mediated by some representational structures (as opposed to purely 'behaviourist' organisms), has object consciousness. This is therefore a *transitive* form of consciousness: it is always a consciousness *of* (something).

Against this background, we can speak of an immediate, organismic subjectivity, consisting of the object consciousness of the infant or animal. Object consciousness results from the representational activity; this activity shapes a purely *objectual* experiential space. As Fonagy et al. (2002) put it, the child's mind is at the very beginning of life characterized by the principle of *psychic equivalence*, the identification of inner reality with external reality. The principle can be put as follows: 'Originally, only the world is given to the subject' (Lyyra 2009, 76). The principle states that there is no distinction between mind and world or inner and outer realities in consciousness at the outset. One cannot tell primordially whether the content of the experience arises from within or without, insofar as no such distinction can be made. What is often taken to arise from within, be it pain, hunger or any other affective state, is experienced as a property of the world among external objects.

The principle of psychic equivalence is the psychological and developmental counterpart of a *first-order* representational view of phenomenal consciousness, according to which the latter consists in *analogue* or *fine-grained contents* that are available to the first-order processes that guide thought and action (Dretske 1995; Tye 1995). So, a phenomenally conscious percept of red, for example, consists in a state with the analogue content *red* which is tokened in such a way as to feed into thoughts about red, or into actions that are in one way or another guided by redness.

According to first-order representational theories, phenomenal consciousness presents us with nothing except for external objects and their properties:

> Conscious mental states – experiences, in particular – are states that we are conscious *with*, not states we are conscious *of*. They are states that make us conscious, not states that we make conscious by being conscious of them. (Dretske 1995, 100–1)

In justifying the claim that conscious experience does not involve awareness of experience, the argument from *transparency* is often invoked. We normally 'see right through' perceptual states to external objects and do not even notice that we are *in* perceptual states; the properties we are aware of in perception are attributed to the objects perceived.[14]

Against the background of this first-order representationalism, we can introduce the notion of bodily self-consciousness. When infants, from birth, explore the environment, they entertain a rich collection of objectual conscious states; and in exploring the environment they soon discover a particular object, that is, their body. Or, more precisely, they discover parts of their body: they are conscious, for instance, of their hands (without 'knowing', of course, that they are their hands). This is the beginning of a crucial step, since, for an organism to achieve self-consciousness, its consciousness must first apply to a particular object, which is precisely the body. Indeed, we will argue that the most elementary form of self-consciousness is the capacity to represent one's own body as an entire object while considering it as a subject, that is, as the source of the representation.

Once again, this way of conceiving self-consciousness is already in Brentano's descriptive psychology. Among the possible objects of consciousness, Brentano says, there is a very special one, which is the subject itself, and this is bodily self-consciousness. Thus, self-consciousness is not a primary, elemental, simple awareness of the self, preceding any other form of knowing; rather, it is *a variation of our relationship to the world*:

> As Schopenhauer had already noted, and unlike Kant, Brentano thinks that self-consciousness is not a basic modality of consciousness, is not a primary and simple knowing of being there, but consists in watching itself, seeking after itself, and hence it is from the very beginning *a knowing of being there in a certain way*. Indeed, Schopenhauer had already raised the suspicion that this knowing of being there is never exhaustive, in the sense that it is a search for itself always unsatisfactory, and hence interminable. (Jervis 2011, 71; translation ours)

Locke had well seen that personal identity is a matter of work and conquest.

2

The psychological toolkit

More than forty years after the famous confrontation between Noam Chomsky and Jean Piaget at the Royaumont Abbey, today we can retrace the complex history of contemporary developmental psychology with a more irenic and conscious perspective. This is the perspective of our book, which addresses the themes of construction and defence of personal identity backgrounded by a synthesis of ideas classically considered at odds, or at least in friction, with each other. The ingredients of this synthesis are three.

> First: as also some neo-Piagetian psychologists recognized (the most famous case is from Annette Karmiloff-Smith), the newborn can count on a repertoire of competencies that is much wider than what was thought in 1975, the year of Royaumont. Such competencies do not concern only – as Piaget thought – the *sensorimotor* sphere, but also – as Chomskyans claim – the *conceptual* one.
>
> Second: it is possible to use certain elements from a sociocultural perspective on development to incorporate into a Piagetian *individual-based constructivism* the idea that interpersonal relationships crucially affect the dynamics of the mind.
>
> Third: infant research – an area crosscutting developmental psychology and psychoanalysis of object relations – brought the constructs of motivation and attachment into the systematic research of the child's first forms of cognitive-affectional relationality.

A philosophical and methodological reflection on the hypotheses and data provided by such research traditions will delineate a constructive perspective on development, systematically weaving together cognitive, social and motivational components. This is the framework enabling us to elaborate a model for the construction of personal identity firmly rooted in the Jamesian theory of subjective identity.

1. The Jamesian self in the framework of Darwinian naturalism

James' theory of subjective identity falls within the framework of Darwinian naturalism – the same framework within which James conceived his functionalistic theory of mental processes.[1] The latter is in fact an extensive attempt to model psychology on Darwin's theory of evolution by natural selection; and he can be considered the 'first double-barrelled Darwinian psychologist' since he employs selectionist logic at both phylogenetic and ontogenetic levels (McGranahan 2018, 31, 37).

Moreover, James defined himself as 'a rabid individualist' (1992–2004, vol. 9, 625), claiming several times that the individual is the starting point for understanding the world. In *The Principles of Psychology*, for instance, he wrote that 'the mind which the psychologist studies is the mind of distinct individuals inhabiting definite portions of a real space and of a real time' (James 1981, vol. 1, 183). It is impossible to separate Darwinism and individualism in his work: his use of Darwinian concepts seeks precisely to ground an analysis of individual agency. The individual organism is seen as a real locus of agency in its world environment. In his controversy with Herbert Spencer's Lamarckism, which sets the analysis 'from outside to inside', James claims that ontogenesis or phylogenesis of the mental cannot be reduced to a process where the mind is shaped so that it adapts to a coercive environment: ontogenesis and phylogenesis are in part directed by internal processes.

Therefore, James' pragmatism is *naturalistic* in a Darwinian sense, insofar as it conceives human beings as organisms produced by evolution, organisms developing in a natural world. However, it is naturalistic also in a *Quinean* sense. Indeed, James' rejection of foundationalism is in one respect similar to Quine's denial of the first philosophy, to his claim of the continuity of philosophy with science and to the rejection of what he calls the 'cosmic exile' (Quine 1960, 21).[2] This kind of naturalism professes 'a resolute scepticism in the face of any "higher level" of inquiry that purports to stand above the level of ordinary science' (Maddy 2001, 39). If in the Kantian scheme there are the methods of science, at the empirical level, and the methods of conceptual analysis, at the transcendental level, naturalistic philosophers see themselves as members of the scientific community; they regard the methods and techniques of science as the best way to find out about the world. In light of this rejection of the two-level scheme, the *selfing process* (which we introduced in the *Introduction*) should be viewed as the activity of a *psychobiological system*, and not as a Kantian synthetic function. As argued in the first chapter (Section 3), in Kant's philosophical psychology the person is always given in its unity, as if the psychological level of analysis were always and, in any case, guaranteed by the transcendental level of analysis. This, however, does not hold in light of what, in particular, the psychodynamic clinic tells us about the selfing process: here the empirical subject is primarily *non-unitary* and gains a sense of unity in the act of mobilizing resources against the threat of disintegration (Jervis 1993, 298).

Kantian transcendentalism investigates self-consciousness with the 'top-down' perspective that philosophical psychology traditionally adopted, that is, beginning from introspective self-knowledge. Conversely, naturalism brings us to the idea of a 'bottom-up' methodology. Following Darwin in denying any metaphysical leap from non-human animals to human beings, the naturalist philosopher takes up the Darwinian maxim that '[h]e who understands baboon, would do more toward metaphysics than Locke'.[3] This implies the adoption of a comparative and ontogenetic approach to self-consciousness, seeking to reconstruct how the most basic psychological functions lead to those more complex functions enabling self-awareness in the adult and a socially evolved world.

In such a perspective, the investigation of subjectivity in a child under one year old must take as a model the cognitivist studies on animal consciousness. As we have argued earlier (Chapter 1, Section 5), such studies have claimed the need to explain animal behaviour in terms of object consciousness, understood as the ability to create models of reality as well as schemes of action that enable the cognitive system to interact with things and agents flexibly. In almost all adult animals, and infants under one year old, the cognitive field is provided with objects (e.g. models of places or representations of other agents), but it is extremely unlikely that it includes the subject itself. We believe that cognitive ethology and infant cognition research offer plenty of evidence that non-human animals and infants do not need self-consciousness, not even an embryonic one, to perform the several complex activities of which they are capable.

Still in the footsteps of James, however, it is good not only to avoid a top-down approach to self-consciousness and identity but also to shun an excessively reductionist attitude, providing bottom-up explanations for everything in terms of neuro-cognitive mechanisms. Although at the heart of James' reflection there is an analysis of the individual with firm foundations in neurophysiology (see in Chapter 4 the discussion of his theory of emotions), he does not believe that physiological psychology reduces or eliminates other ways to approach mind and behaviour. It is only a component of a broader investigation of the human individual conceived as a concrete organism intent on pursuing its goals (see Franzese 2008).

Here is where a *contextualist* and *systemic* perspective comes into play. In the nineteenth century, the Darwinian theory had already tried to define the characteristics of animal species, their behavioural characteristics included, as a function of the environmental context. The premises of modern contextualism have indeed a naturalistic matrix and were developed in the work of early ethologists. Nonetheless, the general methodology of the contextualist approach was systematized only by Kurt Lewin in the 1930s and then matured around the years of the Second World War with cybernetic studies and the birth of systems theory. Later, among first-generation cognitivists, Neisser (1976) was the most sensitive to a contextual-environmental perspective on cognition.

The contextualist and systemic orientation in psychology is homogeneous with today's dominant approaches in both biology and sociology. Here, the so-called 'systemic school' accentuates, along particular lines, a more general tendency: that of locating the individual's psychological problems (both behavioural and subjective) in the interindividual and social context in which they arise and obtain a sense. When the tendency is homogeneous with current directions in biology, it takes the form of a *systemic naturalism* which incorporates insights from James' Darwinian psychology and the functionalist school of Chicago. As we shall immediately see, this is the foundation of John Bowlby's attachment theory, namely, the ethological-evolutionary approach to dynamic psychology through which a neo-Jamesian account of the self can take on board the defensive component inherent to the construction of subjective identity.

2. From the Hobbesian individual to the mother–child dyad

2.1. First, the unconscious, then consciousness

The attachment theory is the project of a dynamic psychology within the Darwinian methodological framework, which is nourished by contributions from cognitive psychology and neurosciences. This dynamic psychology gathers the critical content of Freudian psychoanalysis: the development of a theory of the unconscious that can serve as an organ of critique for self-conscious subjectivity. However, some clarifications are in order.

In present-day dynamic psychology the unconscious is 'a cognitive unconscious of beliefs, self, object and interactional representations, and implicit assumptions and expectations regarding how significant others will behave toward oneself' (Eagle 2011, 130). Within this framework, consciousness is no longer an unquestionable assumption, a non-negotiable given fact; the concept of the cognitive unconscious is no longer patterned, as in Freud, after the concept of the conscious mind. Freud's definition of the unconscious is still given by its difference from – and in some respects also dependence upon – the definition of consciousness; and the latter is taken as a self-evident, primary datum, although it is then criticized and diminished in comparison with the traditional, idealistic view.[4] By contrast, contemporary psychological science reverses the explanatory relationship between the conscious and unconscious mind. First, a theory of representational capacities of mind and their role in behaviour control (i.e. a theory of intentionality) is to be built, which is independent of consciousness and more fundamental; a theory able to treat in the same way every form of unconscious representational mentality – and therefore 'in brains, in computers, in evolution's "recognition" of properties of selected designs' (Dennett 1991, 457). Then, on such bases, one proceeds to develop a theory of consciousness conceived as 'an advanced or derived mental phenomenon' and not idealistically as 'the foundation of all intentionality, all mentality' (Dennett 1993, 193). Accordingly, cognitive science's subpersonal processes show features different from those of consciousness: whereas the latter seems to be unitary, serial, language-like and receptive to global properties, the former are multiple, parallel, non-linguistic and oriented to the processing of local properties.

Backed by such methodological overturning, psychological sciences provide cues and notions taking up and elaborating on the themes of psychoanalytic tradition, making its demystifying character stronger.

2.2. The critique of the Hobbes–Freud scheme

The work of demystification of psychological sciences addresses, among other things, what we can characterize as the *culturalist* declination of Cartesian dualism. On the one hand, there is our most noble, least animal part (the soul, the ego, the rational mind), connected to self-conscious rationality and civility, from which only optimal, cooperative and 'mature' sociality can arise. On the other hand, there is our instinctive-impulsive part, less rationally conscious, more immediate, less reflective, asocial and perhaps also destructive.

According to such a premise, sociality is a 'secondary' reality. The individual, instead, is seen as an isolated primary subject, a priori 'given' as autonomous – who 'then' moves towards others, lives socially, and creates structures. This conception of individuals, which found its most radical consecration in

Hobbes' pessimistic anthropology, was laid down by Freud as the foundation of psychoanalysis. The Freudian individuals are primarily isolated organisms, in search of other individuals who enable the discharge of their instinctual energies. Therefore, the bond that newborn infants establish with the mother is seen as *secondary*, that is, *derivative*, in two senses. In the first place, the original condition of newborns is characterized by *primary narcissism*, a sort of monadic self-sufficiency from which infants emerge only under the urge of their primitive sexual drives. In the second place, the bond with the mother (the love attachment to her) is seen as secondary to these drives themselves, that is, subsequent to the cathexis of the mother's breast by the libidinal energy in its original oral modality.

Starting from 1914, with *Totem and Taboos*, Freud develops the anthropological philosophy already implicit in the claims stated earlier, by systematizing some ideas concerning the relationship between the Oedipus complex and the origin of social repression. The individuals, bearers of intrinsically asocial and antisocial impulsive-instinctual tendencies, would tend to discharge these energies. However, first the father ('the tribal patriarch') and then the social world forces them to repress these tendencies. Precarious situations arise from this, namely, a compromise between social repression and the tendency to instinctual discharge, situations that are conflictual and the source of uneasiness.

In the Hobbes–Freud schema, therefore, egoism is natural, cooperation an artifice. Nevertheless, rather than starting from adult self-consciousness, ethologists and developmental psychologists have been engaged in a systematic investigation of the humble life of animals and the simplest and most precocious forms of interaction between individuals. This led them to formulate a new hypothesis: adaptive-cooperative activity is primary, and therefore contextual to the very definition of the individual organism. Complex animals cannot be separated either from their environment or from forms of cooperation. In the human species, neither asocial nor pre-social individuals exist. Contrary to what Freud believed, newborn infants are by no means isolated little beings, laboriously learning to come to terms with the world, but they are social beings wishing to have relationships with others, and above all to interact – in a mutually cooperative way – with the mother and their other caregivers.[5]

These are the socially competent children the object-relations theories and attachment theories talk about. They are individuals whose primordial psychological needs are not about the oral libido, but the physical contact and construction of protective and communicative interpersonal structures – a primary need for ties and protection around which their mental life gradually takes shape. These individuals are then the bearers of a very complex set of motivations, and these are always and from the outset *relational*, that is, they take into account the presence of others and are articulated in an interpersonal interplay of communicative strategies.

Here, it is important to note, the term 'motivation' should be taken in a *descriptive* sense and not in an explanatory sense. It is used in current treatises on psychology to refer to the complex of all those factors that trigger, maintain, intensify, modulate or interrupt any physical activity or psychological event. It is therefore easy to realize that the term groups together a multitude of non-homogeneous factors that are difficult to classify and list. Therefore, its usefulness must be assessed on a case-by-case basis: sometimes it is better to examine the factors in question separately; at other times it is useful to consider them all together under the label 'motivations'.

The latter is the case with Lichtenberg's (1989) taxonomy of motivational systems, which is the most famous among modern classifications of motivations, a point of convergence between the psychoanalytic tradition and the systematic investigations on infancy. These systems are identified by Lichtenberg in clusters of needs relating to (1) psychic regulation of physiology, (2) attachment and affiliation, (3) exploration and assertion, (4) withdrawal and antagonism, (5) sensual enjoyment and later sexual excitement.

Note, however, that the systems (4) and (5) are largely dependent, the former on the exploratory-assertive system and the latter on the attachment-affiliation system. Consequently, there could only be two basic motivational orientations (see Jervis 2001, 84). First, the interpersonal, cooperative, elementarily socializing motivational system of attachment-affiliation – it could be called 'the basic prosocial mode', or 'the system of elementary structures of doing together' (see, e.g., Richerson and Boyd 2005; Hrdy 2009). The second system is dedicated to self-assertion and competition – it could be called 'the system of elementary structures of individual autonomy', 'self-assertiveness' or 'possible competition' (see, e.g., Byrne and Whiten 1988; Whiten and Byrne 1997). Between these two systems, spontaneous compromise situations arise, which can be intelligent, articulate and ingenious, and are characterized not so much by Freudian discomfort as by the fact that they create wealth and culture.

From this emerges an anthropology that is neither pessimistic nor optimistic: individuals are naturally inclined to competition (and sometimes destructiveness) but also to forms of sociality, cooperation and even altruism. What is more: competitiveness and cooperation go hand in hand. There is no cooperation without competitiveness and no competitiveness without cooperation. This is a natural foundation of human as well as animal behaviour.

As we shall now see, bringing order to the sphere of motivations by postulating a dialectic between the attachment-affiliation system and the affirmative-exploratory system is the strategy adopted by John Bowlby to reconstruct the cognitive-affective development of the child.

2.3. The contextualistic and systemic approach in attachment theory

The contextualistic and systemic approach informs the object-relations theory. The credit for founding this theory should be given to Alice and Michael Balint. In their criticism of the Freudian idea of primary narcissism and in speaking of a 'primary love' as a primary bond, in emphasizing the risks of a 'primary deficiency' as a deficiency, indeed, of the foundational mother–child relationship, in stating that the (original) object relation is based on the (dual) relationship and not on the instinctual discharge, the Balints' thought stands as a genuine methodological turning point (see, e.g., Balint 1985, 1992).

It was mainly Donald Winnicott and John Bowlby who built on the foundational work of the Balints. According to Winnicott, what makes sense is not considering the infant in itself, but the mother–infant dyad as an affective communication system. In Bowlby's view, the attachment bond is a crucial constitutive aspect of the mental life of very young children and a grounding theme of subsequent interpersonal relationships.

Taking cues from the ethological researchers of his time,[6] Bowlby (1969–80) identified the necessity to protect oneself from predators as the key to the evolutionary explanation of the infant's tendency to seek proximity to the caregiver. The primary object love theorized by the Balints becomes an inborn attachment system,[7] which operates throughout the entire course of life but it is hyperactive during childhood, given the long period of immaturity and dependence on parental care that characterizes the more evolved species, and especially the human infant.

The attachment system includes 'signals' such as crying or smiling which serve to bring about or maintain proximity to the caregiver. Certainly, these signals can be effective only if an adult responds to them by engaging in caregiving behaviour. The attachment system has therefore its complement in a caregiving system. In Winnicott's parent–infant dyad, the two 'instincts' match perfectly as a lock-and-key mechanism: babies emit continuous signals of weakness and need for protection, promptly heard by adults, who, in turn, effectively show their propensity for care.

Indeed, not only are newborns programmed by their psychobiological nature and the history of their neonatal life to seek the protection and warmth of the primary attachment figure; they are also programmed to venture out from it to explore their surroundings. For infants beginning to move autonomously, venturing away from the caregiver is the purest expression of an assertive-explorative motivational system. This curiosity about the world is in no way reducible to a mere survival drive, and neither to libidinal drives, as hypothesized by early psychoanalysts. Rather, it confirms Piaget's idea that children are learning machines – as well as being machines building affectional bonds.

Now, for babies crawling or attempting their first steps, the better their relationship with their attachment figure is, the more explorative they will be. Infants explore and venture out because the mother is what Bowlby calls their 'secure base' (they know they will be able to come back to her at any time), but also because they, so to speak, carry within themselves the image of their mother and therefore her protective, affiliative quality. After all, the entire cognitive-affective trajectory of the individual is always marked by this dialectic between attachment and autonomization.

Such dialectic was systematically investigated thanks to standardized observational procedures, among which the first and still most used is the *strange situation* (Ainsworth et al. 2015). In a room with toys, the mother (or, more generically, the caregiver) and her baby (typically 12–18 months old) are joined by an unknown adult. The caregiver then leaves the room and comes back after a few minutes.

Four different styles of attachment emerge from the analysis of the strange situation and tend to persist into adulthood, as attested by the *Adult Attachment Interview*, a semistructured interview assessing the features of recalling past episodes and the capacity of self-reflection. While secure attachment is typical of well-attuned dyads, insecure styles occur between a child and a caregiver who is excessively cold and detached (avoidant style), who alternates between excessive involvement and inattention (ambivalent style) or is unpredictable and inconsistent (disorganized style).

These different attachment styles affect the content of *Internal Working Models*, which are mental representations produced by the internalization of relational experiences with parental figures. Throughout the life cycle – according to Bowlby – they will significantly contribute to determining the goals of actions, ensuring (or obstructing) a sense of continuity and consistency with the past, the present and the future self.

Having traced the outlines of object relations theory and attachment theory, we can examine how these theories make use of the systemic perspective to study relationality.

There is a long tradition in theoretical biology – the so-called 'evolutionary systems theory' – where the separation of the individual organism from the environment makes no sense. From this perspective, both the developments of Darwin's theory and the modern concepts of equilibrium, adaptation, innate/acquired interrelation and ecological niche lead us to consider the individual-environment structure as a single systemic whole, where neither of the two poles is primary over the other. In animals as well as in human beings the development of the organism from the fertilized egg to reproduction and death consists in a series of structured interactions, each of which builds itself based on the previous one, and each of which sees the interaction, on the one hand of the onset of new environmental signals, and on the other, the gradual opening of new inner potentialities developed during the previous stages.[8]

As already noted, in the case of biological inspiration the consideration of psychological phenomena in terms of equilibria, and hence of systemic interactions, has a naturalistic origin and is in continuity with James and the Chicago school of functionalism. Things change, however, when the systemic approach to the mind has a sociological origin. Indeed, in sociology the systemic focus on interaction rather than on the individual often takes over, leading to the situation against which it aimed to struggle, that is, a conception in which (individual) biology and (social) relationality are split from each other, in that the former is deleted and the latter becomes all-encompassing. The result is a form of *sociologism* radically opposing systemic naturalism: while the latter views each animal (and the human being itself) as biologically part of the environment before being sociologically and culturally part of it, the systemic approach of sociological origin produces a 'pure', disembodied or formalistic relationalism, where the existence itself of living and real organisms is ignored, with the consequent loss of that 'processing' dimension of the agent, which, instead, is at the centre of our book.

A good example of this unwelcome outcome is provided by those forms of sociolinguistic constructivism in which psychological phenomena are produced in social interaction, and above all in the context of 'conversation', beyond which there is no mental process; mental processes are nothing but our conversational interactions. From here it is a short step to seeing persons not as the actors in or the agents of discourses, but rather as the products of the discursive practices themselves (see, e.g., Harré 1987).

Another path to pure relationism is a radical form of externalism that was put forward by some proponents of the dynamical approach to cognition (or 'dynamicism') – an approach that has been widely applied in developmental psychology (starting with the classic Thelen and Smith 1994). According to some defenders of the dynamical approach to cognitive modelling, the dynamical analysis identifies the critical variables characterizing the state of a system and attempts to construct laws (a set of differential equations) to account for the system's trajectory through state space. The system can no longer be decomposed into subsystems (modules) that involve computations on representations. Consequently, the dynamical explanation is seen as incompatible with the explanatory style of the computationalist mechanism (see Chemero 2009; and references in Chemero and Silberstein 2008, 11–13).

Most important for the current discussion, dynamicism dissolves the boundary between the cognitive system and the system's environment. Coupling between the equations describing a cognizing system and those describing the environment gives rise to complex 'total system' behaviours. In this perspective,

> the cognitive system is not just the encapsulated brain; rather, since the nervous system, body, and environment are all constantly changing and simultaneously influencing each other, the true cognitive system is a single unified system embracing all three. (van Gelder 1995, 373)

The role of the brain thus blurs in a conception of reality in which entities are undifferentiated variables and processes – a Machian view, on some aspects (Marraffa and Paternoster 2012, 35).

In brief, dynamicism puts forward 'the radical embodied cognition thesis': to understand the complex interplay of brain, body and environment we do not need either the concepts of internal representation and computation or the mechanistic decomposition of a cognitive system into a multiplicity of inner neuronal or functional subsystems; all we need are the analytic tools and methods of dynamical systems theory (Clark 1997, 148).

This revolutionary interpretation of dynamicism can be contrasted with Andy Clark's and William Bechtel's reformist projects, which aim to amend the computational and representational framework by drawing together insights from explanatory pluralism, mechanistic analysis and dynamicism. Clark (1997) suggests that dynamical and computational-mechanistic explanatory patterns ought to interlock in a complete explanation of cognition, a claim that has been explored in depth by Bechtel (2008).

Bechtel and Richardson (2010) argue that the study of biological systems reveals a continuum. At one end of the spectrum, we have *fully decomposable* systems, which are composed of subsystems that are completely independent except for the mutual exchange of outputs. If the interactions among the subsystems are weak but not negligible, the system is *nearly decomposable*. As the complexities of interaction among parts increase, the explanatory burden shifts from the parts to the organization of the parts (i.e. the interactions between subsystems). Thus, we reach the other end of the spectrum, where we find *holistic* systems, whose components are functionally equivalent and hence interchangeable. In between the nearly decomposable systems and the holistic ones, there are the 'integrated systems': in these systems, unlike the holistic ones, it is possible to isolate different parts that make distinctive contributions, but also give rise to a complex set of nonlinear interactions, and hence much stronger than those of a nearly decomposable system.

Now, both Bechtel (2008) and Clark (1997) suggest that psychobiological cognition is likely to take up the intermediate space between nearly decomposability and holism, namely that of integrated systems; and in an integrated system, the mechanistic analysis provides the foundation for dynamical analysis since the latter has explanatory force only insofar as it describes the operations of the underlying mechanism, only to the extent that it reveals aspects of the causal structure of a mechanism (Kaplan and Bechtel 2011; Kaplan and Craver 2011). Bechtel and Abrahamsen (2010) refer to accounts integrating the mechanistic decomposition of systems into parts and operations with the quantitative tools provided by dynamical systems theory as 'dynamic mechanistic explanations'.

This attempt to reconcile dynamical modelling and mechanistic analysis is particularly relevant here since Griffiths and Tabery (2013) have convincingly argued that the explanations at which developmental systems theory aims are mechanistic explanations, and often dynamical mechanistic explanations, of the developmental potential of the system. A good example is Greenwood's (2015) epigenetic model of emotional development, which supplements 'classical forms of mechanistic explanation with dynamical explanations' (Griffiths 2017, 389).

Armed with these clarifications, we return to object relations theory. There is nothing in this theory that renders it ineluctably liable to pure relationism. Quite the contrary: it is wrong to think that the theory of object relations is, as such, relational. The notion of object relationship does not strictly and per se imply an interactionist theory, let alone a systemic theory. Indeed, here the subject can still be seen as *primary* to the object. In other words, we can still have a relation in the traditional sense, namely in a one-directional sense. In that case, we still do not have a relational theory in the strict sense, that is, a theory focused on the forms of interactive dialectics that constantly generate new dynamic equilibria. That being the case, the different versions of the theory of object relations fit into different parts of the spectrum that from the classical conception of the subject seen as primary to the object leads to forms of pure relationism. So we should not confuse the claims that minds are shaped by early interactions with others – and that much that goes on in our mind has to do with our relationships with others and representations of these relationships (all claims that we can find in the theory of attachment) – with the radical, social-constructivist claim that 'the basic unit of study' in psychoanalysis is not 'the individual as a separate entity' but 'an interactional field', which can be found in the relational theory of Mitchell (1988, 3).

3. In search of a synthesis

Having distanced ourselves from the various forms of sociological antinaturalism present in the debate on personal identity, we can undertake our investigation of how the living and real information-processing organism constructs its own subjective identity. As anticipated in the incipit of the chapter, this will mean making a synthesis between historically opposed positions, such as Chomskyan innatism and Piagetian constructivism. To this end, a crucial role will be played by the sociocultural perspective of Lev Vygotsky, canonically considered the antagonist of Piagetian egocentricity and about as far from Chomskyan internalism as one can conceive. In particular, some elements highlighted by Vygotsky enable us to downsize the excessive individualism of the Piagetian research tradition by emphasizing those dimensions of identity self-construction of the subject originating from the network of interpersonal relationships. As already mentioned, this is a lesson fully assimilated by the attachment theory.

3.1. Piaget's individual-based constructivism and Chomsky's nativist turn

In the study of the mind, the transition from the traditional top-down approach to the bottom-up one marks a methodological change that Piaget defined as *de-centring of the subject*: 'the subject's activity calls for a continual "de-centring" without which he cannot become free from his spontaneous intellectual egocentricity' (Piaget 1970, 139). Under this approach, in the 1920s Piaget refounded the studies in child psychology by beginning investigations on how children see and explain reality from their autonomous, original viewpoint.

The outcome of this investigation is *epigenetic constructivism*. This theory, attempting to overcome the traditional innate/acquired distinction, states that cognitive competencies are built from the synthesis of two factors: on the one hand, the maturation and differentiation in stages of the intrinsic capacities of the mind and on the other, the active adaptation of the individual to the environment. This adaptation occurs through the construction of *schemes*, organized sets of movements and operations. The processes at the basis of adaptation are *assimilation* and *accommodation*, each complementing one other. Assimilation consists of the integration of a new object or situation into the set of objects or situations already belonging to an existing scheme (e.g. encountering new objects leads to expanding the prehension scheme). Inversely, and at the same time, the pre-existing scheme is accommodated, which makes it more flexible and general (e.g. the different sizes, weights or shapes of new objects determine an adjustment to the modalities of prehension). Thus, the cognitive-operational schemes grow by self-construction, that is, they self-reproduce by enhancing themselves with experience, structure themselves according to different gradients of complexity and then are constantly 'reconstructed' throughout life.

In Piaget's theory of development, behaviour and knowledge, and persons themselves, are individual (rather than social) constructions. This self-construction has as a starting point a repertoire of competencies involving only the sensorimotor sphere. At birth, children are endowed with sensorimotor reflexes and representations which, through reiterated processes of assimilation and accommodation equally innate and precocious,[9] progressively give access to increasingly structured, explicit, symbolic and intentional forms of knowledge and adaptations to the environment.

In the late 1960s Piagetian minimalism about the initial stage of ontogenesis drew cutting remarks from the purveyors of developmental psychology inspired by Chomskyan representational nativism. Piaget – neo-nativist psychologists claimed – was misled by an inadequate experimental methodology which, by requiring the child to actively participate in the experimental setting, validated the image of slow, linear and – as we shall see – 'horizontal' development, namely, independent from the domain of knowledge. Observational data, as well, focused on what children showed of being able to concretely do.[10]

Piaget regarded innatism as 'an easy and rather lazy solution' but predicted that 'after the excesses of explanation by learning alone, a return to nativism is to be expected' (1968a, 978); and so it was. The showdown, so to speak, unfolded with all its drama at the aforementioned Royaumont meeting, with the young Chomsky in the role of a staunch defender of innatist rationalism through his hypothesis of universal grammar: it is only by postulating a component shared by all languages that one can explain the ease and rapidity with which children acquire the syntax of their language, independently of their IQ and essentially without adult corrective intervention.

The Royaumont debate, as high in its theoretical level as in its tone, marked the empirical investigations of the following years. Piattelli Palmarini, an orthodox Chomskyan who published a thorough report on the meeting (1980) and recently recalled it (2019), has no doubt about the victory of Chomsky's neo-nativism.[11] Indeed, forty years of investigations on precocious cognitive competencies have highlighted how much Piaget underestimated the competencies of newborns and infants. To a great extent, as mentioned, it was precisely his methodology, focusing on behaviour, that misled the great scholar. Experimental failures often stemmed more from children's inability to activate patterns of motor organization than from their actual lack of knowledge. It sufficed to employ different experimental methods to shed light on a very different reality, made up of significantly precocious competencies. Instead of asking children to do something, the experimenters decided to observe and measure their attention, as evidenced by their gaze direction or suction force. They then adopted and refined the habituation-dishabituation technique.[12]

A huge number of empirical studies revealed the innate and precocious nature of many other competencies – and not only. If Chomsky views universal grammar as an innate *corpus* of knowledge specific to the language domain, other authors went further, claiming that computational mechanisms – and consequently the underlying brain regions – are domain-specific as well. Some restricted their thesis to perceptual systems alone (Fodor 1983), whereas others extended it to cognitive and metacognitive processes (Sperber 2001).[13]

According to the *core cognition* (or *core knowledge*) hypothesis, infants are born endowed with a system of conceptual representations, that is, representations that cannot be reduced to the perceptual primitives postulated by the Empiricists or to the sensorimotor primitives hypothesized by Piagetians (see Samet 2017, 2.1). For example, Spelke (2022) draws from studies with children and adults belonging to different cultures, as well as from research on non-human primates, the hypothesis of a restricted number of core systems that would make possible an early representation of significant aspects of the environment: inanimate objects, agents, number and space. Each system is domain-specific, that is, it hinges on a set of principles that allow entities belonging to a specific domain (physical objects, agents) to be recognized and reasoned about. For instance, physical objects do not pass through solid surfaces, agents can autonomously set themselves in motion and so on. It is based on these domain-specific systems that agents build more flexible capacities, new concepts and systems of knowledge.

Note that the development of innate cognitive structures is typically understood as a process of maturation, a problematic notion if taken in the logic of genetic determinism. However, it is possible to resist this objection and maintain the crucial point of nativism (i.e. that the endogenous biological structure determines how organisms learn and respond to their environment) by combining it with the viewpoint of evolutionary developmental biology – namely, by arguing that the psychological structures documented by neo-nativist research are *constructed* through the interaction of genetic, epigenetic and external factors (Griffiths and Tabery 2013, 77; Perovic and Radenovic 2011). This perspective is congruent with Piagetian constructivism: Piaget's concept of adaptation is partially based on an evolutionary view anticipating the evolutionary systems perspective (Bjorklund 2015; Campanella 2019; Piattelli Palmarini 2019).

3.2. Vygotsky's sociocultural constructivism and methodological individualism

With due distinctions, methodological individualism is something that Chomsky and Piaget have in common. On the other hand, as mentioned earlier, Lev Vygotsky's sociocultural constructivism is, inter alia, a criticism of Piaget's individualism. Vygotsky (2012) argued against Piagetian egocentrism, being, on the contrary, persuaded that language, and in particular linguistic exchanges with others, precede and ground thought. In the Vygotskian perspective, our mind is to a significant extent a social construction plastically developing in interaction with the elements of the background culture, under the guidance and with the scaffolding of adult members of the community. The guidance of expert adults is essential to the process through which children (who also in this perspective are held devoid of innate competencies) develop their abilities in each cognitive domain. Indeed, each level of understanding is achieved within a social context, and only later is it (progressively) internalized. Taking up a famous example, consider a child stretching her arms out towards an object, trying to reach it (Vygotsky 1997a). The adult, who immediately and spontaneously grasps the communicative meaning of the gesture, satisfies the desire of the child and hands her the object. This meaning, which has been suggested and made explicit by the adult, is shared and internalized by the child: through a social negotiation of meaning, a failed movement of reaching to grasp becomes a concept available to inferential processes.

The idea of progressive internalization (or interiorization) of competencies coming from the outside is also the key to understanding the development of self-consciousness: '[T]he social moment in consciousness is primary in time as well as in fact. The individual aspect is constructed as a derived and secondary aspect on the basis of the social aspect and exactly according to its model' (Vygotsky 1997b, 77).

In positing the primacy of the interpersonal over the intrapersonal, Vygotsky is very close to Georg H. Mead (see Bruner 1962; Valsiner and van der Veer 2000). According to Mead (1934), too, subjective identity, as well as every other aspect of mental life, is forged by society through symbolic communication. Thought arises from the internalization of external conversation, made up not only of words but also of gestures. Hence the hypothesis of the sociogenesis of the self: we see ourselves, and define ourselves, essentially through a process of active internalization of how significant others see and define us. As Mead (1934) puts it, the basic mechanism for the development of self-consciousness is 'the individual's becoming an object to himself by taking the attitudes of other individuals toward himself within an organized setting of social relationships' (p. 225).[14]

In a clinical context, Harry Stack Sullivan (1953) was the first to grasp the significance of the concept of self as developed by Mead, exploiting it in the study of interpersonal relationships and the inner dialectics associated with these relationships. More recently, the constructivist approach has been consolidated in developmental psychopathology, taking the form of the thesis that 'unrealistically negative dysfunctional self-attributions are seen to arise from attempts to rationalise the abusive or seriously neglective child-directed behaviors of attachment figures' (Gergely 2002, 42).

For our part, we will adhere to a constructivist model in which social scaffolding is inextricably linked with the maturation of the endogenous psychobiological system. We will investigate those neurocognitive mechanisms that enable children to immerse themselves into the social world, making it so that social interaction works as scaffolding for their development. As Gerrans puts it,

> individualism is not inconsistent with social interaction; it is required to explain it. Social exchanges, evidenced in gaze monitoring, social referencing, emotional responses, protodeclarative and imperative pointing, pretence, play, and conversation all play a role in development, but the nature of that role is opaque without an understanding of the cognitive mechanisms on which they depend. (2004, 107)

Couldn't have said it better. In the remainder of this book, we shall thoroughly articulate such constructivism, starting from the processing individual. We shall propose the image of an individual who is born 'pre-wired' for interpersonal relationships. Such wiring is the basis of the construction of an identity that is *contextual* and *interactive* from the outset.

3

From bodily awareness to bodily self-awareness

After outlining the bottom-up and systemic-relational naturalistic approach within which we aim to build on the Jamesian theory of the self, this chapter begins to investigate the process of construction of subjective identity.

The external world, the inner world of the mind and the visceral world enclosed within the confines of the body constitute the three primary existential spaces in which the universal field of human experientiality is distributed and ordered. Against this background, the concept of self-consciousness (or, equivalently, self-awareness) implies different levels of complexity. At the (relatively) simplest level, self-consciousness is bodily self-awareness: our capacity to form a body image of ourselves as an entire object and associate this with ourselves as a subject – the active source of the representation of ourselves. On the other hand, at a maximally evolved level, self-consciousness is something more complex: it is the introspective recognition of the presence of the virtual inner space of the mind, separated from the other two primary experiential spaces, namely, the bodily and the extra-bodily space.

Our view of the ontogeny of bodily self-awareness is constructivist through and through.

Numerous experimental data show that from the very first weeks of life, self-specifying proprioceptive and kinaesthetic information is precociously available to infants. These findings have been interpreted as evidence in favour of the thesis that long before the acquisition of a conceptual and objective form of self-consciousness, a *pre-reflective sense of ownership* for one's body is already present in preverbal infants. To this thesis we will oppose a more cautious reading of these same findings, arguing that postnatal infants are immersed in a subjectivity that they are unable to objectify; they are already agents but do not yet know it, because, in place of a unified representation of their body as recognizable as their own body, they possess only fragmented and incomplete perceptions of their bodies.

It is only in the second year of life that infants become able to construct a body image of themselves as *an entire object*, while at the same time considering this image as *a subject*, that is, as an active source of self-representation. Here the subject recognizes a new type of object of consciousness: the object is the subject itself, or rather the objectified image of it ('I am there'). This occurs through mediation with the caregiver within the attachment environment; bodily self-awareness is therefore a cognitive acquisition that requires seeing oneself through the eyes of the other, that is, identifying oneself in someone who is looking at us. As Winnicott puts it, '[i]n individual emotional development *the precursor of the mirror is the mother's face*' (2005, 149). The other is thus alter-ego, the mirror function through which the body recognizes itself and is accepted as a whole.[1]

Self-consciousness in its simplest form, namely, as awareness of existing, is, therefore, the representation of a physical self.[2] We access the idea of existing only because we become able to identify ourselves 'in the flesh', namely, insofar as we 'know' that we are individuals with certain characteristics, which are primarily physical, physiognomic and bodily characteristics.

More in general, we know that we exist only insofar as we know that *we exist in a certain way*, that is, with determined characteristics, as a *describable identity*. Observing and studying infants during the second year of age, we realize that there is no difference between the construction of their self-awareness (now corporeal, physical, but then also psychological, introspective) and the construction of their identity.

1. The initial state: Sensitivity for contingency

A large set of studies have demonstrated that very young children can estimate the degree of causal relatedness between responses and stimuli, and detect visual-proprioceptive temporal contingency arising from their movements. Here are some influential examples.

Infants' contingency detection is commonly tested using the preferential-looking method. In a seminal study by Bahrick and Watson (1985), three- to five-month-old infants were presented with two screens side-by-side. One screen displayed a live transmission of the infant's legs and feet (perfectly contingent display), while the other screen showed either the legs and feet of a peer wearing the same clothes or a video clip of the infant's movements recorded shortly before the experiment. In these cases, the level of contingency is certainly not perfect, but neither is it a noncontingent event: the child makes a movement and sees a different but not entirely unrelated one, since the experimental context is uniform (same place, same clothes, extremely limited possibilities of movement). The results revealed an age-dependent preference for visual orientation. Specifically, three-month-olds were in a developmental transition from a preference for perfect contingencies to a preference for high-but-imperfect degrees of response-stimulus contingencies, whereas five-month-olds had by then consolidated a propensity to explore high-but-imperfect contingency.

The finding that young infants can discriminate differences in visual-proprioceptive temporal contingency has proven robust, corroborated by experiments that reach the same conclusions with a slight variation in the investigation paradigm. In Rochat and Striano (2002), four- and nine-month-old infants were placed facing video images either of themselves (in real-time or delayed) or of another person (an experimenter) imitating them. After the first one-minute presentation, the video image (of either the self or the other) was suddenly frozen for one minute (still-face episode); this was followed by one minute of a live presentation. From four months of age, infants appeared to perceive and act differentially when facing the specular image of themselves or the mimicking other. When looking at the video image of the other, infants smiled more, watched more intensely, and showed longer first-look duration. And at nine months of age, infants have taken more social initiatives towards the other compared with the self during the still-face episode.

Rochat and Morgan (1995) extended Bahrick and Watson's investigation of temporal contingency to the domain of spatial contingency. Three- and four- to –five-month-old infants were presented with two live films of their own legs side by side. The legs were presented from different perspectives, including an ego versus an observer view, with or without a right/left reversal. In one study, infants saw two ego views of their legs, one normal and the other with a right/left reversal. This caused a discrepancy in the spatial mapping and the direction of movement of the video image, with respect to the infants' legs. Results indicated that infants at both ages demonstrated a significant preference for the incongruent display with the right/left reversal. This shows sensitivity to a spatial contingency; in particular, the directionality of the leg motion. A further study found no evidence of sensitivity to spatial orientation *per se* when right/left was not reversed. These results extend those of Bahrick and Watson (1985) by demonstrating that infants detect the visual-proprioceptive contingency generated by their motion based on spatial as well as temporal information.

Before questioning what the underlying computational mechanism for these infant performances might be, we note that all the experimental data cited refer to the recognition of body parts; the parts/whole distinction will be examined in Section 4.

Based on the data described earlier, Gergely and Watson (1996, 1999) hypothesized the existence of an innate mechanism, the *contingency detection module* (CDM), designed by natural selection to detect and represent causal contingency relations between responses and stimulus events (see also Gergely 2004; Frankenhuis, Gergely and Watson 2013). The CDM would already be operational at three months (but perhaps earlier: see Rochat and Striano 1999), with the function of attracting attention to *one's* movements. In the following months, the CDM would vary the mode of operation, fulfilling a second and no less useful attentional function towards other agents and interpersonal relationships.

The CDM is specialized to automatically and quickly estimate the conditional probability that a given event will be followed by a response; the estimation is accomplished through a kind of automatic algebraic summation of the value of two indicators. The *sufficiency* index emerges from an assessment that registers the prospective probability that a given type of event (A) will be followed by a second event (B). Conversely, the *necessity* index captures the retrospective probability that an event (B) will occur in response to an event (A) that precedes it.

It is easy to appreciate that the maximum contingency index is reached by observing the movements of one's body in real time (in a mirror or on a screen), which are perfectly predictable. However, we have seen that children turn early to prefer a high but not a maximum level of contingency. If in the experimental context reviewed earlier such a suboptimal value is achieved when children observe their own delayed image (or their peers), in a more natural context the imperfection is typical of social interactions.

Indeed, it is precisely the analysis of the most typical context of interaction, namely the protoconversational exchange between children and adults, that helps to clarify how the temporal relationship between two events is not the only index considered. Causal dependence is spontaneously calculated on two additional elements: affective intensity and similarity of structure. To a stimulus from infants (e.g. a vocalization) the caregiver, who in front of them is engaging in an emotional dialogue still without words, does not perfectly echo, but spontaneously responds with an at least partially different gesture – a smile or gentle touch but having equal intensity and a similar dynamic structure; and this is enough to raise the degree of contingency.[3]

On the other hand, the negative consequences of excessive lowering of contingency are well known. In the *still-face* procedure (Tronick et al. 1978), a mother who is interacting with her child suddenly freezes her expression: the collapse of the contingency value resulting from the detuning causes obvious signs of stress in the child and, consequently, induces primitive self-regulatory strategies designed to recover the sense of well-being and security that was naturally found in the dyad (see Adamson and Frick 2003).

In the delayed feedback procedure (Murray and Trevarthen 1985), six- to twelve-week-olds are observed while interacting with their mother's live image through a TV monitor. After a certain period, the TV image is switched to a noncontingent image of the interacting mother recorded earlier. The infants react with dissatisfaction and negative affect to the loss of contingency.

2. Ecological self and pre-reflective self-consciousness

2.1. The ecological self

Commenting on the investigations just described (with particular reference to the study of Rochat and Morgan 1995), Rochat writes:

> In all, this research suggests that by moving and acting, infants from at least 3 months of age manifest an intermodal calibration of the own body, developing an intermodal body schema. This body schema is an implicit, perceptually based 'protorepresentation' of the body as specified by the intermodal redundancy accompanying perception and action. (2010a, 328)

Here the reference is to a *body schema* (and not to a *body image*, a distinction that will become clear in the next few pages), a representation that encodes information concerning parts of one's body in a procedural form, primitive but sufficient to control movements and maintain posture. This is 'self-specifying' information (see Bermúdez 1998, ch. 5; Musholt 2015, 48–9). Nothing Rochat writes, however, justifies the assumption that infants automatically construct a unitary experiential space, a self-awareness of their whole body. This is an important point; to fully grasp it, it is necessary to clarify the meaning of the term 'self' that appears in the locution 'self-specifying'.

In English-language philosophical, sociological and psychological literature, the term 'self' has two main meanings: the first is subjective, experiential; the second objective, structural. As mentioned in Chapter 1, Locke and James employ the word 'self' in an experiential-reflexive sense: what 'self' designates is neither the person nor the mind, nor even a part of the latter, but rather our way of grasping and considering them introspectively.[4] In its objective meaning, on the other hand, the term 'self' refers not to a subjective experience, but rather to an inner structure, a set of functions of the mind. In that case, we cannot help but observe that this objectified self often replaces, without any clear need for it, terms such as 'person', 'personality', 'mind' or even 'ego'.

Armed with this distinction, we can say that as regards the body schema, there is no reason to understand the self occurring in the locution 'self-specifying' as the self in the subjective sense. Rather, it must be the self in the objective-structural sense: an acting organism, a psychobiological system endowed with mechanisms that subserve the perception of the external world and also with mechanisms for self-monitoring. This 'neonatal self' is therefore in relation to the environment through representations, but these make up a subjective world that coincides with the object field, and in which any self-image is therefore absent (see Chapter 1 , Section 5).

Let us now examine another passage in Rochat (2010a):

> In summary, from the earliest age, perception and action specify the body as a differentiated entity among other entities in the environment. Early on, infants appear to calibrate their own body based on intermodal (that is, perceptual) invariants that specify the sense of their own ecological self: a sense of their own bodily self that is differentiated, situated, and acts as an agent in the physical environment [...]. This may form the perceptual origins of what will eventually develop as an explicit or conceptual sense of self by the second year of life. (330)

This passage is flawed by the ambiguity of Neisser's notion of the ecological self itself, on which we should therefore pause. In an article as famous as it is full of terminological and conceptual stumbling blocks, Neisser (1988) sets out to describe five kinds of self-knowledge. Despite ambiguous terminology, the first two kinds – the ecological self and the interpersonal self – are not objects of knowledge, but rather of perception, available to the child from the earliest months of life. The genuinely epistemic level will intervene later, with the (temporally) extended self, the private self and the conceptual self. The theoretical frame of reference is Gibson's ecological theory of perception, according to which every perceptual act automatically provides information about the self, understood as the limit of the perceptual field. For example, the fact that we cannot see beyond a certain angle informs us at all times, among other things, of the existence of body parts, starting with the nose and cheekbones; self-specifying information also comes from the proprioceptive and kinesthetic feedback of every action. Such proprioceptive sensitivity could be innate: as observed by Rochat and Hespos (1997) 24-hour-old infants turn their heads three times more frequently towards a stimulus (a finger pressure at the corner of the mouth) produced by others than towards a self-produced stimulus.

According to Neisser, this information constitutes the ecological self and the interpersonal self. The former is 'the individual situated in and acting upon the immediate physical environment' (Neisser 1995, 18); the latter, which appears from earliest childhood just like the ecological self, is 'the same individual considered from a different point of view: namely, as engaging in face-to-face interaction with others' (Neisser 1993, 4). In both cases, we are dealing with a corporeal-agentive self in interaction with the physical world or, more specifically, with that physical world made up of agents. But it is necessary to be more precise to highlight any critical points.

Immediately after introducing the first type of self-knowledge in the terms mentioned earlier, Neisser suggests that 'infants perceive themselves to be ecological selves from a very early age' (1995, 18). Recalling once again the ambivalence of the word 'self', we note how in the definition of ecological self (the individual situated in and acting upon the immediate physical environment) Neisser is using the self in an *objective* sense (the self as the object of perception), while in the last quotation, he seems to switch to the self in an *experiential* sense (the self as the subject of experience). However, that same statement, despite its objective ambiguity, does not seem to mean more than this: the embodied individual from the very beginning has mechanisms that process not only information about the external world but also information about parts of one's own body. Thus, the ecological self refers to the fact that the experiential object field can be structured in different domains. For example, there will be certain objects that will be perceived as 'near' or 'domestic' precisely because children have self-specifying information about them. A peripheral somatic segment, such as a hand, is as much an object of gaze as it is an acting, active and non-passive part in the manipulation of objects: and therein lies the dual status, objective and subjective, of every part of the body. In very early infancy, however, this status prepares but does not yet translate into that boundary line between an inside and an outside in the experiential sense, which will instead take shape in the second year of age. Neisser writes that the infant 'has, and perceives herself to have, an extended body that is capable of interacting with the environment in a purposeful way' (1995, 21). But experientially, infants under one year *are* their body but do not *have* their body.⁵

On this track, we can frame Bermúdez's (1998, 2011, 2018) use of Neisser's expression 'ecological self' to describe a type of non-intellectual and non-conceptual self-awareness – pre-reflective – that would reveal itself in the perception of the external world and through the information provided by the proprioceptive or somatic system. Now, there is no doubt that proprioception is important for self-awareness, but Bermúdez goes much further when he argues that it *is* a form of self-awareness. In addition to providing information about the self, in the sense of providing agents with information that has their body (or parts of it) as its object, proprioception also automatically provides the representation of the self as an acting physical unit.

2.2. Pre-reflective self-consciousness

Gallagher and Zahavi (2019, 2020) proposed, within the framework of scientifically informed phenomenology, the thesis that all conscious experience involves an implicit awareness of oneself as its subject without explicitly representing the self as an object of awareness.⁶

In other words, this form of self-consciousness, far from being a second-order representational state, is immanent or intrinsic to first-order mental states. It is a non-cognitive and non-explicit self-consciousness: the idea is that for example, any state of perceptual experience is systematically associated with a sense of ownership of the experience; the experience in question is given to me immediately as mine, as something that belongs to me (*mineness*). This sense of ownership is not to be thought of in the form of a relationship between the subject and the experience – in which case it would be a second mental state in addition to the experience – but rather as a trait intrinsic to the experience itself. The form of self-consciousness in question 'is not intentionally structured; it does not involve a subject-object relation. It is not just that self-consciousness differs from ordinary object-consciousness; rather it is not an object-consciousness at all' (Gallagher and Zahavi 2020, 59).

Being a structural, intrinsic feature of experience itself, the self-awareness in question is tacit: non-conceptual, non-reflective and non-observational. It manifests itself in the mere sensation of possessing experience. The authors call it 'pre-reflective self-consciousness' and use it as a basis for formulating the so-called 'ubiquity thesis': necessarily, an organism that is in a conscious mental state (i.e. possesses phenomenal consciousness) is also self-conscious (i.e. possesses a primitive form of self-consciousness).

Now, unlike other philosophers who have defended the ubiquity thesis with a priori arguments, Gallagher and Zahavi defend it in the context of an empirically informed philosophy of mind; thus, their concept of pre-reflective self-consciousness cannot merely be the result of transcendental arguing. Within a naturalistic framework, we need to know which psychological capacities or processes are to be considered instances of pre-reflective self-consciousness; and we need to find empirical evidence of their existence. Furthermore, since it is theorized that such capacities/processes are intrinsic to 'primary' states of consciousness, evidence is required in favour of the hypothesis that such capacities/processes are ontogenetically very early.

And here we come to the point that interests us most. According to Gallagher and Zahavi, the literature on developmental and ecological psychology attests to 'a primitive form of self-awareness, proprioceptive in character, being already present at birth' (2019, section 1). Of the same opinion is Rochat (2012): infant research of the past forty years would show that infants' from birth manifest 'unity in the Kantian sense' (4), namely, a 'primordial sense of embodied self-unity' (3). Here it is difficult to escape the impression that this primitive form of self-consciousness is the result of a psychologistic hypostatization of Kantian synthetic unity: one could say that the integrating function of experience has been mistaken for the experience of integration.

We believe that developmental and ecological psychology provides no evidence that a primitive form of self-awareness, proprioceptive in character, is already present at birth (see Di Francesco, Marraffa and Paternoster 2016, ch. 2).[7] Such a description of infants' subjectivity under one year of age is undermined by an 'adultist' perspective, which projects the construct of pre-reflective self-consciousness onto the infants' behaviour. Historically, in developmental psychology, adultism has taken two forms. It may be discriminating or excluding: the newborn is an animal-like creature lacking any kind of mind and true interpersonal life. Or it may be a top-down approach to neonatal psychology involving empathic identification or projection: newborns are then viewed and evaluated not from the standpoint of their world but from the standpoint of the adult (Peterfreund 1978). It is this adultomorphization of infancy that afflicts the interpretation of developmental psychology data in terms of the construct of pre-reflective self-consciousness.

In conclusion, the notion of innate pre-reflective self-consciousness, understood as a tacit, non-intellectual sense of self that renders every conscious state a first-person phenomenal state, turns out to be an empirically void construct, connoting itself rather as the artefact of a top-down approach to self-consciousness, in which the philosopher's self-experience is (anti-naturalistically) taken as an explanans rather than an explanandum.

Against this regressive shift, our approach is built around a clear-cut distinction between object-consciousness and self-consciousness as this is drawn by a representational approach to consciousness (see Chapter 1, Section 5). This affords to view bodily and psychological forms of self-consciousness as the result of a process of self-objectivation which requires conscious (but not self-conscious) representational activities.

Within this framework, the first, minimal condition required for the development of the self is the possession of a simple or primary object consciousness. As seen at the end of the first chapter, the methodological ground of this distinction comes from a certain way of reading Brentano's theory of intentionality. If ordinary intuition takes consciousness as a phenomenon fully 'internal' to the mind, Brentano conceives of it in relational terms: consciousness is not so much a primary and essential quality or character of the mind, but rather a collection of heterogeneous forms of active relations, involving the construction of representations, between an organism and its environment. Against this methodological background, we can speak of an immediate, organismic subjectivity, consisting of the primary (object) consciousness of the infant or animal. Primary consciousness is the result of the representational activity. This activity shapes a purely *objectual* experiential space.

2.2.1. Pre-reflective self-consciousness and the Jamesian I

Pre-reflective self-consciousness is the cornerstone of the theoretical framework proposed by Prebble, Addis and Tippett (2013; Tippett, Prebble and Addis 2018) to support the investigation of autobiographical memory and sense of self. Within this theoretical framework, pre-reflective self-consciousness is seen as a key to understanding the Jamesian distinction between I and Me. We will now argue that this interpretation of James' duplex self has no basis.

The three researchers propose a model of the sense of self based on two properties that vary along two axes or dimensions. The first axis consists of the opposition between a subjective and an objective aspect of the sense of self: the former is the phenomenological experience of selfhood (the 'subjective sense of self' identified with the Jamesian I-self); the latter is self-representation, the content of which encompasses all that subjects perceive and know about themselves (the 'self-content' identified with the Jamesian Me-self). The second axis consists of the contrast between those aspects of the sense of self that are connected to the present moment ('present self') and those aspects that are extended in time ('extended self'). In each moment I experience a sense of (synchronic) unity both in the conscious experience of selfhood and in the mental representation of who I am ('self-concept'). In time, I experience (diachronic) unity both in my subjective experience of selfhood ('phenomenological continuity') and in the way I represent myself ('semantic continuity').

The model distinguishes between two hierarchically related forms of conscious self-experience associated with the present moment: pre-reflective self-experience and self-awareness. Both are necessary (though not sufficient) for autonoetic consciousness (autonoetic recollection and imagination) and episodic memory, but pre-reflective self-experience precedes and grounds self-awareness.

Prebble, Addis and Tippett (2013, 820) introduce the concept of pre-reflective self-experience by starting from the observation that most people, at the heart of what they conceptualize as their essential self, feel that there is 'an experiencing "thing" inside their heads' that is the recipient of their thoughts, feelings and experiences (Leary and Tangney 2012, 5). The primary intuition here is that phenomenal consciousness involves a subject–object polarity: there is no such thing as the mere non-relational phenomenal appearance of an object or quality; rather, anything that phenomenally appears, appears to someone or something. Admittedly, this is not an unchallenged intuition: as seen in the first chapter, although 'the idea, or rather impression of ourselves is always intimately present with us', Hume (1739–40, book II, p. I. sect. XI) denies that a distinct subject relatum is phenomenologically accessible. But – one may reply – what the Humean 'no-self' intuition challenges is the existence of a subject of experience understood as a metaphysical entity that observes the stream of consciousness from the outside – the self in the Cartesian theatre, as Dennett (1991) puts it. And the doctrine of pre-reflective self-consciousness aims to get rid of any little ubiquitous homunculus by understanding pre-reflective self-experience as a *phenomenological* (and not substantialist) guarantee of personal identity: what characterizes this mode of consciousness as a 'self' experience is that it is imbued with a particular phenomenological 'flavour' that confers an 'immediate and automatic full ownership of experience' (Vandekerckhove and Panksepp 2009, 1022). No matter what modality we are experiencing (e.g. sight, sound, taste, interoception), or what type of experience (e.g. thinking, remembering, knowing, feeling, dreaming), all our experiences are pervaded by a subjective *mineness* that leaves us in no doubt that they are our own.

Let us now compare this theoretical framework with James' theory of the self. It is a serious mistake to assume that the Jamesian I has at its core the intuition on which the doctrine of pre-reflective self-consciousness rests. Prebble, Addis and Tippett write that the Jamesian I-self is 'the psychological process that is the subject of knowing and experiencing', whereas the Me-self is 'the object of this awareness' (2013, 817). The Me would thus be the product of a process that has a source: the I-subject, the primordial starting point of experience. The pre-reflective experience of self as experiencing and acting subject is then given in full autonomy from the Me, that is, from the overall identity of my person as I can describe it according to the three forms of material, social and psychological self.

This interpretation, however, does not hold. For James, as we have seen in Chapter 1 (Section 4), the egoic centre of conscious subjectivity is not the I-self but the 'pure Ego'. Each of us spontaneously envisages the reality of this ego, but if we then, looking inside ourselves, set out in search of it, we realise that every part of our mind is the object of this alleged ego; as a consequence of this, the pure Ego is reduced to being a pure grammatical artifice, a point without dimension. What remains then is the I-self construed as a process with no egoic centre of conscious subjectivity; a process by which the subject (cognitivistically understood by us as a psychobiological system capable of representational activity) seeks itself, and in doing so presents oneself to oneself – a self-presentation that is a description of identity. Consequently, there can be no 'subjective sense of self' (not even a 'brute' first-personal experience) without a 'content of self'; our conscious, phenomenological experience of selfhood is our feeling of being here as being here in a certain way, according to a mental representation 'comprising all the things that we perceive and know about ourselves' (Prebble, Addis and Tippett 2013, 817).

In light of the essential link established between self-consciousness and identity, we will say that the ontogenesis of self-awareness is the story of the construction of different forms of identity; and first comes the construction of bodily identity.

3. Bodily self-awareness

3.1. The second year: That body is mine

In the previous section, we criticized the claim that the infants' very early ability to discriminate visual-proprioceptive contingency arising from their movements implies that they can recognize these movements and body parts as belonging to the self (i.e. Neisser's ecological self taken in a phenomenological sense). To this, we add here a criticism of the hypothesis that newborn humans are provided with innate representations of body components. Contrary to ecological and nativist accounts of the development of body representations (e.g. Butterworth 1995; Neisser 1995; Rochat 2010b), we conceive many documented abilities to perceive the body in early life as small pieces of a much larger puzzle. As Bremner puts it, the evidence, where it exists, indicates that 'postnatal infants' early perceptions of their bodies are fragmented and incomplete, and that fully-fledged abilities to represent our bodies take significant developmental time to emerge, likely as a result of experience' (2022, 281). In this perspective, crucial elements of body representations possessed by adults develop gradually through prenatal and postnatal life as a result of the experience gained in sensorimotor contexts.

This constructivist approach applies not only to the development of body representations but also to the process through which these body representations support the development of self-awareness or self-recognition. Bodily self-awareness originates from the *recomposition* of representations of parts of the body (the limbs, the belly, the head, etc.) into a single closed spatiality, which encompasses the source of perceptions. The fact that a hand is an object of the gaze and at the same time an active, rather than passive, agent in the manipulation of objects, refers to the double statute, objective and subjective, of every part of the body: and thus poses the need to define the global corporeal space in its 'ambiguous' experiential unity (Merleau-Ponty 1945). This body is a space experienced as ambiguous because it is neither properly external nor properly internal, a source but also an object of representation.

This re-composition process takes time. Infants do not yet have a full awareness of their body as a unit that is hierarchically structured into interrelated parts (Brownell, Svetlova and Nichols 2012). The explicit visual-spatial representation of one's own body is formed through an initial awareness of its parts, gradually leading to the representation of the body as a whole, in which these parts constitute a typical configuration that corresponds to the bodies of other individuals.

Inspired by previous impressionistic findings gathered from numerous informal observations, Brownell, Zerwas and Ramani (2007) carried out rigorous tests showing how considering one's own body as something that occupies a large space, and that can impede the movements of surrounding objects, represents a slow achievement. It is only towards the end of the second year (22–26 months) that children become steadily capable of assessing the size of their bodies, ceasing to make mistakes such as trying to sit on toy chairs, while at around 18–22 months they can take into account that their bodies can obstruct the movement of objects, for example, by preventing the movement of a mat on top of which they are placed. Thus, the infant's awareness of oneself as an acting physical unit is perfected over time, reaching a stable point around the age of three.[8]

A crucial segment of this re-composition process is intercepted by the best empirical indicator of bodily self-awareness, the *Mirror Self-Recognition* (MSR) test, which was independently developed by Gallup (1970) for chimpanzees, and Amsterdam (1972; a study conducted in 1969) for children. In Gallup's original investigation, the MSR test entailed placing a red spot on the chimpanzee's forehead and testing whether, when faced with a mirror, the animal attempts to reach for and remove the spot. In Amsterdam's revised version of the MSR test (the 'rouge mirror task'), infants were unobtrusively marked with a spot of rouge on their faces (a part of the body that cannot be seen without the aid of a mirror). Mark-directed behaviour (instead of mirror-directed behaviour or no reaction) was interpreted as evidence that the infants infer from the mirror image that they have a mark.

The MSR test has evidenced that from eighteen to twenty-four months, infants show a specific set of mark-directed (e.g. touching the mark) and self-conscious (e.g. coy/embarrassment) behaviours (Amsterdam 1972; Bertenthal and Fischer 1978; Brooks-Gunn and Lewis 1984; Lewis and Brooks-Gunn 1979). According to Nielsen, Suddendorf and Slaughter (2006), toddlers who pass the MSR test can recognize features of their whole body, not just their face. Stably at twenty-four months, and already as a tendency at eighteen months, children recognize a mark not only on their forehead but also on their leg.

The MSR test is a technique which appears regularly in textbooks and standardized tests of cognitive development but is also criticized and debated. We are assuming here that it is a valid indicator of bodily self-awareness, for the following reasons.

As to its validity, Bulgarelli et al. (2019, 2020) showed that performance on the MSR test in infants is strongly related to the activation of the so-called 'default mode network', a network of brain regions[9] which is activated during resting-state[10] and is recruited during self-related processing – it is, therefore, an important marker of self-awareness in adults.

As to the interpretation of the MSR test as an indicator of *bodily* self-awareness, alternative interpretations are either too 'rich' or too 'poor'. An example of an overly rich interpretation is offered by Keenan, Gallup and Falk (2003): agents pass the MSR test only if they can reflect on their private mental states – that is, if they possess an introspective type of self-awareness and a self-concept inextricably linked to an understanding of the intentional states of others. Various reasons cast doubt on this interpretation: to give just one example, persons with autism spectrum disorder, despite well-known difficulties with mentalization, have no difficulty in passing the MSR test (Williams 2010).

An example of an excessively poor interpretation is offered by Mitchell (1993): agents pass the MSR test if they can compare postural changes observed in the mirror with kinaesthetic and proprioceptive information. However, there is no doubt that there is much more to passing the MSR test than simply calculating contingencies.

Certainly, the cognitive prerequisites for passing the MSR test also include the infant's capacity to detect the perfect contingency relation between its body movements and the corresponding movements of its mirror image.[11] The perceived contingency between one's behaviour and the movement of the mirror image enables infants to determine the source of the image in the mirror (Lewis 1986); however, without the ability to represent this source of movement as oneself, contingency awareness alone would not enable children to pass the MSR test.

The aforementioned experiment by Nielsen, Suddendorf and Slaughter (2006) helps to clarify how the reaction in front of the mirror involves not only the calculation of contingencies but also the *sense of ownership*, that is, the ability to represent one's image as one's own. Returning to consider children who, between eighteen and twenty-four months, perfect the ability to recognize a mark placed on both forehead and leg, it is enough for them to be surreptitiously made to wear unfamiliar trousers for a clear dissociation of competencies to emerge: in the new condition they touch their forehead, but not their leg, which although moving contingently they have not recognized as their own. Significantly, it is sufficient to allow children to see the new clothing for 30 seconds for the two performances to become aligned again.

In addition to sensory-kinaesthetic matching, two additional prerequisites are required to pass the MSR test – that is, to understand that the mark one perceives on the mirror image of one's not-directly visible body parts is, in fact, on the corresponding part of one's body surface (Gergely 1994, 54–5). First, children must be able to construct a visual representation of how the typically unseen parts of their bodies appear. Second, upon detecting the mismatch between this visual representation and the corresponding image in the mirror, children must be able to re-establish the correspondence relation between the mirror and reality. They achieve this by modifying their self-representation and attributing the mismatching visual features (the mark) in the mirror image to the representation of their own body.

To fulfil these two prerequisites, infants' representational system must include both the ability to modify the primary representation of reality based on information coming from sources other than direct perception, for example, through conceptual inference, and the ability to represent reality in multiple models (see Gergely 1992; Leslie 1987; Meltzoff and Gopnik 1989; Perner 1991).

We can then assume that infants placed in front of the mirror have a primary model of reality that contains representations of external objects as well as a representation of the self. When confronted with a mirror, with experience children learn to map the visual information in the mirror onto their primary model of reality. However, this perfect correspondence relation breaks down when the visual features of the image of the non-visible parts of the body are mapped onto the representation of the corresponding object in space:

> The systematic correspondence between the primary model of reality and the mirror image can be salvaged only by attributing to the self-representation the mismatching visual features of the corresponding object in the mirror. This, however, can be done only inferentially, through analogy to other external objects: Because the spatial position and visual features of objects in the mirror image correspond perfectly to those of the objects in the primary representation of reality, and because the self is represented as one of these objects in space, therefore, just as other objects at other locations, the self must also be truthfully characterised by the visual features of the corresponding object in the mirror image. (Gergely 1994, 56)

That is to say, when infants notice the mismatch between their normal self-representation and the visual features of the corresponding object in the mirror, they attribute to themselves the unusual feature (the mark) by adding it to their self-representation; and this is supposed to explain why they reach up to touch or remove the mark that they have discovered in the mirror.

According to Perner (1991), the use of multiple models or 'secondary representations'[12] is a common factor that explains why other cognitive capacities develop at nearly the same time. Infants who pass mirror tests also show the first signs of empathic responses (Bischof-Köhler 2012), pretence and invisible displacement (Perner 1991; Gergely 1994), synchronic imitation (Asendorpf 2002) and personal pronoun use (Lewis 2014).

These changes in the second year may arise due to distinct developmental processes. Perner (1991) notes that such changes might emerge due to the maturation of a new cognitive architecture. However, he alternatively argues that secondary representations are present early in development but infants have to learn how to use them meaningfully. This latter explanation seems to be confirmed by Nielsen and Dissanayake's (2004) longitudinal study on the emergence of pretend play, mirror self-recognition, synchronic imitation and deferred imitation. Infants learn how to apply secondary representations in one developmental realm (e.g. synchronic imitation) but must then learn how to apply this knowledge in another (e.g. pretence). Thus, all secondary representational skills are not expressed at the precise same stage in development and learning how to apply secondary representations in one realm does not automatically mean that secondary representations can be applied in another.

3.2. Bodily awareness versus bodily self-awareness

One may wonder whether after all the picture sketched so far does not leave a margin to talk about pre-reflective self-consciousness. Infants under one year of age possess a pre-reflective object consciousness. Suppose then that this very young child sees a cat and is ipso facto conscious of it, even without knowing what a cat is, that is, without having any propositional knowledge of cats. Once this is recognized, it seems that one must also recognize the possibility of pre-reflective self-consciousness, since the latter is but a particular case of object-consciousness: the consciousness of that particular object we call 'self'. Therefore, at least in principle, there must be a pre-reflective self-consciousness in the sense of a non-conceptual experience of the self: infants experience themselves without knowing themselves, without having a self-concept. This is exactly the view proposed by Bermúdez (1998, 2018), who identifies the non-conceptual self-experience with the (objectual or transitive) consciousness of one's own body: 'bodily awareness is a basic form of self-consciousness, by virtue of which percipient agents are directly conscious of the corporeal self' (Bermúdez 2011, 157). He sees this view as a 'deflationary' account of mineness as opposed to the 'inflationary' view proposed by Gallagher and Zahavi (see earlier, note 33).

The discussion conducted in the previous section, however, invites us to raise doubts about this proposal. The representations involved in the precocious proprioceptive states referred to by Bermúdez are representations of single parts of the body, not of the body taken as a whole. And when an infant of, say, six or eight months perceives, for example, her hand, she perceives it *as an object among the others*, not as a *part* of her body. Indeed, to perceive it as a part of her body, she ought to possess the ability to represent her body as a whole, which is not the case – as seen, there are no empirical grounds to assume that infants under one year of age can construct a representation of the unity of their own body. Indeed, we have reason to think that, around one year of age, the young child is in the process of bringing together some parts of her body. Before then, her body can be made up of 'close' and 'domestic' objects; but these being part of the world, the kind of agentive and phenomenological relation between the infant and, for example, her thumb is similar to the relation between her and, say, her little, soft pillow, imbued with her smell.

But then could it not be said that a pre-reflective self-consciousness emerges when infants become able to represent their body as a whole? This statement, however, is still too strong since the self is not a simple object like any other. The notion of self involves, to say the least, the whole body of the organism *experienced as one's own body*. Indeed, the notion of self (or of self-consciousness) brings with itself an aspect of subjectivity that is missed in the objectual representation of one's own body. This is clear when infants become able to pass the mirror self-recognition test: mirror self-recognition involves being able to form a bodily image of oneself as an entire object and simultaneously taking this image as a subject, that is, as an active source of the representation of oneself. Here the subjects recognize a new kind of object of consciousness: the object is the subject itself, or better the objectified image of the subject – 'it is *me* there'. MSR onset indicates therefore the emergence of a new modality of cognition compared with the ability to build the image of any external object that is characteristic of animal consciousness in general, one that is unique to humans and only a few of the higher non-human primates.

At most, we could concede that it is possible to distinguish between an objective self (i.e. the whole body of the organism) and the subjective self; yet it is the latter that fits better the ordinary concept of self-consciousness. Referring to the organism as a 'self' is misleading to a certain extent, although the claim that the 'objective self' is a necessary condition for the development of a subjective self is certainly correct. But, to repeat, to ascribe a (subjective) self, the representation of the body as a whole must somehow make explicit that the represented body is one's own body, that is, children must be able of taking the representation of their body both as an object and a subject which is the source of the representation, and this is not the case before the age of (at least) eighteen months. Further developmental stages are required.

What we have just said is much in agreement with Musholt's (2015) claim that the possession of non-conceptual or implicit information about the self does not amount to possessing a form of self-consciousness. Indeed, she argues against Bermúdez that self-consciousness requires explicit representations of the self, whereas infants' perception and proprioception involve merely implicit self-information. As she puts it, Bermúdez conflates the notion of being related to the self with the notion of *referring* to the self. The latter, but not the former, is explicit. Let us elaborate on this point a little bit.

According to Musholt, bodily self-consciousness requires an explicit representation of one's own body. The opposition between explicit and implicit is equated to the distinction between knowing-how and knowing-that; and this, in turn, is the way she spells out the distinction between non-conceptual and conceptual. Therefore, Musholt's claim is eventually that (bodily) self-consciousness requires the *concept* of one's own body.

We are defending here a close position, namely that bodily self-consciousness requires the representation of one's own body *as one's own*; with the following difference, due to the different requirements that one can impose on the notion of concept. We conjecture that representing something *as a certain thing* does not necessarily involve knowing-that. There is a sense of 'seeing as' such that one can see a duck as a rabbit without believing that it is a rabbit. Since, according to a quite standard account of concepts, these are the constituents of the content of propositional attitudes,[13] representing something as a certain thing might not involve mastery of concepts, after all. To the extent that one takes 'pre-conceptual' to imply 'pre-reflective' (what seems to us reasonable), this position leaves room for the possibility that there is a sort of pre-reflective self-consciousness, which is a very basic form of bodily self-consciousness. It is worth pointing out, however, that there are no empirical grounds to assume that this form of self-consciousness is achieved approximately at eighteen months of age – presupposing, as we did earlier, that the mastery of the mirror self-recognition task is evidence for the ability to represent one's own body as one's own. Therefore, this view is different from both Gallagher's and Zahavi's and Bermúdez's ones. Pre-reflective self-consciousness turns out to be a developmental stage in the second half of the second year of life in which children can represent their own body as their own, and, at the same time, have not yet a (full-blown) concept of the bodily self.

Alternatively, it could be argued, in a slightly different way, that possessing a concept is not an all-or-none matter: the difference between non-conceptual and conceptual styles of representation is a question of degree. There is a 'grey region' between the clear cases of non-conceptual abilities and the clear cases of conceptual thought. In this case, it is hard to say whether bodily self-awareness requires mastery of concepts (specifically, mastery of the concept of one's own body) since taking one's own body as one's own seems to fall in the grey region. As a consequence, there is no definite answer to the question of whether there exists or not a form of pre-reflective self-consciousness. Much as in the previous view, our point is that (more or less) eighteen months-old children who recognize themselves in the mirror have a bodily self-awareness, whether or not they have a full-blown *concept* of their body.

Therefore, we are disposed to concede to Bermúdez that there might be some forms of pre-reflective self-consciousness (after all), but merely in the sense that it is hard to say whether the representation of one's own body as one's own is definitely conceptual. What, by contrast, we do *not* concede to him is the legitimacy of talking about bodily self-consciousness before the age of eighteen months (more or less), since before this age infants do not possess the relevant kind of representation. Thus, for instance, their ability to maintain balance and their feeling to lose it are not instances of (bodily) self-consciousness, because they lack the involvement of the representation of the whole body as their own body.

To recapitulate. We have explored two ways of defending the existence of pre-reflective self-consciousness – two partially different accounts of it. On the one hand, in the line of Gallagher and Zahavi, pre-reflective self-consciousness is a phenomenologically salient sense of mineness (arguably depending on very precocious bodily representations); on the other hand, according to Bermúdez's version, pre-reflective self-consciousness is the implicit, non-conceptual knowledge of self-specifying information carried by (precocious) proprioceptive states. We have seen that, in both cases, empirical evidence does not warrant the claim. At most, it might be conceded that there is a relatively short developmental stage in which children have bodily self-awareness but have not a full-blown concept of their bodily self.

4

The origins of affective self-awareness and self-regulation

We argued in the previous chapter that newborns, like infants at six months or one year of age, produce rich subjectivity, but, being immersed in it, cannot objectify it. That is, infants are active subjects in the sense of being functional centres organising action, but they cannot have themselves as active subjects. And when, for instance, infants' eyes are exploring the environment, they 'are', so to speak, their eyes, but certainly they do not 'have' their eyes – and neither, actually, do they have the slightest inkling of their existence.

This picture of the subjective world of the child under one year of age led us to the rejection of the thesis that since affordances, visual kinesthesis and bodily invariants all carry self-specifying information that is very early available to children, the latter often and usually do have an agentive, first-person experience of, say, their hand as their own – as the one they are actively moving, for example. In phenomenological terminology, this is the *body-as-subject* or the body-as-agent (the *Leib*), which is associated with body-schematic processes, in contrast to body image, the *body-as-object*, or the objective perception of one's body. Against the claim that a pre-reflective sense of ownership for one's body is available to the 0–1 year-old infant, then, we argued that before agents can have a sense of their body-as-subject (before they can sense that their whole body is moving as they crawl around or start to walk), they must have developed a body image for their whole body. They just do not have a sense that this hand is their hand until a point in development when they have a developed body image for their whole body. For infants to be able to experience their body (or body part) as their own body, they require a developed, objective bodily self-awareness which comes at around eighteen months with mirror self-recognition, when infants can form a body image of themselves as an entire object and associate this with themselves as a subject – the active source of the representation of themselves.

In this chapter, we begin to examine a more advanced phenomenon than bodily self-awareness, namely, *introspective reflexivity*. As noted at the beginning of the book, the modern definition of this concept is Locke's: persons as rationally and morally conscious and responsible individuals are such because they are capable of introspectively appropriating their actions, that is, representing and recognizing them as their own, thereby considering their meaning. But to do this, agents must be able to represent not only bodily actions, but also the intentions and affections that they produce within themselves, and therefore must be able to represent their inner world, objectifying the latter but at the same time making it their own. This is introspection: knowing that one is considering, objectively, the various aspects of one's subjectivity. The place of reflexivity is here no longer only the body as a *real* dimension, but the mind as an internal *virtual* dimension.

Like bodily self-awareness, the mind as an internal virtual dimension is the result of a process of construction. We begin here with the construction of an introspective consciousness of 'discrete' emotions, that is, emotion episodes designated by an individually separate and distinct category such as fear or anger. We will argue that there is no data to suggest that in the early stages of development, infants can introspectively access their own affective life; and we will point to the well-tuned relationship with significant others as the factor that promotes the path that, starting from a *core affect* phenomenology (an initially undifferentiated structure of valence and arousal dimensions), leads to the internalization of a repertoire of discrete emotions. This inaugurates a new dimension of subjectivity, which will gradually expand until it shapes subjects' entire mental life.

Thus, as well as what happens in the construction of bodily self-awareness, early interactions with the attachment figure play a decisive causal role in the establishment of the mind as an internal virtual dimension. It is the first dialogue without words, rich in emotions to negotiate with the caregiver, which allows infants to grasp their own affective experience, form separate categories of their affective states and form associations between these categories and their developing knowledge of the causal roles of emotions in other people's behaviour.

At the same time, in reconstructing the process of building introspection of discrete emotions, we will find that such introspective knowledge hinges on bodily self-awareness; the first form of psychological self-awareness is therefore made possible by the construction of a representation of the self that is both bodily and emotional.

1. Emotions: Bodily feelings and embodied appraisals

The scientific study of emotion begins with William James' answer to the question 'What is an emotion?' (the title of an essay that appeared in *Mind* in 1884 and later, in 1890, flowed into *Principles of Psychology*).

The starting point of James' theory of emotion is that upon introspective observation, emotions turn out to be 'a unique class of related experiential qualities that can occur in different intensities' (Reisenzein and Schmidt 2022, 237). To account for these intuitions about emotional experiences, James draws attention to the fact that the description of emotions suggested by introspective evidence precisely matches the phenomenological definition of sensations (e.g. of tone, colour or taste). Given the similarities between emotions and sensations, it seems natural to try to explain the phenomenal properties of emotions by assuming that they are analogous to sensations, or even *are* a group of sensations. This is the core idea of the sensory theory of emotion, often called the 'feeling theory' by philosophers.

James offers the classical version of this theory by arguing that emotional experiences are identical to bodily feelings, namely, sensations produced by the bodily changes evoked by emotional stimuli. Thus a bodily feeling is not 'a primary feeling, directly aroused by the exciting object or thought'; it is rather 'a secondary feeling indirectly aroused; the primary effect being the organic [muscular and visceral] changes in question, which are immediate reflexes following upon the presence of the object' (James 1894, 516). Defining emotion as a 'secondary' feeling caused by muscular and visceral changes is tantamount to reversing the commonsensical conception of the order of sequence of feelings and bodily changes:

> Our natural way of thinking about these standard emotions is that the mental perception of some fact excites the mental affection called the emotion, and that this latter state of mind gives rise to the bodily expression. My thesis on the contrary is that *the bodily changes follow directly the* PERCEPTION *of the exciting fact, and that our feeling of the same changes as they occur* is *the emotion*. (James 1884, 189–90; italics in the text)

Thus, bodily changes cause our feelings, and not vice versa as common sense would have it (James 1884, 194). So, for example, fear is the feeling resulting from the perception of autonomic bodily changes such as quickened heartbeats, shallow breathing, weakened limbs and visceral stirrings.

James' theory of bodily feelings would set the agenda for philosophical and scientific debate on emotions in the twentieth century, representing for better or worse the starting point in the process of building new theories. This is exemplified, in the bad, by the 'cognitive turn' of the 1960s, which used James' theory as a clear example of the inadequacy of the conception of emotions that prevailed at the time (Deigh 2014). For the good, it is illustrated by the fact that contemporary neo-Jamesians and psychological constructivists have both singled out James as a central predecessor, but they have found inspiration in different aspects of his work. As we shall see, neo-Jamesians like Antonio Damasio and Jesse Prinz have focused on the bodily side of James' theory, whereas psychological constructivists like James Russell and Lisa Feldman Barrett have focused on the constructivist side – that is, they have followed James in assuming that 'emotions are psychical compounds that are constructed out of more basic psychological ingredients that are not themselves specific to emotion' (Gendron and Barrett 2009, 317).

One of the strongest objections to James' theory is that it is unable to deal with a central explanandum for emotion theory: emotions are subject to norms of fittingness, namely, they can be appropriate or inappropriate, reasonable or unreasonable. For example, imagine someone who feels fear at the sight of a teddy bear: you would certainly criticize his fear by judging it as unreasonable. This criticism would consist of reprimanding that person for misrepresenting the object of fear as dangerous. But in James' feeling theory, there is no room for this kind of evaluation. If that emotion is a phenomenal state lacking an intentional object, the idea of misrepresentation cannot be formulated; if instead, the emotion *is about* bodily changes, intentionality is misplaced: the only misrepresentation that can be assumed concerns how the emotional feelings represent these bodily changes.

In the 1960s Anthony Kenny was the most prominent of several philosophers to argue that emotions are subject to normative standards of 'fit' to the world – they can be appropriate or inappropriate, reasonable or unreasonable. Kenny (1963) distinguishes two types of objects to clarify in what sense an emotion can represent an object correctly or incorrectly. The 'particular' object is any entity X in respect of which I can experience emotion; the 'formal' object, on the other hand, is the property I implicitly attribute to X insofar as I experience emotion in relation to X. An example: the particular object of fear is anything that an individual may fear (a vicious beast, war, falling down stairs, etc.), while its formal object is dangerousness, based on the assumption that one can only fear what one considers (perceives/judges/represents as) potentially dangerous.

Formal objects are 'values', in a neutral sense of the term including both positive and negative evaluative properties. They are often referred to as 'core relational themes', using the expression introduced by Lazarus (1991) to designate some relationships that the organism has with the environment that are important to its well-being – e.g. anger represents 'a demeaning offence against me and mine', fear represents 'an immediate, concrete and overwhelming physical danger', sadness represents the experience of 'an irrevocable loss', guilt represents the transgression of 'a moral imperative'.

For Kenny, the particular object and the formal object constitute the two main aspects of emotional intentionality: emotion is *object-directed* to the extent that it has a particular object, and it is *appropriate* to the extent that its particular object instantiates the formal object represented by the emotion. If – say – my anger represents an offence I received, my antagonist's offensive tone can be offered as a rational justification for my anger since an offensive tone instantiates the very property (the offence) that the anger represents. Or, to take up the example given earlier: it is inappropriate to be afraid of something that is not dangerous (like the teddy bear) because fear represents a thing as dangerous.

To recapitulate, if an emotional state is an intentional state, there are norms of fittingness under which the state is appropriate only in the case where its formal object is instantiated. But then – some philosophers and psychologists have argued from the early 1960s onwards – since sensation-like feelings are not the kind of things that can establish conceptual relations with formal objects, emotions must be (or imply) some kind of evaluation – a cognition, an interpretation, a judgement, a thought or some other kind of representation of the eliciting situation – that allows them to be included in this kind of relation.

This emphasis on the evaluative dimension of emotions has been declined in at least two different ways. The constitutive version (henceforth 'constitutive cognitivism') asserts that emotions *are* a particular type of evaluation; the causal version (from now on 'aetiological cognitivism') asserts that emotions are *caused* by a particular type of evaluation (see Scarantino 2016, 24).

The historical referent of constitutive cognitivism is Stoic psychology. Ancient Stoicism has a strongly intellectualistic character, being a radical development of Socratic intellectualism, polemic towards the Platonic theory of the tripartition of the soul. In this view, emotions are identified with a subform of belief: emotions are (occurrent, and usually conscious) evaluative beliefs, or evaluative judgements.[1] This identification has inspired the work of philosophers such as Jerome Neu, Martha Nussbaum and Robert Solomon.

Nussbaum offers her version of constitutive cognitivism in *Upheavals of Thought* (2001): the image of '*soulèvements géologiques de la pensée*' is taken from Proust; and Nussbaum's intent is to develop the Proustian image, arguing that several phenomena of our emotional life are well explained by a theory that has its antecedents in the ideas of the ancient Greek Stoics: 'this view holds that emotions are appraisals or value judgments, which ascribe to things and persons outside the person's own control great importance for that person's own flourishing' (2001, 4). Emotions are thus not 'non-reasoning movements', 'unthinking energies that simply push the person around, without being hooked up to the ways in which she perceives or thinks about the world' (24–5); rather they are beliefs that call into play 'Aristotelian' value judgements: when an individual experiences a positive emotion towards an object, there is not only the judgement that the object has value, but also the eudaimonistic judgement that the object is valuable to one's well-being.

Nussbaum's modified neo-Stoic cognitivism exhibits flexibility and an internal articulation which makes it very different from the more standard versions of constitutive cognitivism. However, the view that emotions are judgements creates a dilemma even for Nussbaum. Agents lacking verbal language cannot make judgements if a judgement is assent to representations with propositional content. This is the position of the Stoics; certainly of Chrysippus, for whom emotions involved 'the acceptance of *lekta*, proposition-like entities corresponding to the sentences in a language' (Nussbaum 2001, 91). But the problem generalizes to all versions of constitutive cognitivism. As seen, formal objects are often referred to as core relational themes; but if anger, for example, is the judgement that the agent has suffered a demeaning offence against me and mine, the content of the judgement involves sophisticated social and normative concepts. The intentionality of emotions is thus placed in tension with the plausible claim that adult human anger has something deeply in common with anger in frustrated infants or the anger of a dominant monkey towards a subordinate. Either these agents possess the concepts of demeaning and self, or they are not angry in the true sense of the word. Nussbaum tries to correct constitutive cognitivism on this point; however, to understand her proposal and the difficulties it faces, we must first say something about the aetiological version of cognitivism.

While philosophers had focused on the inability of James' theory to explain how emotions can be object-directed and normatively assessable, psychologists focused on its inability to account for how emotions are *caused*. Aetiological cognitivism is the claim that emotions are caused by a particular type of evaluation. It was pioneered by Magda Arnold and Richard Lazarus in the emerging cognitive psychology at about the time (the early 1960s) when constitutive cognitivism was taking hold in philosophy.

Arnold (1960) begins by noting that psychological emotion research since James has mainly focused on clarifying the causal relation between bodily changes and the experience of emotion; however, it has been mostly silent about 'the problem of how cold perception can cause either the felt emotion or the bodily upset' (1960, 93). To come to a solution to this problem, Arnold proposed the idea that 'to arouse an emotion, the object must be appraised as affecting me in some way, affecting me personally as an individual with my particular experience and my particular aims' (171).

Arnold coined the term 'appraisal' to designate this evaluation process. The process mediates (or, as Lazarus would later say, 'actively negotiates') between, on the one hand, the demands, constraints and resources of the environment and, on the other hand, the individual's hierarchy of goals and beliefs. This allows one to continually assess the significance of what is happening for one's well-being.

In a way that again is reminiscent of the Stoics, Arnold thought that appraisals comprise several dimensions. Thus, she moved from a 'molar' conception of emotional appraisal as a unitary mental state to a 'molecular' analysis, in which appraisal is decomposed into some individually investigable components (Smith and Lazarus 1990, 617). Arnold's molecular analysis brought to light three dichotomous dimensions of judgement designed to determine whether the eliciting circumstances are beneficial or harmful, present or absent, and easy to attain or to avoid. An example: the cognitive cause of fear is the appraisal of an event as harmful, absent but possible in the future, and difficult to avoid.

However, it soon became clear that the three dimensions postulated by Arnold were not sufficient to distinguish emotions from each other. Take, for example, anger and disgust: both are about things that are harmful, present and difficult to avoid. Hence the proposal of other (and alternative) dimensions of appraisal by Lazarus (1991) and Scherer (2009). With these authors, we move more and more sharply from a personal to a subpersonal level: emotions are no longer judgements about the significance of a situation for a person; they are states of mind that are identified in behavioural, neurological or neurocomputational terms, and their aetiology is analysed as a causal process rather than an inferential one.

We are now in a position to discuss Nussbaum's attempt to amend constitutive cognitivism on the matter of emotions in animals and pre-linguistic humans. Nussbaum clarifies that Lazarus' theory of appraisal is 'in all essential respects' the conception of emotions defended in *Upheavals of Thought* (2001, 109). After that, she makes use of something like a multilevel appraisal to correct classical Stoicism that makes room for animal and infant emotions: the propositions which are the intentional objects of a judgement can be 'preverbal', so as to be attributable to pre-linguistic humans and animals. Nonetheless, emotion remains primarily an intentional phenomenon. Despite the existence of low-level appraisal that cannot be expressed in language, 'emotions include in their content judgments that can be true or false, and good or bad guides to ethical choice' (1).

However, if we examine how the notion of low-level appraisal is theorized in the psychological sciences, it becomes difficult to consider it reconcilable with Nussbaum's constitutive cognitivism. Consider Robert Zajonc's affective primacy thesis. 'Affective primacy' means that emotional responses are independent of the rational evaluations we make of things; that we can be afraid of things that we know are not dangerous and angry about things we firmly believe to be just (cases of 'recalcitrance to reasons' in D'Arms and Jacobson 2003). One explanation for this phenomenon is, precisely, to postulate a low-level appraisal, which would occur when our emotional responses are independent of – or conflict with – appraisals that guide action, and which are explicit and verbally reportable. Zajonc (1980) provided evidence supportive of the psychological reality of this type of low-level appraisal by showing that subjects can form preferences for stimuli to which they have been exposed subliminally so that their ability to identify those stimuli remains at chance levels. Subsequently, many experimental results (e.g. Öhman 1986; Öhman and Soares 1994) confirmed Zajonc's work, going beyond simple 'like/dislike' preferences and demonstrating the existence of real unconscious emotions (Winkielman 2010).

These experimental dissociations between cognition and emotion therefore effectively reveal the existence of separable, low-level processes that are capable of triggering what we will shortly refer to as 'an affect program response' (see Section 3). The construct of multilevel appraisal, however, raises a major difficulty for Nussbaum: the representational states involved in low-level appraisals are very different from those involved in high-level appraisals. Millikan (1984) suggested that primitive mental representations of elementary organisms may unite the functions of beliefs and desires in a single undifferentiated functional role; well, low-level evaluation in human cognition manifests the same 'collapse of attitudes'. Thus it is simply misleading to describe appraisal processes as judgement-like (let alone conscious); indeed, it is what characterizes a multi-level theory of appraisal – as Nussbaum's would like to be – to assume that various mechanisms can underlie it and that they can operate on a wide range the body. Prinz incorporates a plausible account of the intentionality of emotions into James' theory of bodily feelings, whereby emotions are seen as involving valenced representations of core relational themes via registrations of bodily states. This allows the theory to take a step beyond the contributions that emotions make to the organism's internal, psychological economy and to accord role to the environment: core relational themes are features of our natural – what interests us most here – social environments that relate to or bear certain typical aspects of our well-being. This is an important point since social interaction will play a pivotal role in the next pages: the emotion-eliciting situations that we will soon consider are microsocial situations; situations in which emotions arise, evolve and subside in the course of actual communicative exchanges (Hinde 1985), sometimes only imagined but hardly ever absent.[2]

Thanks to Prinz's theoretical elaboration of James' seminal perspective, we are well-equipped to tackle the investigation to which the following pages are devoted. We will begin with the theoretical model that in our opinion, best accounts for the ontogenetic formation of the introspective space relating to emotional states: the social biofeedback model. As we shall see, this model gives ample space to the body and its introspective space; the concept of appraisal, in its perceptual form accessible to infants as young as a few months old, will also play a role in our subsequent conceptions aimed at analysing the theories of emotions on which the social biofeedback model is based: emotional constructivism and emotion theory.

A socio-constructivist model of emotional introspection

The social biofeedback theory of parental emotional mirroring (henceforth only 'social biofeedback theory') is the core of a socio-constructivist model of emotional introspection (Gergely and Watson 1996, 1999; Gergely 2002, 2007; Fonagy et al. 2002; Gergely and Unoka 2008a, 2008b; Gergely, Koós and Unoka 2010). It is elaborated within the broader ethological and evolutionary framework characteristic of the contextualistic and systemic orientation of attachment theory; the starting point is therefore the caregiver–child dyad and its bidirectional and reciprocal exchanges, such that each element can both influence and be influenced by the other. The social biofeedback model, which applies contingency detection theory (see Chapter 3, Section 1) to the interpersonal domain, reveals further, previously undisclosed functions of parental affect-mirroring in early infancy.

of representations: conceptual and/or propositional vers
embodied; symbolic versus subsymbolic; locationist vers
et al. 2013).

Against this background of the debate, Jesse Prinz's (200
appraisal is extremely interesting as an attempt at a synth
approach and feeling theory. Following in the footsteps of I
neuroscientific version of James' theory, Prinz suggests tha
a dedicated system within the somatosensory system. T
reactions', that is, perceptions of bodily changes, either at
and musculoskeletal levels or in the form of changes in th
areas. To defend this view, Prinz argues that emotions ar
the traditional sense of philosophical emotion theory: tl
nor do they essentially involve propositional representat
cognitive in Prinz's preferred sense of the term: they a
organismic control by executive systems in the brain.
are not cognitive in either of these senses, Prinz concl
representations. More specifically, they are representat
core relational themes as proposed by Lazarus. Thus, alt
propositional representations, their content is assumed to
by the propositional descriptions with which we are fa
content of anger is that a demeaning offence to me or m
To assign such complex intentional contents to gut rea
form of teleosemantics, which is the view that the cont
state is the state of affairs that is the function of that rep
Dretske 1988; Millikan 1989; Rupert 2018; Shea 2018).

Now, according to the neo-Lockean conception ela
the vehicles of representation are always perceptual in
to represent the whole range of topics about which v
thoughts. Gut reactions are therefore perceptual images
their representational content derives from their broa
core relational themes. It is the function of fear to de
the body so as to detect dangerous situations. Fear i
acceleration of the heartbeat (its 'nominal content'), b
a dangerous situation (its formal object/core relation
virtue of its representing dangerous situations – and
them – that the emotion of fear has been selected.

Prinz's theory of embodied appraisal provides a corr
approach, with its exclusive emphasis on the percep

The expression 'social biofeedback' aims at recalling the terminology employed in the physiological domain to denote what happens when someone is made sensitive to the variation of an internal parameter (e.g. blood pressure) through the continuous exposure to a monitoring system that connected to a pressure detector makes externally perceptible what happens internally. Transposed to the social domain and contextualized in parental affect-mirroring, the biofeedback process would ultimately lead children to become sensitive to their internal states through the monitoring of external indices manifested during the interaction.

Social biofeedback theory is directly opposed to the rich mentalistic interpretation of early caregiver-infant interactions which Gergely (2002) calls 'the strong inter-subjectivist position'. According to strong intersubjectivists, in interactive contexts infants manifest their innate ability to (1) attribute mental states, such as intentions and feelings, to others; (2) introspect a broad set of differentiated mental states, such as emotions, intentions and goals, and (3) recognize their mental states as being similar to corresponding mental states of the other, thus experiencing a feeling of 'mutually sharing'. For example, Trevarthen (1979) made the hypothesis that the richly structured early affective exchanges between mothers and infants imply what he calls 'primary intersubjectivity'. In light of the data contained in the earlier study by Murray and Trevarthen (1985; see Chapter 3, Section 1), Trevarthen (1993) makes the hypothesis that infants are born with a 'dialogic mind', an innate sense of 'the virtual other', and can interpret the other's effectively attuned interactions in terms of the same wide set of underlying motives, feelings, intentions and goals they use in interpreting themselves.

In a more overtly cognitivist context, Meltzoff and his colleagues hypothesize a specific innate mechanism underlying intersubjective attributions during early imitative interactions. The affective/intentional behavioural acts of the other are mapped onto infants' supramodal body scheme that allows them to recognize the other person as 'just-like-me' (Meltzoff 2013). By imitating such acts, infants generate the corresponding subjective intentional and/or feeling states in themselves. These are then introspectively accessed and attributed to the other by inference.

The assumption that infants' starting point is characterized by direct introspective access to internal primary emotion states can be traced back to a tradition in developmental psychology holding the view that infants are initially more sensitive to internal than external stimuli. Against this idea, the social biofeedback theory suggests that at the beginning of life infants' *perceptual system is set with a bias to attend to and explore the external world and builds representations primarily on the basis of exteroceptive stimuli*' (Gergely, Koós and Watson 2010: 145; italics in the text). According to this proposal, the dispositional content of discrete emotions is learnt first by observing the affect-expressive displays of others and then associating them with the eliciting situations and behavioural outcomes that accompany these emotion expressions.

And indeed, consistent with this, numerous studies show that very young infants can discriminate and respond consistently to facial, bodily and vocal manifestations of specific primary emotions (for a review, see Grossmann and Johnson 2007) – let's call it a *third-person competence*. Conversely, there is no evidence that the set of internal (visceral as well as proprioceptive) cues that are activated when being in and expressing a dispositional emotion state (e.g. fear) are, at first, detected or perceived consciously by the infant or, at least, grouped categorically in such a manner that they could be perceptually accessed by introspective monitoring as a distinctive dispositional emotion state that has been induced in oneself in the given context. More likely, very young infants' awareness only occurs as part of an experiential field that is differentiated by interoceptive sensing along the dimensions of high/low arousal and negative/positive valence (Gergely and Unoka 2008b, 62). In the transition from such valenced feelings with some degree of arousal to the subjective awareness of discrete emotion states – the transition, for example, from just experiencing some undifferentiated negative state of tension to the awareness of being angry – an essential role is played by protoconversational interactions, which create the microsocial context in which social-biofeedback takes place.

2.1. Social biofeedback theory

The most common context of dyadic, affective relationships involving children and their caregivers are turn-taking protoconversational interactions. The two partners actively interact, reciprocally exchanging information during non-linguistic (or, later, only partially linguistic) 'conversations' made up of imitations (but also of episodes of subtle desynchronization), improvisations, search for eye-to-eye contact and sensitivity to those features of actions that Daniel Stern has called 'forms of vitality' (see later, Section 4).

During protoconversational turn-taking, infants' contingency detector readily registers the highly contingent relations between the internal cues (i.e. changes in physiological states and proprioceptive stimuli) corresponding to their yet unrecognized affective states[3] and caregivers' affect-mirroring displays. (Recall that the degree of contingency is calculated based on different heterogeneous indices, such as the temporal relationship between two events, affective intensity and structural similarity.)

As illustrated earlier (Chapter 3, Section 1), at around three months of age infants begin to prefer less than perfect degrees of contingency, which are typically related to interpersonal contexts and, specifically, to protoconversations. This may help explain how, beyond simple proximity to well-tuned primary caregivers, protoconversations provide an ideal *milieu* for generating and maintaining well-being. Not less importantly, such cooperative, well-attuned contexts may provide 'the experiential basis for the establishment of a sense of self as self-regulating agent' (Gergely and Watson 1999, 114). That is to say, the perception of causal control over caregivers' behaviour contributes to increasing the sense of efficacy.

Protoconversational contexts, together with the affect-mirroring that characterizes them so profoundly, can also be crucial for the process we are specifically concerned with, the construction of emotional introspection:

> It is the experience of one's current internal states being externally 'mirrored' or 'reflected' back through the infant-attuned contingent social reactions of the attachment environment that makes it possible to develop a subjective sense and awareness of one's primary affective self-states. (Gergely 2007, 60)

To understand the constructive process by which children gradually come to represent the affective states they are experiencing as their own emotions, we have to pay attention to something that might at first glance appear strange: in well-tuned pairs, adults are spontaneously inclined to mirror children's emotional expressions *markedly*.

An action is marked if it is somehow differentiated from its realistic expression and transformed in a perceptually salient way (e.g. exaggerated, slowed down, schematic or only partially performed). In the case of affective mirroring, marking consists of subtly transformed (and thus less contingent) versions of children's emotional expressions. It involves exaggerated (even emphatic), slowed-down executions of the children's original expression – similar to the marked 'as if' behaviour that is characteristically produced in pretend play. On other occasions, caregivers' marked responses are schematic, abbreviated or only partial; or again, the mirroring of the original emotion is mixed with simultaneous or rapidly alternating components of other emotion displays. Think, for example, of a caregiver who responds to a crying child with an expression that, although initially very sad (as expected by a perfect mirroring), turns rapidly to a subtle smile; or think of the same adult who responds to a happy child with an expression mixing joy (i.e. the original child's expression), tenderness and possibly surprise. Indeed, as remarked by Gergely and Watson, when 'we look at the structural relation between the stimulus features of the parent's mirroring expression and those of the infant's state-expressive behaviour, it becomes clear that the term "mirroring" is a seriously misleading one' (1999, 113). (As far as we are concerned, we will continue to use the term, aware that healthy mirroring is always imperfect and marked.)

On their part infants, who still lack an introspective self-awareness of their discrete emotional states, never stop automatically computing the (suboptimal and therefore particularly appreciated) contingency degree between parental affect-mirroring displays and the still undefined, procedural affective states they can detect in themselves.

The process of marked affect-mirroring, with its typical and spontaneous trends on both sides of the dyad, achieves two important outcomes.

First, marked affect-mirroring reinforces the regulatory power of protoconversational contexts, specifically in particular situations. A caregiver who responds to a very sad child not by displaying inconsolable sadness (as would be the case with non-marked mirroring), but by inserting marked signals such as attestations of empathic participation, small grimaces and openly serene expressions, will probably succeed in avoiding an escalation of discomfort in a child still lacking effective tools for affective self-regulation. Through this mode of communication, caregivers indicate a possible 'way out' of infants' confused but no less intense discomfort; an opportunity to find consolation. At the opposite extreme, marked responses to expressions of intense joy tend to mitigate an otherwise probable escalation towards states of excessive arousal, equally – though for opposite reasons – deflagrating.

At the same time, marked expressions have a second crucial function: a 'teaching' function. When adults respond markedly to infants' expressions, they signal that the emotions they are displaying are 'not for real'. On their part, infants repeatedly experience caregivers' behaviour both in its realistic and in its marked form, day after day, and have the occasion to represent the two forms as qualitative variants, each one with peculiar features. Such a kind of situation encourages them to 'decouple' the perceived emotions (i.e. the emotion manifested in caregivers' face and body) from their referents: most natural referential links are suspended, and caregivers' marked expressions are represented as 'not being about' their (i.e. that of caregivers) ongoing emotional state. Adult marked expressions, however, remain similar enough to the 'normative' expressions of caregivers to suggest to children that there is something relevant to think about. Specifically, this situation prompts them to take the next step: the search for the true referent. Once decoupled, in fact, adult affect-mirroring displays still need to be interpreted as referring to 'someone's emotion'. A particular role in this step is played by the adult's gaze: ostensively and continuously directed to the infants, it induces them to '*referentially anchor* the marked mirroring stimulus as expressing their *own* self-state' (Gergely and Watson 1996, 1199; italics in the text).

Gergely and Watson suggest that such a process of referential anchoring is determined by the high degree of contingency between caregivers' affect-mirroring displays and infants' emotion-expressive behaviour: based on the degree of contingency they perceive, infants come to anchor adults' marked mirroring stimulus as an expression of their own state.

To credit infants with a verbal competence they have not yet matured, we can redescribe the entire process by imagining them asking themselves questions like these: 'Why does daddy behave like that?'; 'Whose emotions are painted on daddy's face, on his body and in his behaviour?'. The fact that adults address their gaze, words and gestures to infants with emphasis and continuity, witnessing affectionate attention to them in a variety of ways, helps infants to referentially anchor the marked mirroring stimulus as an expression of their self-state: 'Those emotions are mine!' To return to technical terminology: based on decoupling and referential anchoring,[4] the social biofeedback process has led to emotional self-awareness.

The result of biofeedback in the social domain, thus, is nothing less than the phenomenology of one's basic emotion states. In an interpersonal context characterized by a primarily third-person interpretive competence, infants finally succeed in giving a form to their confused feelings. Infants' representations of the caregiver's affect-mirroring displays become associated with their primary, nonconscious and procedural basic emotional automatisms; thus, children form cognitively accessible second-order representations (or metarepresentations) that are about those emotional automatisms[5] and provide the basis for their emerging ability of affective self-control. Knowing what exactly one feels is not sufficient, but it is certainly a necessary condition for analysing oneself in one's relationships with others, inhibiting immediate responses and allowing oneself the time to identify the best action in a given context.

Of course, however, everything can work at its best only if the relationship is well-tuned. When, as not infrequently happens in insecure forms of attachment, some disorder of communication comes to disturb the dyad, the whole process becomes much less effective, and consequently, access to self-knowledge becomes more difficult to achieve. In particular, one can easily understand how disturbing is the repeated absence of marking typical of caregivers who, in the grip of their suffering, are unable to stay in the relationship and become infected by the state of their children or show absence, disinterest. In the first place, the work of emotional hetero-regulation is disturbed and infants remain abandoned to themselves. Moreover, being unable to notice anything strange, infants have no reason to look for another more likely referent of adults' expression and therefore have no way to activate the process of biofeedback that would slowly lead them to perfect their introspective capacity. Consequently, in many situations children will run the risk of attributing to others the mental states that they cannot recognize in themselves, in a process that Winnicott (2005) has effectively described through the image of the *alien self*.

An interesting hypothesis about the causal origins of disorganized attachment styles is the *flickering switch* hypothesis proposed by Gergely, Koós and Watson (2010). Both parental maltreatment and unresolved loss and trauma, which are highly statistically correlated with disorganized attachments (Carlson 1998; Liotti 1992), could be causally related to a 'deviant contingency environment' to which infants are exposed, particularly during the critical period of the contingency detector's resetting taking place soon after the three months of age. In such dysfunctional relational contexts, the mechanism devoted to the analysis of contingencies continuously flickers between situations of high contingency degrees and sudden drops of contingency (when the caregiver is in some acute suffering state or becomes abusive). This continuous, chaotic flickering generates experiences of significant loss of control power in infants, as their very same responses to the caregiver trigger different kinds of reactions. To defend themselves from painful feelings of helplessness and anxiety, children may then react by triggering a strategy based on 'switching back' the contingency detector to its original preference for perfect contingencies. This reaction has the palliative advantage of providing some temporary relief (e.g. through the adoption of repetitive, stereotypic body movements); nevertheless, not only hinders the development of emotional introspection but even promotes the progressive development of a dissociative organization.

2.2. Social biofeedback as natural pedagogy?

The marking that characterizes protoconversational contexts is the signal that suggests that 'here is something important to learn'. Csibra and Gergely (2009; Gergely and Csibra 2013) trace the dual propensity of parents to teach and children to learn back to the activation of a specialized system – natural pedagogy, precisely – selected in humans for its usefulness in facilitating the transmission, reception and sharing of theoretical and practical knowledge, encouraging epistemic trust in the truth and actual relevance of a certain piece of information (Sperber et al. 2010).

According to Gergely and Csibra, a natural pedagogical relationship establishes a kind of two-way game in which each player has a role to play. On their part, adults are spontaneously led to signal to children that there is something interesting and useful to learn – for example, by accentuating gestures and prosody, or by exaggeratingly opening their eyes and looking into the eyes of their young interlocutors; these ostensive signals are followed by actions, such as the gesture of pointing or the emphatic gaze shift towards some nearby object, that help children to orient attention and find the appropriate referent, that is, what the (not necessarily verbal) information that adults are conveying refers to. In turn, from the very first months of life, learners spontaneously develop the ability to read the signals that help them grow by taking advantage of the culture in which they are immersed and understand, for example, that if daddy looks at them with a smile and then turns his ever-smiling gaze towards a nearby puppy dog (perhaps saying 'Look what a nice puppy'), then he probably wants to communicate something about that nearby object, and in particular wants to convey trust in the meekness of that dog (as well as teach them a new word, 'puppy'). The authors make the further hypothesis that natural pedagogy induces in learners the double assumptions of generalization and universality. The first assumption states that what is learnt about something (an object, a fact) generally applies to all tokens of that kind; the second assumes that the information learnt becomes shared knowledge.

Gergely and Unoka (2008a, 2008b) have suggested subsuming social biofeedback theory under the model of natural pedagogy, as a special case of functioning in which marking plays the role of those ostensive signals that precede the transmission of information. In developing a more refined analysis, Gergely and Király (2019) observed that caregivers' responses often are marked by precisely those ostensive-communicative signals, such as direct eye contact, referential gaze direction, eyebrow flashing, slightly tilted head or exaggeratedly open eyes, that typically characterize teaching contexts. According to them, marked emotional displays are pedagogical signals designed to spontaneously teach infants that the emotional states they are expressing (and which they perceive in an altered form in their adult partner) belong to a set of categorical emotions socially shared by members of the cultural community they are part of. As is typically the case in pedagogical contexts, what children learn about the role of emotions in their society, together with the set of behavioural dispositions that connote them, is generalized and universalized. Yet, emotional protoconversation serves the second, 'private' function of sensitizing children to their emotional experiences and identifying what was only a generic experience of core affect as a specific, categorical experience of a certain emotion.

Bringing social biofeedback back to natural pedagogy is a very interesting hypothesis (but see Loria 2020, for a radical critique). Concerning the first function of marking, that is, that of 'cultural teaching', the authors' analysis does indeed stress aspects that bring social biofeedback closer to naive pedagogy as originally described by Gergely and Csibra, although shifting it – most interestingly – towards a less exclusively cognitive dimension. Still, we are inclined to see some differences whose effective relevance should deserve further investigation. For example, in the emotional domain, and specifically when protoconversational contexts are involved, the dimension of negotiation becomes primary in comparison to the more assertive, so to speak 'directive' context which is typical of adult teaching.

Turning then to the second alleged function of marked affective mirroring – the creation of a mature discriminative awareness of one's emotional experiences – an analysis in terms of 'traditional' natural pedagogy risks generating deeper issues. The authors' theoretical move is interesting and admirable: attempting to bring together under a single description two phenomena that have aspects in common. However, in this case, contrary to what is usually the case in pedagogical contexts, it is the *absence* of universality and generalization that is a distinguishing feature. Moreover, the emotional protoconversational context lacks the overtly triadic (adult-child-external object) context of 'traditional' natural pedagogy; on the contrary, here the object is the most private thing, fully inaccessible to others: our private *quale* – what it is like to feel a certain emotion.

3. Basic emotions as evolved affect programs

Having presented the main features of the social biofeedback theory, we turn to consider this approach in the light of the philosophical and psychological debate on the nature of emotions which we started discussing in the first section.

Although recent publications have presented the point as a more open issue and adopted a more agnostic attitude (Gergely and Király 2019), the social biofeedback theory accounts for third-person emotional competence of very young children basically in terms of *basic emotions programs*:

With regard to an infant, the *constitutional self* [. . .] designates a complex prewired affective structural organization. In other words, it is characterised by genetically-based individual differences in temperamental traits [...] and it also contains innate specifications of the core physiological and motor components of a number of basic emotion programs [...]. (Gergely and Unoka 2008a, 59)

The authors' reference to basic emotions requires careful examination. In the first section we examined two of 'the three ideas that have historically constituted the primary attractors in the project of defining emotions', namely, the idea that emotions are *feelings* and the idea that emotions are *evaluations* (Scarantino 2016, 4). The third idea is that emotions are *motivations*, and the Basic Emotion Theory (BET) is an influential evolutionary variant of the motivational tradition in affective science.

In the 1970s, Silvan Tomkins' pioneering work, which hinged on the idea that 'the primary motivational system is the affective system' (Tomkins 2008, 4), gave rise to two interconnected developments. The first is the birth of the BET, precisely, which gave full development to Darwin's (1872/1998) experimental work on facial expressions of emotion. Ignored by behaviourist psychology, Darwin's work was rediscovered by classical ethology, and continued by Paul Ekman and Carroll Izard (both Tomkins' students). These researchers abandoned the hydraulic metaphors that classical ethologists had used to describe psychological processes – the best-known being Konrad Lorenz's famous drive-discharge or 'hydraulic' model of instinctual motivation. Already under attack since the 1920s, the idea of instinct as a definite quantity of energy that 'discharges itself' waned in the 1950s on both the biological front, owing to the British school of ethology's study of behaviour in terms of signals (see Griffiths 2007), and the experimental front, in relation first to the development of studies on the mechanisms of learning, and subsequently to the appearance on the scene of information theory (with cybernetics and systems theories, and later with computer science). Since the 1960s, with the rise of cognitivism, psychological functions have been defined in terms of information.

The second development was the application of evolutionary psychology to emotions. Evolutionary psychologists aimed to integrate neo-Darwinism with computational and modularistic psychology. So, it is true – as sociobiologists had argued in the 1970s – that genes influence behaviour, but this occurs only through the construction of brains populated by a plurality of *modules*, which are conceived as information-processing systems characterized by domain specificity (see Chapter 2, Section 3.1) and the possession of proprietary algorithms. These modules are adaptations, that is, algorithms forged by natural selection to solve problems posed to our ancestors by the physical and social environment of the Pleistocene (the period between 2.5 million and 10,000 years ago from which our direct ancestors emerged). The task of the evolutionary psychologist is therefore to formulate and test hypotheses concerning 'Darwinian algorithms' (see Griffiths 2007).

Since the 1990s, the BET has merged with the evolutionary psychology of emotions. So, when Ekman states that basic emotions have evolved because of their adaptive value in coping with basic life tasks, he draws from a list compiled by evolutionary psychologists: 'fighting, falling in love, escaping predators, coping with sexual infidelity, experiencing a loss of status due to failure, reacting to the death of a family member' (Tooby and Cosmides 2008, 117).

Within this cognitive-evolutionary framework, basic emotions are *evolved affect programs*, namely, complex, coordinated and automated reactions to environmental events, intimately related to survival-critical functions. These reactions are complex because they involve two major structural components: (1) a specific pattern of physiological arousal responses (e.g. changes in the endocrine system, activation of the autonomic nervous system); (2) prewired emotion-specific motor routines which consist of two types of fixed behavioural automatisms: (a) stereotypic action tendencies (approach/avoidance, fight/flight, etc.) and (b) emotion-expressive facial-vocal displays and bodily postures. These reactions are coordinated because these elements recur in recognizable patterns or sequences, and they are automated because they are activated outside of conscious control.

This array of fast and mandatory physiological and behavioural reactions is triggered by information coming from an extremely limited range of perceptual inputs and – as already said – is coordinated by a computational subsystem (a module) that draws on a limited database and works independently of more conceptual processes, such those underlying action planning. In emergency conditions, facing environmental threats to survival, the modular architecture permits the affect programs to work as fail-safe systems that seize behaviours when having little time, the agent must generate adequate coping responses immediately, even at the price of trusting quick and dirty information. Correspondingly, in certain situations we cannot avoid perceiving basic emotional expressions in others, effectively and quickly, exposing ourselves to the typical false positive errors that are the price to pay for the advantage of having selected mechanisms to save our skin and of which there are traces even in phylogenetically distant animals.

We have therefore a limited number of innate, hard-wired affect programs, the input side of which must, however, be distinguished from the output side. The output consists of a specific sequence of pancultural somatic changes. The triggering stimuli, on the other hand, show individual variability – for example, the sight of a spider may trigger the fear program in some individuals but not in others. It is precisely to account for such individual variability that Ekman postulated an 'automatic appraisal mechanism', a specialized neurocomputational system that applies its own distinctive rules for evaluating stimuli to a limited set of data derived from the early stages of perceptual information processing.[6]

This hypothesis of an automatic appraisal mechanism has obvious similarities to that formulated by Zajonc of the existence of direct pathways from the perceptual system to the limbic areas involved in emotional responses. The latter hypothesis seemed to receive a confirmation by the mapping of the neural pathways underlying fear conditioning carried out by LeDoux (1996), which is a neurobiological theory of multilevel appraisal (see Teasdale 1999). According to his *dual pathway model*, stimulus information elicits many aspects of the emotional response through a 'low', fast pathway that activates subcortical structures, among which the amygdala is particularly important; a 'high', slower, pathway activates cortical structures and is essential for responses to the same stimulus that are longer-term, planned and often accompanied by conscious awareness.[7] Against this background, at least for certain basic emotions, the idea that emotions require one appraisal of the stimulus must be replaced by the idea that emotions require two appraisals, which may conflict with each other and have complementary but independent cognitive functions.

The classic source of evidence for BET, however, is cross-cultural research on facial expressions. Using as stimuli photographs corresponding to six emotions (fear, anger, surprise, sadness, joy, disgust/contempt) that appeared in Tomkins' list of basic affects, Ekman, Sorenson and Friesen (1969) and Ekman and Friesen (1971) attested that a range of Western facial expressions of emotion could be reliably classified by members of an isolated, non-Western culture, and vice versa. Around the same time, ethologists showed the early appearance of some of these expressions in human infants (Eibl-Eibesfeldt 1973), and primatologists reaffirmed Darwin's postulated homology between human and non-human primate facial expressions (Chevalier-Skolnikoff 1973).

Ekman's studies, along with those carried out in parallel by Carroll Izard, inspired dozens of similar studies hinging on emotion recognition from a photograph of facial movement. Elfenbein and Ambady (2002) conducted a meta-analysis on emotion recognition, taking into account 87 articles, totalling

97 studies, involving the responses of more than 22,148 participants from 42 different countries. Some of these studies required the decoding of emotions from short video clips or voice; but the majority (66 out of 97 studies) used the same method as Ekman and Izard: showing photographs of facial expressions and asking participants to associate them with a specific emotion. This huge sample essentially confirms the results of Ekman, Sorenson and Friesen's first study: emotions conveyed through photographs of facial expressions (*as well as other communication channels*) are recognized with a significantly higher level of accuracy than mere chance.[8]

3.1. Pluralism in the theory of emotions

The mandatory, fast and passive character of affect programs makes them good candidates for instantiating basic folk emotion concepts. However, folk psychology also recognizes other types of emotions which are much more cognitively complex than basic emotions. These are the complex emotional episodes that figure in folk-psychological narratives about mental life; episodes involving, for example, self-conscious emotions such as embarrassment, pride, shame and guilt. Contrary to what some researchers have claimed (e.g. Tooby and Cosmides*et al* 1990), there are good reasons to hold that such complex emotions rest on psychological mechanisms that are different from affect programs (see Griffiths 1997). The latter possess some salient features that complex emotions lack, and vice versa. On the input side, complex emotions are sensitive to a much wider range of information than the encapsulated affect programs. Thus, they cannot be automatically triggered as one would predict by assimilating them to affect programs. Moreover, on the output side, complex emotions are responses that fail to display stereotypical physiological effects, persist longer and are much more integrated with cognitive activities such as long-term planning.

The general category of emotion subsumes a third kind of psychological state: socially constituted patterns of acting out that are characterized as 'disclaimed action emotions'. A disclaimed action emotion is 'a transitory social role' that is 'interpreted as a passion rather than as an action' (Averill 1980, 312). These social roles are transitory because individuals play them exclusively in short-lived and stressful situations. Social roles allow behaviours that would be unacceptable in other circumstances – in these cases, the passive character ordinarily ascribed to strong emotions and sudden passions (love or aggressive) is exploited to avoid responsibility for the action. Moreover, such roles are 'covert' in the sense that they take shape only insofar as society recognizes neither their function nor the social practices which include them. Culture-bound syndromes such as running amok or 'wild man' syndrome are cases of disclaimed actions modelled on emotion. Thus, disclaimed action emotions differ from basic and complex emotions not only because they are culturally local but also by their psychological mechanisms: they are unconscious attempts to take advantage of the special status usually accorded to emotions because of their passivity. This means that their aetiology involves the mechanisms that subserve social cognition rather than the perceptual mechanisms underlying basic emotions or the conceptual mechanisms that subserve complex emotions (Griffiths 1997, 245).

Up to this point, the result is that the folk concept of emotion is a cluster concept, which does not pick out a natural kind that can be used to ground inductions or projections across the range of emotions (Griffiths 1997, 2004). The collection of features that characterize emotions are explained by various causal mechanisms in different cases. Basic emotions are psychological states involving isolated modules; complex emotions are special adaptations of higher-level cognition. Building a theoretical category based on the similarities between these two classes of mental phenomena would not be justified by any promising explanatory project. As to the disclaimed action emotions, they are manifestations of higher cognitive activity, namely the understanding and manipulation of social relations. Consequently, they cannot be placed in a single category with the other emotions because they are in substance 'pretences'.

Furthermore, Scarantino and Griffiths (2011) have convincingly argued that there is as much need for pluralism in the theoretical treatment of subordinate categories of emotion as there is in the treatment of the superordinate category: some instances of anger, disgust or surprise may be adequately accounted for within the affect program framework, but others may require different theoretical perspectives, and the same holds a fortiori for episodes of guilt, shame or embarrassment (which, in their opinion, sometimes can also be simpler, non-cognitive emotions). In many cases the very same basic emotion (as individuated by folk terms) seems to be much more cognitively penetrable than expected by BET: we are afraid of the approaching dog, but we cease to fear it as soon as we recognize Snoopy, our neighbours' dog. Not to say that we are also afraid of Dow Jones' drop.

Taken together, these remarks have at least two implications for a scientific theory of basic emotions.

First, the theory should not use folk emotion categories such as anger, fear, disgust, happiness or sadness. These folk categories do not designate basic emotions in the sense of the affect program tradition; indeed, some of these categories lack at least some of those physiological, expressive, behavioural and cognitive features that are regarded as the markers of basic emotions. Moreover, behavioural manifestations of a given basic folk emotion are too heterogeneous to be amenable to a single program. And yet some members of the anger, fear, disgust, happiness and sadness categories *do* meet basic-ness criteria. For example, the kind of fear produced by the sudden loss of support does meet Ekman's (1999) criteria of affect program 'fear'. Consequently, as an alternative to the use of folk terms, Scarantino and Griffiths (2011) suggest that one could coin neologisms (e.g. 'threat-coping system'), or use modified versions of the folk categories, making it clear that what is referred to is not the whole folk category, but only a part of it (e.g. $fear_b$ or $fear_{basic}$).

Second, basic emotion theorists should embrace an *anti-essentialist* approach to natural kinds (Boyd 1991) and reformulate their definition of a basic emotion accordingly. In this perspective, Ekman's criteria for being a basic emotion belong to a property cluster and co-occur imperfectly due to some yet-to-be-understood mechanism that may have a dedicated neural basis. No cluster properties are individually necessary, and a significant amount of variability is permitted among instances of the same basic emotion. In this view, 'what is distinctive about basic emotions is not the specific responses they involve but the programs that recruit such responses in a task-oriented and (often) context-dependent fashion' (Scarantino 2015, 335). In different contexts, different patterns of emotional reactions are produced by the mechanism. But, despite superficial dissimilarity, these reactions often involve functional equivalents. Facing a snake, we can run away or be frozen, two superficially different reactions that share the deeper property of being avoidance strategies. On the contrary, at no place or time are avoidance strategies implemented by approaching the danger.

Importantly, this revised basic emotion theory may be integrated into the contextualist and systemic perspective from which the psychodynamics of object relations and attachment approaches caregiver-infant relationality. The activation of affect programs may be seen as part of longer emotional episodes where emotions are social signals designed to change the behaviour of other organisms. Here emerges a view of emotional behaviour as a form of *negotiation* that can be traced to the ethologist Robert Hinde (Griffiths and Scarantino 2009, 446). Human beings, as well as other animals, usually express emotions in interpersonal contexts that trigger and shape what could be seen as an affective dialogue. Emotional manifestations depend on the individuals' internal states, but in most cases also depend on the response of the individuals facing them, in a sort of communicative emotional cycle (Hinde 1985). An episode of disagreement in a couple of persons, as well as in a couple of other animals, does or does not escalate depending on the reciprocal reactions of both partners. The same is true of a couple constituted by a child and her caregiver: the first reacts emotionally to an event perturbing her homeostasis, thereby sending a signal to the adult who, in turn, reacts and continues the emotional dialogue.

We will pursue the analysis of Scarantino's proposal in the following pages, after discussing two – in our view, fundamental – contributions to understanding the nature of the early developmental stages of emotional life: Daniel Stern's reflection on the role of forms of vitality in emotional understanding; and the psychological constructivist views of emotion.

4. Forms of vitality

Let us return to the social biofeedback model's commitment to BET.

The claim that each affect program has a unique bodily response profile (see Griffiths 1997, 79–84) is an open question. We have seen that there is no single way to have or show fear, nor a unique manifestation of joy. Still, it seems plausible to maintain that each basic emotion has a limited set of typical expressions that human beings (probably together with many other animal species) are innately able to detect.

Certainly, the evolutionarily plausible fact that human beings are endowed with innate affective programs and parallel innate discriminative capacities does not imply that such competence is present at birth, at least in its full-fledged form (Sroufe 1996). Indeed, understanding other people's emotional expressions is a complex matter. For example, one has to detect differences among emotional expressions, as well as among emotional and neutral expressions (Camras and Shutter 2013). Moreover, different behaviours, somatic manifestations and vocal cues must be taken into account. The most precocious sensitivity probably concerns vocal expressions: newborns respond differentially to vocal expressions of emotion, manifesting a listening preference for a text read with happy rather than sad, angry or neutral intonation (Mastropieri and Turkewitz 1999). By four months of age, infants become able to discriminate, both in protoconversation and in more structured settings, among happy, angry and neutral facial expressions (Serrano, Iglesias and Loeches 1992, 1995; D'Entremont and Muir 1999). Multiple studies have confirmed that between five and twelve months of age infants display an increasing capacity to perceive, interpret and differentially perceive, interpret and differentially respond to other people's positive and negative facial expressions (Ruba and Repacholi 2020). Eighteen-month-olds not only are capable of distinguishing dislike/disgust from joy/interest facial-vocal expressions directed towards objects, but they also exploit that information to modulate their cooperative behaviour: in a controlled environment, when children perceive different attitudes of experimenters towards two objects through voice and facial expressions, they tend to offer the object towards which the experimenter expressed a more positive attitude (Egyed, Király and Gergely 2013).

In all likelihood, the refinement of these biologically based skills occurs precisely in protoconversational contexts: protoconversations are areas of negotiation in which adult help to discriminate multimodal stimuli, for example, by using the emphasis of prosody and the slowing down of expression that characterize the language addressed to children (IDS, *Infant Directed Speech*).[9] Although ignored by the social biofeedback model, the most important contribution to elucidating the nature of these early developmental stages comes from the paradigm of infant research, most notably from Stern's analysis of the role of vitality forms in the process of emotional understanding.

Decades of microanalytic research on mother-infant face-to-face communication led Stern (1985, 2009, 2010) to conclude that since infancy humans give sense to other people's basic emotional manifestations by detecting their *forms of vitality* rather than their components. Although it is difficult to give a precise definition, vitality forms are multimodal expressions of the temporal contour of actions, structures that unfold the dynamic manifestation of inner states:

> For instance, a minute variation in the temporal contour, force, or direction of the actions may let the recipient of the action, as well as a neutral observer, to understand whether the agent is gentle or angry, whether he or she performs the action willingly or hesitating, and so on. (Rochat et al. 2013, 1919)

Forms of vitality are perceived as wholes through unitary acts of apprehension; they are 'good forms' (*Gestalten*) originating from five components: movement, force, temporal contour, space, and directionality exploding, surging, accelerating/intentionality. To consider some examples, there are explosive forms, forms that surge, accelerate, fade away, and so on.

In many passages, Stern remarks that vitality forms are *not* emotions, and this conviction even moves his lexical choices; the expression replaces the original 'vitality affects' (Stern 1985). Rather, they are structures of dynamic behaviour, which can contain emotions as well as fantasies, streams of thoughts, desires and so on. For example, the desire to eat a pizza may generate a rather explosive action of approaching the table, while the imaginative act of getting out of bed at 6 a.m. to go to school will take a rather different form. We observe, however, that emotion is what more than other states tends to convey vitality forms (think, e.g. of explosions of joy or anger) or to take energy away from them (in the case of emotions such as sadness); consequently, it seems legitimate to assume that there are forms that convey an 'emotional vitality' as particularly frequent and salient. Moreover, emotions 'creep in' even in forms that would not be primarily emotional: think of how a child can show joy in recounting a fantasy, or how a desire can be permeated with emotions – but we will come back to this.

We, therefore, believe, distancing ourselves somewhat from the 'second Stern', that forms of vitality are indeed manifestations that correlate significantly with emotions, thus playing a decisive role in emotional recognition. Certainly, it is to be expected that the first 'exercises' of recognizing emotions in forms expose children to false positives: what is not an emotion is mistaken for it. In front of a surging form, for example, young children may mistake as anger the emotion related to an action that is instead dictated solely by hunger. Yet the pervasiveness of emotions offers many opportunities for learning and refinement. Moreover, and not least, far from being a theoretical problem, the existence of false positives is exactly what is expected from an evolutionary perspective: a few too many alarms make us waste time and energy, but often save our lives.

It seems plausible, therefore, that infants precociously represent other people's emotional manifestations mainly as forms of vitality; or, in other words, that vitality forms are one of the major components of infants' third-personal emotional competence. We stressed earlier that an initial relatively high degree of competence in detecting other people's emotions contrasts with children's very limited phenomenology of their inner states, and the social biofeedback model was proposed as a promising account of the process that leads to emotional introspection. What we intend to argue now is that vitality forms also play a central role in that process. But first things first.

5. Primary appraisals and core affect

The social biofeedback theory states that access to one's own emotions is not guaranteed by any *ad hoc* neurocognitive mechanism, but must instead be formed based on an already (at least partially) developed third-person emotional competence and the analysis of causal contingencies.

We have seen that BET has little to say about the phenomenological dimension of basic emotions. The central empirical hypothesis of the theory is that each basic emotion corresponds to a bodily signature consisting of highly correlated, emotion-specific changes in facial expressions, autonomic changes and preset and learnt actions. Ekman's (1999) inclusion of 'distinctive subjective experiences' in the list of the markers of basic emotions remains an underdeveloped point.[10] Without further specification, the only available phenomenology associated with discrete folk emotion types is some version of the feeling theory – paradigmatically, James' version (or Damasio's and Prinz's neurobiologically updated version of it).

We also mentioned earlier that psychological constructionism has followed James in emphasizing that emotions are put together out of building blocks that are not specific to emotions. In arguing for this, constructivists set up a systematic critique of the BET. In their view, the empirical data do not support the existence of hard-wired emotion mechanisms specifically associated with anger, fear, happiness, sadness, disgust and so on, which are causally responsible for coordinating patterns of tightly associated components with a one-to-one correspondence with the relevant folk emotion categories.

As an alternative to the BET, constructivists propose a 'dimensional' approach to emotions. Since 1980 James Russell has been developing the *affect circumplex* model (Russell 2003, 2015); psychometric studies of self-reported moods and emotions show that all affective states can be represented as varying along the same two orthogonal dimensions. One is *valence*, an elemental, binary, antinomic dimension of the agent's dispositional orientation towards reality which varies through the endless gradations of the positive affect (i.e. the various intensities of what is joy, pleasure, acceptance, availability, lust and so on) and of the negative affect (i.e. the variable intensities of suffering, depression, closure, rejecting and possibly aggressive unavailability and so forth). The second dimension is *arousal*, which ranges from complete bodily quietude or sleepiness at one end, to extreme excitement (pounding heart, intensified breathing and so on) at the other. Crossing the axis positive-negative with the axis quiet-active, we get a fourfold field, or quadrant, which can be regarded as the basic structure of emotions. In practice, any subjective experience of emotion can be located, at any given moment, somewhere in a two-dimensional valence-arousal space. Here one can feel euphorically aroused and excited; blissfully calm and soothed; or unpleasantly excited (i.e. at the mercy of anxious restlessness, which can turn into panic or aggression); or immobile and almost frozen in an insensitive and closed hostility, or in the distress of depression.

This is the kind of phenomenology that psychological constructivists call 'core affect'. Or rather this applies at the psychological level of description, where core affect is 'the most elementary, simple, primitive affective feeling' (Russell 2015, 197). On the other hand, at a neurophysiological level, core affect can be characterized as 'the constant stream of transient alterations in an organism's neurophysiological state that represents its immediate relationship to the flow of changing events' (Barrett 2006a, 48; see also Russell 2003, 147). Taking both description levels into account, core affect is a neurophysiological state that is available to consciousness and is experienced as feeling good or bad (valence) and to a lesser extent as feeling activated or deactivated (arousal).

Psychological constructivism – should be noted – is not specifically a developmental theory: according to constructivists, *every* subjective experience of emotion at any time of life – and hence also in adults – is taken as the outcome of a constructive, conceptual process. Nevertheless, it is precisely from this developmental perspective that we are now interested to look at it, in the conviction that it can help explain the early construction of children's subjective world.

Let's delve into the construct of valence. Valence is used by the rest of the cognitive system to confer value on the objects at which it is directed and to motivate their pursuit or avoidance.[11] In other words, valence is a primary form of low-level appraisal (positive-negative) that covaries with a measurable somatic state such as arousal (activation-deactivation). When one is attending to one's bodily states and changes, the presence of positive valence will make those events seem good (as in the case of a sensation appraised as attractive or liked); the presence of negative valence will make those events seem bad (as in the case of pain). When one attends to some object or event in the world, the presence of positive valence will make that object or event seem good or attractive; and negative valence will make it seem bad or repellant.

In all non-human animals, the relationship with the external world is mediated by basic alternatives such as approaching-withdrawing, accepting-rejecting and incorporating-expelling. Even the simplest animals deal with objects and events according to the good–bad dyad. The same holds for newborn humans. From birth, valence as a primary appraisal of the world enables infants to discriminate whether an object or situation is helpful or harmful, rewarding or threatening, requiring approach or withdrawal; and the presence of positive valence will give rise to feelings of acceptance-pleasure-reassurance-incorporation, whereas the presence of negative valence will give rise to feelings of rejection-insufficiency-distress-expulsion. It is based on this kind of fundamental distinction that newborn infants begin to organize relationships with the world.

In brief, the original form of differentiation of the human organism's purely objectual experiential space would occur according to a dimension of positive vs. negative valence. Or equivalently: at the beginning, the infant's subjective world is characterized exclusively by a core affect phenomenology.

The richer and more discriminative experience of folk emotions is given only later, starting from basic emotions up to more complex affective states. Unlike core affect, which is automatically felt, the experience of folk emotions is constructed by the individual who superimposes a conceptual grid over the flow of rough feelings (Barrett and Russell 2015). Although different constructivists describe how affective episodes are built out of core affect and other ingredients in different ways, all versions of psychological constructivism reject the very basis of the affect program hypothesis: there is no specific causal mechanism staying in one-to-one correspondence with folk-psychological emotion terms and automatically delivering a certain output whenever the organism faces a certain input. Of course, evolutionary processes have shaped neural circuitries allowing rapid and mandatory reactions to environmental changes, such as LeDoux's (2015a, 2015b, 2017) *defensive survival circuits*. But, importantly, these neural mechanisms are not specific to emotions; rather they are just a component in a causal pattern leading to an emotional experience, so LeDoux's threat conditioning system should not be confused with a (non-existent) fear system. As LeDoux himself admits, it is now time to get rid of a misunderstanding induced by an unfortunate terminological choice widespread in the scientific studies of emotions – starting from his pivotal research on fear (see Section 1). A firm point should be established: 'mechanisms that detect and respond to threats are not the same as those that give rise to conscious fear' (LeDoux 2014, 2871). Rather, each survival mechanism is triggered by a large set of inputs and gives rise to a set of heterogeneous physiological and behavioural reactions that once permeated by contextual non-emotional elements, produce an emotional experience. As a consequence, emotional experience is not immediately available to young children: 'Infants can react in "emotionally" long before they can feel emotion' (2876).

This distinction between automatic reactions and feelings is crucial in the constructivist framework: to have an emotion is in a very fundamental sense to have a feeling, and each emotional experience is constructed (i.e. built out of core affect and other ingredients) rather than triggered (Barrett and Russell 2015, 15).

The categorization of core affects gives rise to an emotional meta-experience, that is, to the conceptualization of oneself as having a certain emotion.

Barrett's (2017) theory of 'constructed emotion' (Barrett, 2017; Hoemann, Xu and Feldman Barrett 2019) – formerly, the 'conceptual act' theory of emotion (Barrett 2006a, 2006b, 2015) – takes a more radical stance. Emotions are exclusively constituted by the individual's categorization (through a conceptual act) of core affect, as determined by personal memories and cultural concepts. Concept knowledge about emotion is considered necessary for an instance of emotion to occur: to *have* an emotional experience x one must subsume an ongoing affective feeling under the emotional concept X.[12] While everyone is always in a (changing) state of core affect, one experiences emotions only when parsing the ongoing affective flow through an emotional concept. The relativistic impact of Barrett's theory fully emerges when we think about the role of language in the transmission of emotional concepts. Indeed, Barrett admits that her theory 'is consistent with a strong version of linguistic relativity [. . .]. In the case of emotion, language shapes core affective phenomena into the emotional reality that we experience' (2006b, 37).

On our part, we can concede that there are some reasons to wonder whether language could exert a (strong) influence on the meta-experiential level. Nevertheless, it is worth bearing in mind that Whorf's views fell into disrepute among cognitive scientists through much of the second half of the twentieth century; and although since the early 1990s a weakened form of Whorfianism has been undergoing something of a revival, the claim that different natural languages have differing effects on non-linguistic cognition remains, to put it mildly, open to very serious doubt (Carruthers 2011b).

This is only one of the problems in Barrett's approach. The theory has also been criticized for conflating emotions with verbal labelling, for making it impossible for adult humans to mislabel their own emotions, and for preventing infants and animals from having emotions in the first place (see, e.g., Scherer 2009; Scarantino 2015; see Barrett 2015 for a reply).

Thus, in evaluating the interest of constructivism, we will refer only to Russell's idea of the conceptual nature of emotional meta-experiences: without the relevant concept, one can have an emotional episode but cannot be aware of that experience.

Russell's constructivism explains the variability within folk emotion categories in terms of the fact that several different combinations of components can match the script associated with each folk emotion category (e.g. there will be cases of fear that include facial signals and cases that do not, cases of fear that include autonomic bodily changes and cases that do not, etc.).[13] The central challenge for this model is to explain what underlies the correlations among components of fear, anger and so on. He advances the hypothesis that the components instantiating folk-psychological emotion categories are brought together by non-emotional means. In contrast, Scarantino's revised version of BET posits multiple causal emotion mechanisms associated with each folk emotion category *E*, which are causally responsible for bringing about the components that instantiate *E* (Scarantino 2015, 49). On the one hand, in discussing the critical arguments Scarantino comes very close to constructivism: there are no one-to-one associations between folk psychological emotions and affect programs (or their physical implementations). Still, the core of his theory remains very close to BET. Indeed, he proposes a 'new BET', that is, a revised Basic Emotion Theory that preserves some central intuitions of what he calls '(traditional) BET' while taking into account some critical points issued from the constructivist *milieu*. In particular, in the new BET theoretical framework pancultural basic emotions programs, elicited by an automatic appraisal of the stimulus, are selected by an evolutionary process and present since birth. Yet, the new BET does not underestimate the heterogeneity, flexibility and context-dependence of inputs and outputs. Rather, these superficial differences, which tend to hide a much more important functional equivalence, are a consequence of the evolutionary origins of affect programs. Moreover, the causal mechanisms do not stay in one-to-one correspondence with folk emotional categories such as those individuated by emotional terms (Scarantino 2015, 340).

New BET accepts most critical instances moved against traditional BET but does not get rid of specific emotional mechanisms. Scarantino (2012, 2015) reads LeDoux in an essentialist manner. Taking for granted that LeDoux has revised his terminological choices as discussed earlier, Scarantino still believes that his neural adaptation circuits, which are conserved across animal species, are 'hardwired circuits for orchestrating responses to the sort of challenges basic emotion evolved to solve' (2015, 338). Therefore, survival circuits are emotional circuits, provided that one adopts a functionalist perspective: beyond superficial differences, emotional responses share functional similarities (see earlier). These considerations are followed by a constructivist-like claim: 'These circuits combine with learning and other forms of higher cognition to give rise to the full panoply of context-dependent manifestation of basic emotion' (2015, 338).

As already discussed earlier, another promising issue raised by Scarantino concerns the idea that emotions are forms of negotiation. This is exactly the perspective defended by the social biofeedback model: emotions are social signals, part of interpersonal communication which, while being present all the life long, is probably particularly important in infant-adult communication.

It is, therefore, time to pull the strings on the intertwining of relations among affect programs, core affect and the social biofeedback model.

(1) The social biofeedback model assumes that young children are already able to recognize basic emotional manifestations in people facing them. That is, they have some third-person emotional competence while lacking the correspondent first-person competence. In contrast, there is no phenomenology associated to affect programs (in the new BET version). In the initial stage, basic emotions are packages of somatic, motor and motivational components elicited and coordinated by causal mechanisms (affect programs) which play the role of social signals in the negotiation between infant and caregiver.

(2) Gergely and collaborators endorse traditional BET as a good candidate to explain third-person emotional competence concerning basic emotions. But traditional BET has some important problems; it is too 'rigid', and does not take account of many phenomena – the social (Averill) and openness-to-negotiation (Scarantino-Griffiths-Hinde) dimensions of emotions, not to mention the nature of complex emotions, nor the input-output variability. Last but not least, traditional BET underestimates phenomenology.

(3) Many of those critical issues for BET lay at the core of psychological constructivism, which puts forward a radically alternative view. Specifically, being deeply interested in the phenomenological dimension constructivism is in a good position to account for the second cornerstone of the social biofeedback model, that is, the initial first-person emotional incompetence and its development through protoconversation.

(4) An approach inspired by psychological constructivism can take charge of the great complexity of the development of emotional introspection. It may be supposed that from birth, information about the environment is translated into core affect, namely coded as mental representations of bodily changes that are sometimes experienced as valenced feelings with some degree of arousal. This affective coding enables newborns to discriminate whether an object or situation is helpful or harmful, rewarding or threatening, requiring approach or withdrawal, acceptance or rejection, incorporation or expulsion (Barrett et al. 2007, 377). Core affect is both the product of two neurophysiological systems (one related

to valence and the other to arousal) and the subjective experience of this neurophysiological activity as feelings of acceptance, pleasure, reassurance, incorporation or feelings of rejection, insufficiency, distress, expulsion, which are all to some extent arousing or quieting.

(5) It is based on these kinds of primary appraisals that very young children begin to organize their relationship with the world. In other words, the first form of differentiation of newborn infants' purely objectual experiential field is that of positioning their dispositional orientation towards the world at some point on the map drawn by the axes of valence and arousal. This happens after all in every animal; unlike other animals, however, human infants continue the process of emotional development – thanks to the intervention of social biofeedback, we believe. And again, life forms and body knowledge would seem to play a significant part in the story.

(6) Actually, the mixed model proposed by Scarantino is the most promising theoretical framework to sustain the social biofeedback model, as the new BET accepts some central issues of traditional BET (thus explaining third-person competence about basic emotions) while advancing important constructivist instances which explain first-person initial incompetence.

(7) It is affect-mirroring that gradually adds a phenomenological component to basic emotion packages. As seen, marked mirroring displays are interpreted self-referentially by the infant. As a result, they are referentially anchored (in the form of internalized second-order representations) to those procedural basic emotion states that the mirroring displays contingently reflect. This process will lead to the internalization of discrete emotions into the infant's own inner life when – in the second year of life – the phenomenology of basic emotions is embedded into bodily self-consciousness, making the infant's bodily self-image an affective bodily self-image. The affective bodily self-image is the first form of the internal experiential space.

(8) Two aspects of the social biofeedback approach to the development of emotional self-awareness are particularly remarkable. First, knowledge of one's mind rests on interactions with the attachment figure, who displays emotional expressions whose meanings children already know. Even at this basic level, therefore, we find the primacy of third-person cognition: at any level of complexity, knowledge of the self requires at least an equivalent stage of knowledge of others. Second, this approach to the emergence of the introspective awareness of one's basic emotions supports the claim that bodily self-awareness is a necessary premise of

the further development of the ability to identify the presence of the inner experiential space of the mind. While aware of the limits of the peripheralist tradition founded by James and Lange, somatovisceral feedback is certainly one of the determinants of the formation of discrete emotion categories.[14] Thus, the earliest cognition of mental events requires the acquired capacity of interpreting primary somatic data specific to categories of affective states and of attributing them to the self. In this respect, basic emotions are events that are originally detected in the body, and subsequently internalized in our mental life.

Nonetheless, a critical issue remains for our developmental perspective: while in adult humans core affect feelings are only the starting point of a constructive process leading to the awareness of discrete emotional states, very young human infants – and non-human animals – are unable to refine their low-level, pre-conceptual knowledge. Still, while the cognitive limits of non-human animals will permanently impede progression, in the case of human children the gap will be filled by social biofeedback. This long-lasting, reiterated process starts from core affect experience and progressively structures the conceptual self-knowledge necessary for full-fledged introspection. We argue that forms of vitality and bodily knowledge both have a role to play in this story.

6. Forms of vitality and background feelings

According to both the social biofeedback model and psychological constructivism, emotional introspection does not emerge from anywhere but is, on the contrary, a long and arduous endeavour. Nonetheless, the nature of experience – at its various levels – still is not clear. In particular, it is not clear which role, if any, the body plays in the construction of emotional introspection. To tackle this point, the notion of forms of vitality may be helpful again.

Stern introduced his theoretical construct not only to describe the dynamic forms we perceive in others' behaviour; he also stressed – notably in his last writings – the role of vitality forms in the early self-experience organization: pre-conceptual experience, namely, 'the experiencing of the dynamics of a happening' (Stern 2009, 308; see also 2010) that precedes the two forms of conceptual experience (respectively, non-verbal and verbal reflexive experiences). To say that gestaltic forms of vitality are the form of experience amounts to saying that what very young infants experience is a mix of their (aforementioned) five components: movement, force, temporal contour, space and directionality/ intentionality. And it seems clear to us that these five dimensions once grasped pre-conceptually as a Gestalt, can be traced back to the dimensions of valence and arousal that characterize the phenomenology of affect in early childhood. Indeed, once grasped through a multimodal, perceptual process, movement and its contour, as well as space and intentional direction, jointly convey information about pleasantness/unpleasantness and relaxed/activated behavioural attitudes, both when perceived in others and registered in our own body. At the same time, they convey information about the temporal development of actions, thus adding some important cues about the dynamic of our basic feelings. Yet, according to constructivists, states defined uniquely through low-level appraisal leading to a raw antinomic dimension correspond to a sort of proto-emotions, that is, extensively under-differentiated states that are experienced by young infants still deprived of the emotional conceptual repertoire necessary for full-fledged, recognitional experiences. We can therefore conclude that although not explicitly taking part in the constructivist debate, Stern defends a position which is perfectly coherent with it.

Moreover – and crucially for our reasoning – Stern explicitly acknowledges the resonance between his forms of vitality and Damasio's notion of *background feeling*, defined as the feeling of what is happening, moment by moment, to our own body.[15] A couple of quotes from Damasio will clarify the point:

> Most of the time we do not experience any of the six emotions [. . .]. But we do experience other kinds of emotions, sometimes low grade, sometimes quite intense, and we do sense the general physical tone of our being. (1999, 285–6)

A few lines as follows:

> Background feelings arise from background emotions,[16] and these emotions, although more internally than externally directed, are observable to others in myriad ways: body postures, the speed and design of our movements, and even the tone of our voices and the prosody in our speech. (1999, 286)

To recapitulate. Background feelings are the mental images that arise from neural patterns representing biological changes in our body and brain, such as inter alia, fatigue, energy, excitement, wellness, tension, relaxation and stability. Nevertheless, limiting ourselves to noticing Damasio's proximity to Stern would lead to seriously underestimating a crucial point for us. By explicitly endorsing Damasio's well-known position, Stern emphasizes the role of the body in the construction of psychological introspection. What we feel – the emotions we experience – issues in an important sense from representations of states of the body. The echo of James' theory of emotion cannot but be perceived, interlaced with a point that conversely, distinguishes Damasio from Stern: while originating from the external world – often, from the external relational world – what background feelings represent is the 'internal side'. More precisely, they represent the ongoing states of a body that is connected to the external (be it physical or social) world without conveying representations of the world itself. On the contrary, in Stern's view vitality forms are more explicitly intentional and relational. They not only represent a state of our own body, but they are the consequence of our being in interaction with the vitality forms of another agent (in most cases, a real agent, but also with agent-like objects such as music, waves, bouncing balls and so on). In this sense, the interpersonal nature of self-construction appears more neatly in Stern's approach. But, thanks to Damasio, Stern's selfing processes are now supplemented with a stronger emphasis on the corporeal dimension.[17]

7. Beyond emotions: Simple desires

Remaining within an interpersonal framework, we would now like to cast a glance beyond the emotional world, thus anticipating the work of investigation on the process of enlargement of the experiential space to which we will devote the next chapters. In doing so, we will draw a parallel with our investigation of emotions, which began with basic emotional states.

Being primarily interested in volitional states, we will then focus on *simple desires*; that is, we are interested in those states that correspond to the agent's tension towards an external object or situation or, vice versa, to the propensity to move away from it ('Liam desires candy', 'Evelyn does not want cheese'); we will exclude instead complex states such as 'Emma desires her father to come and play with her', 'Elijah does not want his father to go to work'. So: are there reasons to believe that introspection of simple desires is achieved through a process that somewhat resembles social biofeedback?

Let us start with one of the most interesting computational models of the development of mindreading, that is, the human propensity to interpret behaviour by postulating mental causes (we will elaborate on this later): the mindreading system proposed by Baron-Cohen (1995). Among its earliest maturing components is the *Intentionality Detector* (ID), an amodal mechanism that activated by the perception of stimuli with direction or that manifest self-propulsion, represents their behaviour in terms of volitional states ('X wants Y'). The other component of very early maturation, the *Eye Direction Detector* (EDD), instead works only in the visual modality: it detects the presence of eye-like stimuli and represents gaze direction as 'X sees Y'.[18] Despite what Baron-Cohen claims, an agent can't determine the direction of one's gaze by detecting the shape of one's own eyes, except in very particular and ecologically insignificant situations (mirrors, videos); rather, these cases of self-attribution involve proprioceptive mechanisms. This architectural detail, as well as the overtly evolutionary framework of Baron-Cohen's research, make it clear that EDD is a system aimed primarily at exploring the external world: in the ancestral world in which cognitive faculties evolved, it was much more important to determine what others are looking at than to explicitly represent ourselves looking at something.

For ID, the situation is prima facie different: being an amodal system, it allows agents to perceive the onset of movement and its direction both in themselves (through proprioceptive cues) and in others (through external cues). However, does the fact of perceiving our movement in a certain direction mean ipso facto that we perceive the movement as our own What has been repeatedly observed so far suggests extreme caution: experiencing the body as one's own body is a hard achievement, a process that begins with the representation of a purely objective experiential space. But then, the fact that the same computational mechanism represents one's own and others' direction of movement is not enough to guarantee that agents have recognized their own goals and desires as their own: more simply, the agents could have detected such states without experiencing themselves as the subject of experience.

If, therefore, the subjective experiential space of simple volitional states does not exist at birth either, but has to be constructed, we can ask the initial question again: is it reasonable to bring this constructive process, too, under the social biofeedback model, that is, an explanatory model created to account for the development of emotional introspection?

Although not infrequently confused with emotions (Liljenfors and Lundh 2015), simple desires must be distinguished from them. It is clear that the desire for a chocolate ice cream has (for us, at least) a phenomenal correlate very close to that of joy, or perhaps even coincident; and it is also true, as widely remarked earlier, that emotions are also intentional states, that is, internal states referring to something else. But it seems equally clear that the external object plays a more essential role in desire attribution than in emotional attribution: often a state of joy can be recognized by perceiving only the face or body of the happy person (possibly our own body), whereas the recognition of a simple desire requires considering the propensity towards an object. Therefore, if we are to argue that social biofeedback is indeed the way to achieve volitional self-awareness, we must admit that this process is much more overtly triadic with volitional states.

Imagine a relational context typical of early childhood, with a mother and her child who desires a ball nearby. The child wants it (looks at it, reaches for it), but he is not aware of his psychological state: he represents the ball, but he is not yet able to represent his mental representation (the desire). The mother, for her part, looks in the direction of the child's gaze, understands his intention, looks at the ball, moves towards it and grabs it to offer it to her child. In short, she allows her son to activate EDD and ID in a mode directed towards others: EDD represents Mum as looking at the ball, whereas IDD represents Mum as wanting the ball. Moreover, her behaviour probably contains a mark of pretence that is soon recognized by the infant: 'Mommy wants the ball, yet she smiles and hands it to me'. Thus, some elements of social biofeedback are undoubtedly present, but the inherently triadic dimension brings the process of self-awareness of simple desires closer to the situation that triggers processes typical of natural pedagogy. Therefore, the empirical question already posed in Section 2.2 should be reiterated: are social biofeedback and natural pedagogy two processes that can be traced back to the same computational mechanism? Pending a definitive empirical answer, we can once again recognize the crucial role of socialization, which 'trains' the child to recognize previously undetermined internal states.

8. What about beliefs?

If we were also to attempt to explain the self-attribution of beliefs through the social biofeedback mechanism, we would be faced with (at least) a double difficulty. On the one hand, there are typically no particular bodily expressions corresponding to a state of belief, which can thus be recognized in the behaviour of others; at least, there is nothing comparable to the florid expressiveness of emotions ('Mummy smiles') and simple desires ('Mummy reaches for the ball and looks at it'): believing X generally does not correlate with a behaviour that is so detectable that it can trigger social biofeedback. On the other hand, beliefs rarely have phenomenal correlates strong enough to be the object of biofeedback: generally speaking, beliefs are not recognized through their introspective, experiential qualities. Thus, there seems to be no room for an explanation in terms of biofeedback. Instead, a theoretical construct such as natural pedagogy could be better suited to account for this; the risk, however, is that of watering down the meaning of such a theoretical proposition too much, bringing everything that is taught by the adult to the child back into its scope. It is certainly plausible that the social context strongly influences the process that leads to the introspection of one's beliefs; nevertheless, these are overtly verbal and dialogical contexts, far more detached from the overtly ostensive contexts to which natural pedagogy is linked.

Leaving open a point of no easy empirical resolution, in the next two chapters, we will turn our attention to two different, complementary issues. In Chapter 6, we will try to understand how the experiential space inaugurated with emotional introspection (and in which social biofeedback would play a crucial role) expands to contain more complex states. Instead, in Chapter 5 we will explore the human propensity to attribute mental states to others to explain and predict their behaviour. This analysis will allow us to fully emphasize the anti-Cartesian nature of our overall proposal.

5
Naïve psychology

As emerged from the previous chapters, becoming aware of one's mind is a highly complex process. From their initial knowledge of the physical and social world, through the acquisition of bodily self-awareness during their second year, children come to know the first mental states accessible to them: discrete emotions, as well as simple volitional states. The construction of emotional introspection occurs through social biofeedback. In examining the social biofeedback model, we took an integrative approach that challenges traditionally opposing perspectives such as BET and psychological constructivism. Our multidisciplinary analysis unveiled a development path composed of the following main steps:

(1) The first form of differentiation between infants' object field and their subjective world occurs based on valence dimensions: positive valence gives rise to feelings of acceptance-pleasure-security-incorporation, while negative valence gives rise to feelings of rejection-insufficiency-anguish-expulsion. At this initial point, no phenomenology is associated with the experience of basic emotions.

(2) The distinctive phenomenological component of basic emotions is added in a microsocial context, largely through interpersonal affect-mirroring. Infants, who possess innate and precocious competence in recognizing the basic emotional expressions of others, notice that adults typically address marked expressions to them. Through social biofeedback and the process of contingency detection that is part of it, infants gradually come to anchor marked parental expressions to their own as yet undefined emotional experience, thus producing second-order representations of their affective states.

(3) The complete internalization of discrete emotions in infants' subjective world is produced when the phenomenology of basic emotions takes shape in bodily reflexivity: bodily self-images become emotional bodily self-images. We could also say that first-person emotional mentalization

consists of the acquired ability to group primary somatic data into categories of discrete emotions, which are then attributed to oneself and thereby internalized in one's subjective world.

Having internalized simpler states, there is still a lot of hard work to be done. Children must learn to recognize and self-attribute other types of mental states and activities, as well as to form the conceptual network that links these phenomena together: self-consciousness is initially the phenomenological seat of emotional life but must then expand considerably to become what James calls 'spiritual self' and Locke assumes as a precondition of personhood. During this further development, the social dimension retains its crucial role. We will suggest that the expansion of the virtual space of the mind occurs mainly because children, under the socio-communicative pressure of adults, become capable of turning onto themselves a repertoire of socio-cognitive skills that were originally focused on others. These abilities consist primarily of those naïve psychological skills that we use spontaneously in everyday life. This is the theme of the chapter.

1. Attachment and mindreading

In the previous chapter, we criticized the strong intersubjectivist approach, according to which introspective access to one's internal states is guaranteed and provides first-person authority over the contents of one's mental life. This Cartesian perspective, which assumes that the ability to interpret the mind of other people (i.e. third-person competence) is an achievement based on the primary capacity of introspection, has been widely subscribed in the infant research tradition. In the search for the primary causal factor in the acquisition of the ability of third-person mindreading, special attention has been devoted to those relational elements that correlate with secure attachment: for example, the parental propensity to discuss with their children what the mental causes of a certain behaviour could be (Meins et al. 2002),[1] or their habit of examining together possible conflicts between feelings and emotions (Dunn 1996), or, more basically, of talking about mental states (Heyes and Frith 2014).

Those who disagree with such a Cartesian approach generally defend a parity thesis, which assumes a parallel development of knowledge of other minds and one's mind. More radically, Gergely and Unoka (2008a, 2008b) defend a third-person-first position. According to them, attachment only exerts an influence on the more advanced aspects of third-person competence, as early third-person mindreading is the expression of a domain-specific system that matures independently of relational styles. On the other hand, attachment strongly influences introspection from its early development: understanding of one's mind develops progressively as children, under the pressure of interpersonal relationships in the attachment environment, redirect towards themselves what they already knew about the mind of other people. Gergely and Unoka's stance is deeply rooted in one of the most flourishing experimental paradigms in contemporary developmental psychology, concerned with investigating early understanding of others' minds. Before delving into this vast literature, let us make it clear that, unless otherwise stated, we will use the terms 'mindreading', 'mentalization', and 'naïve psychology' as synonyms. For simplicity, we will also use these terms as a shortcut for *third-person* mindreading/mentalization/naïve psychology.[2]

2. Naïve psychology: The initial level

From their earliest days of life, infants engage in interactions using rudimentary skills of naïve psychology. Attracted from birth by eye-like stimuli (hence Baron-Cohen's hypothesis of EDD considered earlier), they are sensitive to various parameters of the human voice and even to the specific language of the community they live in; they recognize the typical pattern of a human face; moreover. In short, children seem to be pre-programmed to pay attention to the social world, that is, the context that throughout life will provide them with most of the fundamental pedagogical stimuli concerning various domains of knowledge (Gergely and Csibra 2013).

Within a few months, initial knowledge increases significantly. An important milestone is reached shortly after the age of six months: six-and-a-half-month-old babies recognize a goal-directed action and expect it to be performed in the most rational manner (Csibra 2008; Gergely 2011). Such precocity supports the hypothesis of an innate 'obsession with goals' (Csibra and Gergely 2007) that was already attested in older children, as revealed by the seminal study by Gergely et al. (1995). We will examine it in some detail, taking it as an opportunity to explore one of the most important methodologies employed in the studies of very young children's psychological abilities: the *violation of expectation* paradigm. The problem that developmental psychologists had to face was clear: how can we investigate the higher cognitive capacities of babies only a few months old, since we cannot ask them questions? A promising solution is to observe their behaviour, in particular, to monitor those behavioural parameters that correlate with their attentional level, on the assumption that infants will show surprise when witnessing an impossible event.

In its essential elements, the experiment (whose scheme is similar, although not identical, to the 3D version proposed to younger babies in Csibra 2008) goes like this: in the preliminary, habituation phase, twelve-month-old infants repeatedly observe a small circle approaching a larger circle by jumping over an obstacle (a big rectangular form) with a parabolic trajectory. When infants' interest (measured by visual fixation time) decreases beyond a set threshold, the obstacle is removed and the true experimental phase begins, with the infant witnessing two different situations: the 'ball' either makes the same parabolic trajectory as before or moves with a linear trajectory. The analysis of children's reactions suggests that they expect the ball (whose path no longer contains obstacles) to move *rationally*, that is, adjusting its path and following the shortest and most direct trajectory, instead of 'persisting' in a parabolic path that would no longer be the rational way to reach the goal. The linear trajectory does not surprise them, while the parabolic trajectory causes them to recover a high level of visual attention: arguably since their expectation has been disregarded, they look intensely at 'something wrong' (Gergely et al. 1995).[3]

Not only geometric shapes can replace real human beings or biological agents in activating the teleological strategy, but also robots, dolls and even agents that perform biologically impossible actions. This is what happens in Southgate, Johnson and Csibra's (2008) study with infants aged six to eight months: when observing an action of retrieving an object, they are not surprised when an arm takes on shapes that are biomechanically impossible but functional to overcoming certain barriers, thereby effectively achieving the goal.[4]

According to Gergely and Csibra, teleological reasoning is subserved by an innate specialized system. It is therefore interesting to compare their hypothesis with the aforementioned hypothesis of the Intentionality Detector (ID), the early developmental system that Baron-Cohen (1995) proposed as a precursor to mature mindreading. Triggered by multimodal stimuli with a direction or self-propelled, ID would detect an action's goal by generating representations of the type 'X wants Y'. Despite the obvious similarities between the two hypotheses, Gergely and Csibra disagree with Baron-Cohen on an important point: they believe that goal detection is independent of any consideration (however primitive) of the mental states of the agent performing it. In their view, attributions of rationality refer strictly to perceived action and not – as Baron-Cohen suggests – to agents and their mental states. It must be said that Gergely and Csibra themselves recognize that teleological reasoning is complemented, at a later stage, by mindreading; but their concession may not be enough: the surprising naïve psychological skills in early infancy that we will describe in the following pages seriously question their position, suggesting rather that the two competencies interact synergistically from the very beginning.[5]

Another crucial step in development is attained at the end of the ninth month of age – with the significant exception of children with autism spectrum disorder, see Baron-Cohen 1995 – when an action that children have already been practising for about a trimester – the pointing gesture – seem to change their meaning completely. From the fourth trimester onwards, when pointing at something, babies begin to seek out their partners' gaze, expressing pleasure when they get attention sharing (Bates, Camaioni and Volterra 1975). Whereas in early infancy children point at something only to get it and do not carry out any monitoring of others' attention, around nine months of age they begin to make triangulations between themselves, the outside world and another agent. One could say, therefore, that older children realize that everyone has a personal perspective on the world and that for communication to be effective, this perspective must be monitored and addressed. Until then, children had shared with others only emotions; now they can share information about the world.

3. Naïve psychology: Mindreading

3.1. Classical false-belief tasks

'Why are you reading this book?' Even if a sort of modesty keeps us from inquiring further, we are ready to bet that the answer would call into question, more or less explicitly, mental states: goals, desires, thoughts, emotions and so on. As human beings, we function this way: we are naïve psychologists, obsessive 'readers' of other people's minds, always engaged in the systematic search for the psychological causes of actions, with the implicit assumption that people are moderately rational.[6] In Baron-Cohen's (1995) celebrated words, we are *mindreaders*.

The study of mindreading, and particularly the research into its nature and full development, suddenly came to the attention of cognitive scientists in 1978, when the psychologists David Premack and Guy Woodruff attributed to Sarah, an enculturated, language-trained chimpanzee, a *theory of mind*. Their conclusions were based on controlled experimental data. In particular, they presented Sarah with some short films in which a person had to solve practical problems, such as reaching for a banana hanging too high from the ceiling. Each clip was interrupted five seconds before the end and Sara had to find the solution by choosing between three images. She proved to be very skilful, even when the solution consisted of an unusual action for her; however, Sarah's excellent performance does not seem to justify the optimistic conclusions of the two authors, who were inclined to attribute refined psychological abilities to her: a more epistemically rigorous examination makes it clear that it is not necessary to consider the experimenter's beliefs and desires to pass the tasks, but it is sufficient to activate a non-mentalistic problem-solving strategy.

In the article's peer-reviewed commentary, three philosophers – Jonathan Bennett, Daniel Dennett and Gilbert Harman – independently suggested the right way to approach theory of mind: to be credited with genuine mentalistic competence, agents demonstrate that they understand that a belief is a representation of reality, and as such can also misrepresent something. Thus, detecting mistaken beliefs, and understanding their properties and behavioural consequences should be taken as the true hallmark of mindreading. To consider one of the three authors, Harman made the following methodological proposal: imagine a chimpanzee seeing another chimpanzee looking at a banana in one of the two opaque boxes in front of him. When the second chimpanzee is distracted, the banana is moved into the second box. If the first chimpanzee expects the second chimpanzee to try and reach the first box, that is, the box that originally contained the banana, this would seem to indicate that he possesses the concept of belief (Harman 1978, 576–7).

In outlining this scenario, Harman and his colleagues (who made similar claims) inspired one of the most successful experimental paradigms in developmental psychology: the *false-belief task*,[7] originally run by Wimmer and Perner (1983) and soon elaborated by Baron-Cohen, Leslie and Frith (1985), who in turn gave great impetus to the investigation of mentalization in persons suffering from autism spectrum disorder. Let us consider this last version, which was the one most replicated and reworked in the following decades.

Children observe a scene in which a doll, Sally, first places a marble in a basket and then leaves the room. During Sally's absence Ann, the second character in the scene, takes the marble from the basket and places it in a box. Children are asked where Sally will look for the marble on her return. The nature of infantile reasoning is thus verbally investigated by artfully creating a conflict between reality (which coincides with children's knowledge) and Sally's mental states. Those who pass the explicit false-belief task may not necessarily be able to reflect on the notions of belief and desire, but they have certainly understood that behaviour largely depends on unobservable states that represent states of affairs; that is, they have understood the perspectival nature of the mind and its causal power over behaviour, and this is enough to make them naïve psychologists.

Except for certain psychological conditions, notably, children pass the task after 3.5 years of mental age.

Let us elaborate on why it is necessary to prove an understanding of false beliefs to justify the possession of metapsychological abilities. As the three philosophers mentioned earlierhave independently observed, this is in a sense a practical point, but it has profound theoretical relevance. Suppose that there is no 'trick' in the Sally and Anne task, that is, that the marble is indeed in the first container (the basket) when Sally returns. In this case, both Sally and the young participants have true beliefs. Yet, how could we ensure that children's correct predictions issue from a true metacognitive analysis of Sally's (true) beliefs rather than from a mere consideration of the actual state of affairs? To repeat, the marble *is* in the basket (actual state of affairs) and Sally represents it as being in the basket. Moreover, without displacement, how could we rule out the possibility that the response only reflects children's propensity to action (e.g. helping Sally)? In other words: in the simplified version of the test, which we might call the 'true-belief task', children might answer correctly because they do take Sally's beliefs into account; but, without the trick of displacing the marble, there is no way to distinguish a correct answer due to justified reasoning from a correct answer only by chance, resulting from extra-mentalistic inferences.

Data emerging from *classical* false-belief tasks have animated an intense debate, regularly fuelled by new findings. In the last few years, the debate has polarized around the true age of onset of naïve psychology: are classical false-belief tasks able to signal the true moment of onset of the new competence, or are they just a late manifestation of competence that had already matured at an earlier age, which no experimental methodology had been able to pinpoint with precision? The analysis of the 'nine-month turn', with the appearance of declarative pointing, had already raised some suspicions; but controlled data were needed to understand better.

3.2. From initial suspicions to implicit tests

To stress again the crucial point: could it be possible that false-belief tasks merely unveil a competence already established at an earlier age? This temporal clarification would be valuable for our attempt to understand the reciprocal relationship between the capacities of introspection and outwardly directed mentalization.

Surely, requiring the analysis of false beliefs is an ingenious methodological trick to make sure that basic mindreading is established; nonetheless, as we have remarked, it is also possible that children can reason about mental states at an earlier age. Inspired by this possibility, Siegal and Beattie (1991) suggested maintaining the focus on false beliefs while introducing a pragmatic simplification of the task. Noting that the traditional question could be interpreted as a question about where Sally should look, they attempted to avoid ambiguity by adding the adverb 'first' in the crucial question: 'Where will Sally look for the marble first?'. Such an emphasis on the temporal order should force children's attention to Sally's behaviour rather than to the normatively correct situation. This revision had a marginal impact, as children under the age of three continued to fail the test: the time gain, while statistically significant, was limited to one semester or so (see Wellman, Cross and Watson 2001).

Instead, the landscape of early competencies changed dramatically when experimenters decided to avoid verbal communication and started to 'interrogate' the children by observing the direction of their gaze – and thus monitoring their attention – through the aforementioned experimental paradigm of violation of expectation.

In the seminal study by Onishi and Baillargeon (2005; see also Onishi, Baillargeon and Leslie 2007), fifteen-month-old children witness a scene in which an adult observer (O) is induced to form a belief that is sometimes correct, and sometimes wrong. The experimental set consists of two opaque boxes (a green and a yellow box) against the background of a closed window. As soon as the window opens, children saw the observer O manipulate a slice of watermelon toy and soon place it into the green box. Depending on whether the window is open or closed, O can or cannot witness the unfolding of events.[8] Four experimental conditions (two true-belief conditions and two false-belief conditions) are proposed to children, who on their part can always see what is happening on stage. In the first true-belief condition, O is present and the yellow box moves (by its self-propelled motion) towards the green box and back to its starting point. In the remaining three conditions, the boxes stand still while the watermelon moves from one box to the other. Notably, in the second true-belief condition O is present and the watermelon toy moves from the green to the yellow box. In the first of the two false-belief conditions, the window is closed so that O cannot see the toy move from the green box to the yellow one. In the second, more complex false-belief condition, O is present when the toy moves into the yellow box, but then the window closes, preventing O from seeing the toy return to the green box. After the children have witnessed all these conditions, the window opens and O reaches for one of the two boxes with her hand. What emerges from monitoring the direction and duration of gaze is that fifteen-month-old children notice O's incoherence (i.e. look significantly longer) when O reaches for the correct box without having witnessed all movements. Similarly, they are surprised if O looks for the toy in the wrong box despite having always witnessed the unfolding of events. In short, and not unlike older children who pass the Sally and Anne task and other language-based false-belief tasks, fifteen-month-olds seem to be able to detect a violation of the psychological rule that knowledge depends on perception – hence, that knowledge depends on psychological states.

Many other empirical data have corroborated this hypothesis and even lowered the age of success. For example, thirteen-month-old children pass a conceptually similar test involving two objects and a mouse (Surian, Caldi and Sperber 2007).

A similar developmental framework emerges from different experimental paradigms. Let us consider three of them.

Anticipatory-looking paradigm. An eye-tracker is used to monitor children's gaze direction while watching actions. When it comes to analysing mindreading, the focus is on actions that can only be correctly anticipated by attributing false beliefs to the actor. For example, Southgate, Senju and Csibra (2007) took inspiration from Onishi and Baillargeon's experiment to run their study based on anticipatory looking. Children aged twenty-five months are shown a video in which a puppet bear hides a ball in one of the two boxes and an actor retrieves the ball through one of the two windows located behind the boxes. In the test trial, after having seen the ball hidden in the left box, the actor is distracted by a phone call and turns away from the scene. When the phone stops ringing, the actor turns her face towards the boxes, and the windows light up. Most infants correctly anticipate her behaviour, looking at the window above the left box, that is, where arguably the agent falsely believes the puppet bear to be (see Senju et al. 2011 for data concerning eighteen-month-olds; see also Scott et al. 2010 for a review).

Make-belief. It is generally acknowledged that make-believe play, which appears universally around the age of eighteen months, mobilizes naïve psychological skills, insofar as it requires distinguishing reality from fiction (Leslie 1987). When pretending (or witnessing others' pretence) that a piece of clay is a cake, children do not try to eat it, nor do they expect others to do so: visibly, they can distinguish the real world from the pretend one, not unlike how they will later distinguish their epistemic horizon from Sally's. At fifteen months, children do not yet play make-believe games, but the analysis of their surprise attests to their ability to detect inconsistencies in pretended scenarios – specifically, they realize that there is something strange if a person pretends to fill a cup and immediately afterwards pretends to drink from the cup next to it (Onishi, Baillargeon and Leslie 2007).[9]

Active helping paradigm. Many studies show that from the middle of the second year of life (and maybe even earlier: see Grossmann, Missana and Vaish 2020) children understand when it is appropriate to help someone. Consider the research by Buttelmann, Carpenter and Tomasello (2009), which involves two experimental conditions. In the true-belief condition, an adult (*A*) and a child are both present when a third person moves a caterpillar-shaped toy from one box to another; in the false-belief condition, *A* leaves the scene before the toy is moved, and returns immediately afterwards. In both conditions, *A* approaches the box that initially contained the toy (and which is now empty). From eighteen months onwards, children evidence sensitivity to *A*'s epistemic states, manifesting discriminative skills. Only those who participate in the false-belief condition warn the adult of his error and help him open the right box: they know that *A*, being absent during the switch, has formed a wrong belief. In contrast, children participating in the true-belief condition refrain from suggesting anything to *A*: they understand that *A* is in an optimal epistemic state and know where the caterpillar toy is. Therefore, if *A* approaches the wrong box, *A* must have some good reason for doing so and must be left undisturbed. In this condition, the children even collaborate with *A* by opening the wrong box with him. Comparable results have been obtained with seventeen-month-old children by Southgate, Chevalier and Csibra (2010), who ran a modified, more participatory version of the false-belief task in which children are required to help find an object someone who has formed an erroneous belief.

To conclude our overview, let us look at the experiment purported to reveal the most precocious competencies arguably involved in early naïve psychology. Kovács, Téglás and Endress (2010) presented a video clip to twenty-four adults and fifty-six 7-month-old infants (see Figure 5.1).[10] In the video, a Smurf-like Agent *A* places a ball on the table in front of an occluder; the ball starts rolling until it hides behind a screen, while *A* goes to the side of the scene, assuming the role of a passive spectator. The total experimental conditions are four, depending on two variables: the ball stays behind the screen or moves away from it, and the Smurf *A* stays or leaves for a while. Finally, in every condition, the Smurf

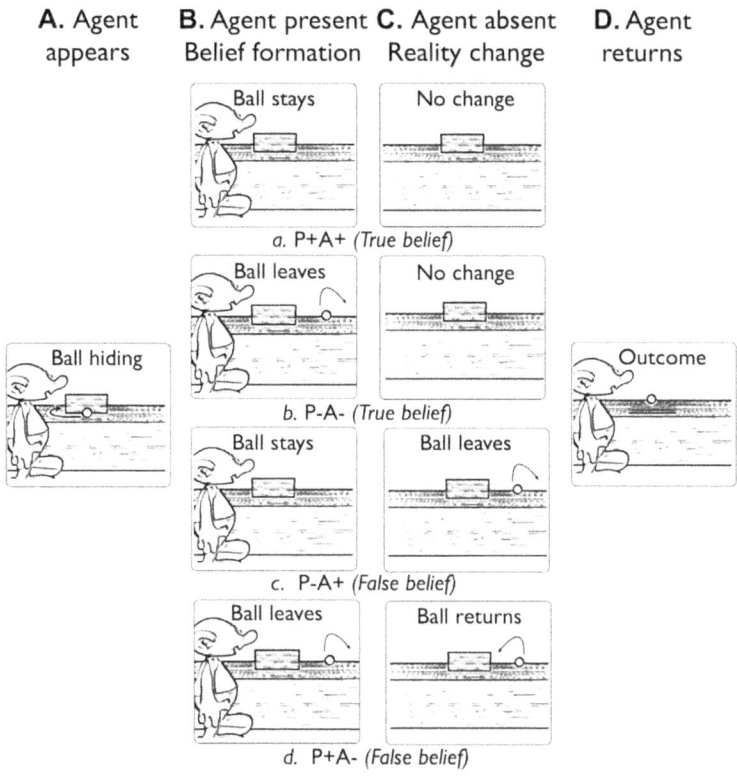

Figure 5.1 From A. M. Kovács, E. Téglás and A. D. Endress (2010), The social sense: Susceptibility to others' beliefs in human infants and adults, *Science*, 330(6012):1830-4. Reprinted with permission from AAAS.

A comes back and the occluder is lowered in his presence, revealing (in two additional conditions) the actual presence or absence of the ball.

Adult participants were asked to press a button as fast as possible if they could see the ball when the screen was lowered.

We will refrain from going into further details of an experiment that appears extremely complex, but which is very salient for those directly involved in the experiment. Rather, let us focus on reaction times. When the lowering of the screen reveals the presence of the ball, not surprisingly P's quicker reaction is in the first condition (*a*), where the ball was where P expected it to be – and one can assume the same happens to the Smurf A. In contrast, the reaction is slower in condition *b*, where neither P nor A expected the ball to be behind the occluder.

But the most interesting things happen when the beliefs of the two observers diverge. In particular, in the third condition (*c*) P does not expect to find the ball and is therefore expected to respond with the same latency as in condition *b*, in which she has the same kind of expectation. But this is not the case: statistically, *P*'s answer in condition *c* is faster. The most reasonable explanation is that the reaction time is accelerated by the fact that *P* automatically takes into account the epistemic perspective of *A*, who (because of the experimental conditions) does expect to find the ball (actually, in this condition the response times tends to be similar to those in condition *d*, in which also *P* expects to see the ball and both *P*).

Let us repeat: Smurf *A* is a mere passive spectator, never involved in the active pursuit of anything; therefore, his beliefs about the position of the ball should have no impact on *P*'s interpretation of the situation. Yet it is not possible to ignore him, not even for seven-month-old children: their reactions of surprise when faced with the violation of an expectation (measured through gaze duration) show a response pattern quite similar to that of adults. We could argue that neither adults nor children can avoid minding other people's business (see also Luo and Baillargeon 2007, for data on 12.5-month-old children). Whenever we perceive something, the mere presence of an agent influences our representation of the situation, even when the crucial point of interest is elsewhere.

Further confirmation of these data comes from a different experimental methodology, namely from neurophysiological studies using electroencephalograms (Kampis et al. 2015). An actor observes an object that from time to time is hidden behind a rotating screen; when the object begins to be occluded from the actor's gaze, the child sometimes continues to see it, sometimes not. The same electrophysiological reaction (measured by the increase in gamma waves) occurs both when the screen begins to hide the object from the view of both, and when it is only the actor's perception that is obscured. Again, the perspective of a character who merely watches a scene is automatically taken into account.

3.3. Interpretations of early data

Although the methodological validity and replicability of some implicit tests have been questioned (see, e.g., Rakoczy 2022), it remains indisputable that something important does indeed happen at least from the end of the first year of life; and this is what we would like to discuss. There are essentially two options: (1) following a constructivist approach, data on early childhood reveal that children possess a preliminary and incomplete version of what years later true mindreading will be. Further development is promoted by symbolic-linguistic interaction with the physical and, above all, social world; (2) according to a nativist interpretation, mindreading is already mature at the age of eighteen months, although it will be enriched later, always through progressively more symbolic and linguistic social interactions.

Given their opposition, the two perspectives face complementary issues. Constructivism must explain the exact nature of early competence and must identify the causes of the conceptual leap that leads to mature mindreading. In contrast, nativism must explain why children already in possession of adequate metacognitive competence take years (i.e. a huge amount of time, at an early stage of development) to pass classical tests; in this latter case, it is a matter of finding an obstacle not to competence (which already exists), but to performance.

A constructivist hypothesis with a strong deflationary character has been put forward by Perner and Ruffman (2005; Ruffman and Perner 2005). In their view, the ability to attribute (false) beliefs is the output of cultural processes tied to language acquisition. On the other hand, younger children can employ two strategies that are not only devoid of a mentalistic nature but also rather primitive.

First, in their view, implicit tests can be overcome simply by paying attention to the spatial relationship between the agent, the object and the place: in one of the most classic formulations of the test, it is sufficient to establish a triadic relationship associating an agent (the observer, in Onishi and Baillargeon 2005) with the object and one of the two containers. Consequently, when false beliefs are induced, children tend to observe the place where the previously established relationship is violated.

Data collected by Surian, Caldi and Sperber (2007) with thirteen-month-old children refute this first associationist hypothesis concerning low-level perceptual properties. The researchers devised the following experimental variant: an agent (a large caterpillar) placed in front of two opaque screens can see an arm repeatedly hiding an apple behind one screen and a piece of cheese behind the other; the caterpillar always goes behind the same screen and eats the food. After a few repetitions, when the caterpillar is absent the position of the two objects is reversed. When the caterpillar returns, it finds one of the following situations: either the screens have been removed, allowing the caterpillar to see the food, or they have been left in place (as in the preliminary habituation phase). Children expect the caterpillar to head for the preferred food – now reversed on the spot – only in the condition of full visibility, without a screen (Surian, Caldi and Sperber 2007: experiment 1). This variant, therefore, renders ineffective the triadic relationship suggested by Perner and Ruffman (see also Csibra and Southgate 2006).

However, Perner and Ruffman advance a second strategy: children can pass implicit tests using behavioural analysis, in particular, by applying the rule that people look for an object where they last saw it and not necessarily where it is. Although in Perner's (2010) opinion this hypothesis implies the possession of an implicit form of mindreading, it is, in fact, an overt behaviourist explanation, as such easily challenged by resorting to the usual arsenal of arguments well-known at least since Chomsky. This is what Surian, Caldi and Sperber (2007), among others, do. A rule can be innate or acquired; in the former case, however, the hypothesis suggested by Perner and Ruffman does not seem any less arbitrary than the fully mentalistic alternative (a rule such as: 'People look for an object where they think it is'). Nonetheless, a naïve psychological rule would have a much broader applicability because, in its abstraction, it embeds several behavioural rules. On the other hand, the assumption that behavioural rules are acquired raises the legitimate question of whether thirteen-month-old children have had time to form a sufficient experiential background to set up an adequate inductive basis for abstraction, not least because they prove capable of reasoning based on wrong beliefs in very different and heterogeneous experimental situations. This is revealed, for example, by Scott and Baillargeon's (2009) experiment based on the violation of expectation, in which the changing element is not the position of an object, but its identity.

In the warm-up phase, eighteen-month-olds see an experimenter (*S1*) with a whole toy penguin and one split in two, like a Matryoshka doll. After hiding a key in the lower part of the split penguin, S1 reassembles it, making it indistinguishable from its whole counterpart. The crucial phase is divided into two conditions. In the true-belief condition, a second experimenter (*S2*) in *S1*'s presence places the whole penguin in an opaque box, assembles the split penguin and places it in a transparent box; in the false-belief condition, *S1* is absent when *S2* performs the same actions. In the final phase, the children see *S1*, again in the scene, searching in one of the two boxes. In the false-belief condition, and only in the false-belief condition, children observe longer when *S1* looks in the transparent box: they seem to have realized that *S1*, who was absent at the crucial moment, should mistakenly believe that the penguin in view is the entire penguin and that consequently, the penguin with the key is in the opaque box. *S1*'s behaviour, therefore, violates an expectation and, as such, is interesting and worthy of observation.[11]

To account for children's skills, one should thus multiply the behavioural rules. This would not only reveal the ad hoc nature of these rules but also introduce the problem of identifying how selection occurs and even some serious theoretical doubts. For example, one might think that another of the proposed rules – 'Ignorance leads to error' – involves naïve psychological elements far beyond a minimal level (we will return to this point by examining Apperly and Butterfill's theory in the next section). Similar doubts arise when considering alternative experimental paradigms based on the analysis of anticipatory gaze or propensity to help. In each of these cases, the behavioural rule invoked should be different, again causing unnecessary proliferation. As Premack and Woodruff (1978) already pointed out when responding to those who questioned the chimpanzee Sarah's theory of mind, the attempt to resort to a behaviourist strategy at any cost in the face of evidence of complex and refined knowledge proves futile. Sarah – but we are by no way different from her – was not intelligent enough to be a behaviourist (for more extensive criticisms, see Helming et al. 2016).

3.4. Min-ToM: Truly minimalist mindreading?

An articulate and interesting proposal that is fundamentally on the constructivist side, albeit crediting young children with some mentalistic skills, has been put forward by Apperly and Butterfill (2009; Butterfill and Apperly 2013; Low et al. 2016): what the dissociation of performances between implicit and explicit tests of false beliefs highlights is the existence of two distinct computational systems underlying two different forms of interpretation, minimally and fully mentalistic respectively. For the sake of brevity, we shall call 'Min-ToM' (from Minimal Theory of Mind) the former system, and 'ToM' (Theory of Mind) the system responsible for full mentalization.

Apperly and Butterfill's dichotomic approach belongs to the family of dual models of human cognition (Evans and Frankish 2009; Evans and Stanovich 2013a, 2013b). These models postulate two kinds of processes: processes of the first type are fast, automatic and unconscious; processes of the second kind are slow, controlled and conscious. Some of these models go further, suggesting that the two types of processes are implemented in distinct neurocognitive systems. Many authors use the label 'System 1' and 'System 2', although it is now widely accepted that System 1 is a set of systems running parallel processes. Systems 1 are fast, parallel, unconscious, not easily altered, universal, impervious to verbal instruction, (partly) heuristic-based, and (mostly) shared with other animals; it is supposed to be efficiently engaged in intuitive reasoning. In contrast, System 2 is slow, serial, conscious, malleable, variable (by culture and individual), responsive to verbal instruction, influenced by normative belief, and can involve the application of valid rules; System 2 is arguably engaged in reflective reasoning.

Consistent with the two-systems approach, Apperly and Butterfill (2009) argue that different levels of mindreading exploit different computational mechanisms. On the one hand, mature theorizing about the mind is flexible, not automatic, and is served by System 2, whose functioning begins later in ontogenesis. On the other hand, Min-ToM is a minimal theory of mind that, automatically triggered, begins to function at an early age and allows one to navigate the social world with a good level of efficiency, despite severe limitations that will only be overcome later. Min-ToM contains knowledge organized in implicit laws that relate behaviour to states of the world, thanks to which it is possible to *trace* mental states such as perceptions, beliefs and in particular right and wrong beliefs (Butterfill and Apperly 2013, 606). Although Min-ToM does not have the conceptual power to deploy true psychological-linguistic competence, it allows children under the age of three to pass implicit tests of false beliefs. However, as is typical of the dialectics between Systems 1 and System 2, even when a mature theory of mind is available, Min-ToM remains involved, at least under certain conditions that need to be empirically investigated.

The rhetorical question from which Butterfill and Apperly's (2013) reasoning stems is provocative: Do beliefs 'stink'? In other words, the question is whether there is something that – like the peculiar smell of many toxic substances – covaries with mental states, and whose identification corresponds to the identification of the corresponding mental states.

As Butterfill and Apperly (2013, 607) argue, Min-ToM makes it possible to represent mental states without representing them as such. Thus, Min-ToM is the computational mechanism capable of detecting something (a mental state) with certain externally perceptible characteristics – its 'smell', in fact – whereas only ToM will allow the mental state to be represented as such, thus leading to true mindreading.

It is not the possibility of functioning in unconscious mode, nor even the possibly automatic character of computation, that distinguishes Min-ToM from the more mature ToM. As far as the unconscious dimension is concerned, both systems can function outside the sphere of awareness: even as adults we spontaneously and habitually evaluate the minds of others to decide how to behave towards people in front of us. On the other hand, the functioning of both systems can be inhibited in certain contexts: precisely the false-belief tasks, in both implicit and explicit versions, require automatically triggered computational processes to be blocked.

It is only by examining the workings of Min-ToM more closely that we will appreciate the nature and – perhaps – the limitations of Apperly and Butterfill's hypothesis. To this end, it is useful to define the three central concepts of the theory: *goal*, *encounter* and *registration*, namely, the notions that young children implicitly possess and use in their reasoning.

> *Goal*: denotes that to which a movement is directed.
> *Encounter*: denotes a relationship between an agent, an object and a place. This relationship is fulfilled when the object is in the agent's field, that is, it is sufficiently close to the agent, and there are no opaque barriers in between. The notion of encounter is extensively equivalent to the notion of perception.
> *Registration*: denotes a relationship between an agent, an object and a place, different from encounter because it continues to hold even when the object no longer belongs to the field. Agents register an object in a place if it was in that place that they last encountered it. A registration, like a belief (with which it shares some important properties), can be correct or incorrect.

These concepts take part in some principles of Min-ToM that – differently from the concepts proper to ToM, such as perceptions and beliefs – deal with goals, encounters and registrations. Notably: (1) body movements form goal-directed units; (2) to have encountered the object is a necessary condition for an action directed towards it; (3) agents correctly register a target at a location if and only if the last time they encountered it was at that location and the object is still at that location – proper registration is a necessary condition for an action to be (not accidentally) successful; (4) when agents perform goal-directed actions, they act as if the object were there where they registered it.

Other principles, in particular, that for tracing states corresponding to desires, are not worked out by the authors, although they are aware that even a minimal theory of the mind such as Min-ToM will have to take them into account. Note, however, the affinity of the notion of goal with the simplest form of desire towards an object present in the perceptual field.

The introduction of abstract concepts, together with the rules that relate them, allows Apperly and Butterfill to refer to an (albeit minimally) psychological theory: the notions of target, encounter and registration allow children to abstract and generalize regarding the immediate aspect of the stimulus, avoiding the limitations and ad hoc rules of Perner and Ruffman's model.

It then becomes immediate to attribute to the characters of the various false-belief tasks thoughts that although not yet fully mentalistic, belong to a minimal theory of mind; and this step will guarantee that Min-ToM possesses the explanatory and predictive power necessary to pass such tests. After leaving the room, Sally no longer encounters the ball; when she last encountered it, the ball was in *A* and there it was registered; it is therefore there (according to Principle 4) that Sally will go looking for it. It thus seems that Min-ToM contains the resources to pass the false-belief tasks involving changing the position of an object.

In Apperly and Butterfill's view, the crucial limitation of Min-ToM is related to its inability to account for the typical *aspectuality* of mental states, that is, the fundamental properties of every mental state to represent something from a certain perspective. Notably, Min-ToM would not support reasoning about changes in identity – false beliefs related to identity, we could say. If Mary believes that the teacher is in front of the school, and if the teacher is John's neighbour, it does not necessarily follow that Mary believes that John's neighbour is in front of the school.

In other words, beliefs express subjective points of view, but Min-ToM would not have the expressive power to account for them. If Mary has registered that the teacher is in front of the school, and the teacher is John's neighbour, it follows that Mary has automatically registered that John's neighbour is in front of the school. In formal terms, contexts created by registrations are extensional, whereas belief contexts are paradigmatically *intensional* – indeed, intensionality and aspectuality are properties of all mental states. It is therefore not surprising that Min-ToM also fails to account for the aspectuality of perceptual states: when both look at the well-known duck-rabbit double image, it is entirely possible that Tom sees a rabbit and John sees a Duck, while it is not possible that Tom encounters a rabbit and John encounters a duck.

It is because of all these characteristics that according to Apperly and Butterfill, Min-ToM could lie somewhere between the total absence of mindreading and the computational power of ToM, with which it shares some important properties but not others equally crucial. The transition to mature mindreading would only occur later, during the years between success in implicit false-belief tasks and the age at which children pass verbal tasks.

But let us now raise an issue: are young children unable to grasp the aspectuality of mental states, as stated by the Min-ToM hypothesis? Childhood make-believe games cast serious doubt on this conclusion; however, it could still be argued that the highly stereotyped situations typical of early make-believe involve purely behavioural routines. An experiment by Buttelmann, Suhrke and

Buttelmann (2015) seems to rule out such a possibility (see also Westra 2017, for a more detailed analysis).

Using the helping paradigm, the authors ask whether eighteen-month-old children understand that another agent can simultaneously entertain two representations, relating respectively to the reality and appearance of an object. The experimental setting involves four deceptive objects having the appearance of something else (a sponge looking like a rock, a box looking like a book, a pencil looking like a twig, and a brush looking like a bath duck); four test objects having the appearance of the deceptive objects (a rock, a book, a twig and a bath duck); and four test objects corresponding to what deceptive objects look like (a sponge, a box, a pencil and a brush).

After a habituation phase useful for ascertaining lexical competence and disambiguating the gestures used to solicit cooperation, an assistant (*A*) shows a deceptive object to the child and the experimenter (*E*), who manifests a great interest in it and shortly afterwards leaves.

Two experimental conditions follow. In the true-belief condition, when *E* comes back, *A* shows the unexpected real identity of the deceptive object to both the child and *E* – for example, if the initially presented deceptive object looked like a stone, *A* now explains to the child and *E* that it is a sponge. Instead, in the false-belief condition, *A* reveals the unexpected real identity of the deceptive object to the child before *E* returns. *A* then puts the deceptive object (in our example, the rock-looking-like-a sponge) on a shelf opposite the child (and *E*), who cannot see it anymore. The experimenter *E* (who, depending on the two conditions, had attended the demonstration or returned afterwards) starts searching insistently for something on the shelf; not finding it, she asks *A* for help, but the latter pretends to be busy. Disappointed, *E* interrupts her search. *A* removes an occluder that prevents a full view of the shelf, thus revealing two objects, corresponding respectively to the two possible identities of the initial object (e.g. a traditionally shaped brush or, vice versa, a bath duck). Finally, *A* asks the child to help *E* by giving her what she wants.

Eighteen-month-olds modulate helping behaviour as we adults would, that is, by offering *E* the object that given her epistemic context, it is reasonable to assume that she wants: when *E*, being absent (false-belief condition), had not been warned of the ambiguity, *E* presumably looks for the duck (or the rock, the book, or the twig); otherwise (true-belief condition), she presumably looks for the brush or another 'real' object (the sponge, the box or the pencil).

Kampis, Fogd and Kovács (2017) come to a similar conclusion. Drawing on the data of Kovács, Téglás and Endress (2010), they ask whether children who spontaneously take into account the presence of someone witnessing an event also assess her point of view. Although marred by the interpretative doubts raised by the original experiment, the answer is again largely in the affirmative (for an extensive critical description of the experiment, see Loria 2020).

To sum up, the experimental data just reviewed not only rule out the possibility that an associationist-behaviourist theory such as that of Perner and Ruffman can explain early competence; they also undermine the hypothesis that Min-ToM is an incomplete theory of mind; at the very least, the burden of proof is therefore shifted to the advocates of constructivism in its various forms.

As extensively argued by many authors (e.g. Jacob 2019b; Helming et al. 2016; Carruthers 2013; Westra 2017; Westra and Carruthers 2017; Kampis, Fogd and Kovács 2017; Loria 2020), one-year-olds prove to be already skilled, genuine mindreaders. If this is the case, the two-systems model cannot account for the ontogenesis of human mindreading: there is no strict dichotomy, as Min-ToM is automatically triggered (i.e. has a property which is typical of Systems 1) but has the conceptual power (typically belonging to System 2) of mature theorizing about the mind. For that matter, it is worth noticing that the whole two-systems approach has come under attack in recent years. For example, Carruthers (2013, 2017a) doubts that Systems 1 and System 2 are truly distinct (see also Westra 2017), observing that many theories committed to the dual approach now recognize that the hallmark of System 2 is only that it exploits the computational resources of working memory.

3.5. Where does the difficulty lie?

The perspective on mindreading outlined so far is in itself a very important point of arrival for explaining the nature of the mind in early childhood, while also marking an important point in favour of nativism. This, however, urgently raises a complementary problem to that of constructivism: it must now be explained what makes the classical false-beliefs tasks so difficult.

The prevalent explanation provided by nativists calls into question the processing load (Fodor 1992; Leslie, Friedman and German 2004; Baillargeon, Scott and He 2010; Baillargeon et al. 2013; Baillargeon et al. 2014), which would compromise the accomplishment of tasks that would otherwise be accessible to younger children. Advocates of this account observe that classical false-belief tasks (i.e. tasks based on the change of objects' location) mobilize at least three processes: (1) a representation of the content of agents' false belief; (2) response selection, whereby the content of the agents' false belief must be accessed; (3)

response inhibition, whereby participants must inhibit the tendency to give responses based on their knowledge. All these processes impose a heavy cognitive load on executive resources to inhibit such propensities. Whereas spontaneous-response tasks passed by younger children involve only false-belief representation, young children fail elicited-response tasks because it is too difficult for them to simultaneously execute the false-belief-representation, response selection, and response-inhibition processes. This overwhelms their limited resources (Baillargeon et al. 2010: 115; for detailed analysis, see also Carruthers 2013).

Other authors doubt that even such an account can represent the whole story. Of particular interest is the proposal by Helming, Strickland and Jacob (2014, 2016), who begin by observing that under certain experimental conditions, even three-year-olds can overcome executive constraints and provide the correct answer (Rubio-Fernández and Geurtz 2013).[12] In line with Siegal and Beattie's (1991) attempts to design a simplified version of the classical false-belief task (see Section 3.2), the three authors call into question the pragmatic dimension of communication. In their opinion, what younger children who pass implicit but not classical tests lack is not a full understanding of beliefs, but the ability to simultaneously handle two antagonistic processes.

First of all, they have to understand from an objective, third-person perspective (i.e. as detached spectators) the instrumental action of the agent who makes the mistaken attribution (Sally, in the most celebrated version of the test). And indeed, they realize that Sally's perceptual deprivation induced by her temporary removal from the scene generated an epistemic gap, whereby she cannot know that the ball has been moved. At the same time, however, they spontaneously realize that the experimenter is carrying out a communicative action, which as such requires them to figure out the intent behind that linguistic act (arguably, to invite them to help Sally); this realization leads them to take a second-person perspective, fulfilling the speaker's communicative intention (helping Sally). Younger children are overwhelmed by the need to manage these two competing processes. Consequently, knowing the actual position of the object and being naturally inclined to cooperate (see Chapter 6), they tend to respond consistently with the request for help. In other words, they tend to interpret the question in a normative sense, as a request concerning where Sally should look to find the ball: the critical point is not mindreading weakness, but rather a specific difficulty in handling two perspectives, which generates a misunderstanding of the communicative goals of the experimenter.

An explanation in full agreement with the one just provided is offered in Carruthers (2013) and Westra and Carruthers (2017). Still focusing on pragmatic processes, their analysis also addresses the specific problem of explaining the different degrees of difficulty found in tests investigating the way people analyse various kinds of mental states – and consequently, the different ages that mark success in the relevant tests. As attested in a large study of seventy-five children (Wellman and Liu 2004) there is a typical temporal progression from the comprehension of discordant desires to the comprehension of hidden emotions and false beliefs.

Carruthers and Westra suggest that the experimental question in classical tests activates not just a pair (as Helming, Strickland and Jacob argue), but a triplet of pragmatic processes, all susceptible to mutual interference. Knowing Sally's perspective and being moved by the cooperative attitude, children tend to interpret the experimenter's question in a normative sense. At the same time, the request activates a pedagogical dimension (see Chapter 3, Section 2.2), which leads children to manifest their knowledge to an experimenter who ostentatiously addresses them by looking them in the eye and activating all the attitudes most typical of attention-seeking for communicative purposes (Gergely and Csibra 2013). But the answer to this pedagogical question is far from obvious. On the one hand, children are entitled to assume (based on the literal meaning of the question, which concerns where Sally will look) that the experimenter wants to verify their knowledge about Sally's behaviour. At the same time, and in the same pedagogical context, the experimenter might also be interested in verifying knowledge of the objective state of things. Altogether, there are thus three possible interpretations in the classic erroneous belief tests: the normative interpretation already stressed by Helming and collaborators, plus two possible (and discordant) pedagogical interpretations. Therefore, grasping the experimenter's goal is a hugely complex issue: 'What is the real meaning of the question the experimenter is asking me? Is it a request for help? Or is the experimenter testing my knowledge? In the second case, does the experimenter want to know where Sally will look, or rather does he want to know what I know about the objective state of things?'. Notice that children would know how to answer all three questions separately, as they possess the necessary mentalistic skills; however, the experimental question, ambiguous as it is, admits only one answer: either here, or there. The victory, 'by 2 to 1', is awarded to the interpretation that suggests children indicate where the ball is. But unfortunately, this is the wrong answer.

Compared to Helming and colleagues' hypothesis, Westra and Carruthers' explanation offers a more articulate interpretation. The children are indeed aware of Sally's mental representation and in principle are also inclined to help her; notably, they have realized that Sally's perceptual deprivation induced by her temporary removal from the scene generated an epistemic gap, whereby she cannot know that the ball has been moved. But they fail to exploit this information, as they are misled by the other competing interpretations of the experimental request. Furthermore, Westra and Carruthers (2017) also explain some notable differences in children's performance in tests that although structurally similar, focus on the attribution of different types of mental states (Wellman and Liu 2004). On the one hand, despite intensive experimental research on belief attribution, children are not familiar with belief questions: they know how beliefs work, but they are seldom asked about them. On the contrary, they are much more familiar with volitional states, as they are often encouraged to express their desires and wills in their daily life. In addition, volitional questions directed at children are generally more accessible to them because they are directly related to the objects ('Do you want milk?' as opposed to 'Do you want to drink milk?'), whereas questions and discourses concerning beliefs can only be indirect ('Do you think Daddy will come soon?'). These simple observations linked to daily practices, rather than a point of real theoretical relevance, could alone explain why desire-related mindreading is significantly earlier.

3.6. A role for language

Throughout this chapter we have argued that the core of mindreading is innate and fundamentally independent of language maturation; moreover, early mindreading has long been hidden by an experimental methodology based mainly on linguistic interactions, which young children cannot access. Last but not least, pragmatic interferences may make the correct attribution of mental states even more difficult. One might therefore be tempted to think that language has no positive role to play in the ontogenesis of mindreading.

This is not the case: language and linguistic communication do have a role, far beyond mindreading tests. Language opens up the possibility of communicating about abstract or other situations (past, future, other worlds, other ways of seeing things); it would therefore be unrealistic to deny that it also exerts an influence on mindreading. Data on large families or parenting styles must be read from this perspective (e.g. Dunn 1996); similarly, data on the mental competence of children with severe congenital perceptual disorders also show the important role of language in development. Deaf children born to hearing parents in most cases achieve full language competence with a considerable delay compared to their peers; even if their parents learn sign language, in the first years of life their speech is primitive, while lip-reading helps only to a certain extent. Not surprisingly, parents themselves report great difficulty in communicating emotions, beliefs, intentions, volitional states and even imaginary situations.

Investigating competence in explicit false-belief tasks around the age of four to five, it turns out that deaf children of deaf parents (and thus exposed to sign language from an early age) perform on a par with their hearing peers, whereas in the case of children of hearing parents the level of failure is very high, equal to that of autistic children of the same mental age. In contrast to children with autism, however, for deaf children adequate exposure to the mode of communication most congenial to them, sign language, is sufficient to make up the deficit (see the review by Peterson and Siegal 2000, which collects the results of eleven studies). Very similar is the situation of congenitally blind children, with whom any communication involving mental states is initially difficult, further complicated by the inability to visually perceive bodily attitudes. The consequences are severe: comparing four different types of erroneous belief tests, Peterson, Peterson and Webb (2000) place the age of test success at around eleven to twelve years.

3.7. The altercentric bias

Let us conclude this chapter with a theoretical hypothesis that touches on many of the issues presented so far, integrating them in an original view which is particularly stimulating: Victoria Southgate's (2020) *altercentric bias* (see also Grosse Wiesmann and Southgate 2021; Kampis and Southgate 2020).

In adulthood, it is now extensively documented that the mere presence of a human agent – but the same happens with an avatar (Samson et al. 2010) and to a good extent even with 'semi-social' stimuli such as arrows (Nielsen et al. 2015) – not only induces automatic imitation phenomena but also interferes with the implementation of various computational processes. Indeed, we spontaneously and automatically take others' perspectives into account when making perceptual judgements. For example, adult participants asked to categorize words that always appear upright from their perspective are slower when the stimuli appear inverted (rather than upright) to a confederate (Freundlieb et al. 2018). Even children are sensitive to others and their attentiveness: Kovács, Teglas and Endress' (2010) experiment is just the best known among the many relevant studies.

Not only do we monitor others, but their presence and attention influence what we remember, in adulthood as well as in infancy. For example, Howard and

Woodward (2019), using a non-verbal eye-tracking paradigm, showed that nine-month-olds' memory increases for events construed as goal-directed actions of an agent compared to those construed as the outcome of an inanimate object.

A cognitive-evolutionary perspective could account for these phenomena. An extrovert perspective is highly adaptive in infancy when children have poor skills to act on the world and are highly dependent on others. Moreover, all life long, a special sensitivity to the attentional focus of others promotes synchronization and coordination and, more generally, makes accessible useful information that might otherwise remain in the background.

But we must be cautious: what emerges overall from this research is that (1) we are sensitive to the presence of others, regardless of whether they pay attention to us; and (2) we spontaneously align our attention to that of others. Southgate (2020) herself clarifies that our spontaneous focus on others does not necessarily imply that we are spontaneously interested in their mental processes. Let us proceed in order, as the point is relevant.

The human sensitivity to others detailed so far does impact perspective-taking tasks; indeed, it could be the factor that leads young infants to solve implicit tasks: in Southgate's view, their spontaneous attention to others, rather than the entertainment of two divergent representations, would be enough to succeed. Consider Onishi and Baillargeon's (2005) test: children pay particular attention to the adult observer (O) who co-witnesses the presence of the watermelon toy in one box and some of its displacements from one box to the other; when O is absent and the toy moves to the other box, children's attention decreases, so that they fail to register adequately the new situation. This is enough to account for their pattern of surprise: basically, they put themselves in O's shoes so that they are surprised when and only when O acts inconsistently.[13]

To repeat, the altercentric bias hypothesis in no way implies that children able to solve the implicit false-belief tasks are true mindreaders. It may be sufficient to adopt the perspective of others and represent the state of affairs from it, rather than genuinely metarepresenting the mental states of others. And indeed, Southgate adopts precisely this deflationary strategy, suggesting that the theory of mind will only develop later. Meanwhile, another developmental milestone is reached and plays a role in our history: the sense of self. This is a point that further qualifies the author's approach; let us see how.

Like adults, young children spontaneously pay attention to anyone in their perceptual space; but unlike adults, they do so without possessing any self-concept. In accordance with what we said in chapter three, Southgate uses the mirror self-recognition test as an index of objective self-awareness, which provides evidence of a late emergence of the latter between eighteen and twenty-four months of age. Self-awareness is considered here as a prerequisite for generating a self-perspective. Before eighteen months, children lack a self-concept that would allow them to generate self-representations enabling them to represent their perspective as *the self-perspective*. As a result, no representation can compete with altercentric representations, which jump to attention unhindered and can be memorized much more easily and effectively. Hence, the success in implicit tasks (Yeung et al. 2022).

Whereas a basic altercentric-based strategy is enough to pass the implicit tests, in classical false-belief tasks children are forced to consider two sources of representations: Sally's representations, but also their own. Unlike implicit versions, which in no way verify whether children correctly represent objects' actual location, classical tests contain reality-check explicit questions. Not surprisingly, then, children's newly acquired subjective self-perspective initially generates the classic error of egocentrism that characterizes performances around the age of three: their first-person representation, finally experienced as one's own and thus becoming salient, comes into conflict with the other-centred representation. The disturbance thus created generates the typical egocentric errors, which are overcome during the following months thanks to the refinement of the ability to manage the conflict between points of view, and the (re)assignment of a privileged role to the altercentric perspective.

To take stock. Although the presence of language connotes classical false-belief tasks, it is not only the linguistic-pragmatic component that needs to be taken into account. Nor does the solution to the problem lie solely in the inhibitory component: in principle, even implicit tests require one to inhibit one's representation of the state of affairs. However, younger children, who already pass these tests, could use a different, pre-mentalistic strategy, based on the altercentric bias, that is, the propensity to pay attention to the perceptual perspective of others over one's own. Please note once again: pay attention to others' perceptual perspectives, not necessarily to their mind. This aspect qualifies Southgate's hypothesis as a two-systems theory, which we have discussed at length and towards which we have put forward issues gathered from the extensive critical literature on the subject. Therefore, if we subscribe to the criticisms of the authors cited in Section 3.6 (among others, Jacob 2019b; Carruthers 2013; Westra 2017), and we accept Southgate's data on the existence of a spontaneous and highly relevant outward focus, then we might conclude that: (1) the altercentric bias is a genuine phenomenon, and (2) it involves metacognitive processes. In this reading, this theoretical perspective is very much in tune with our approach, and as such deserves special consideration.

Having appreciated the richness of children's competencies in the social world, in the next chapter, we will return to look specifically at the construction of their experiential space. As already mentioned, we need to understand how children's experiential space, inaugurated by emotional introspection, expands to contain more complex states. This will allow us to fully understand how children further exploit all their capacities for reading other minds.

6

Expanding introspective space

In the previous chapter, we conducted a comprehensive review of children's naive psychological abilities, primarily based on empirical research focused on understanding the nature of beliefs. We explored different interpretations of these experimental studies and concluded that the altercentric bias hypothesis is the most plausible explanation. Reasons were given to think that children's spontaneous attention to the perspective of others may already have the nature of a true theorization of other minds. This would support the hypothesis that in the epistemic domain as well as in the domain of the discrete emotions discussed in Chapter 4, the first space of mentalistic analysis that opens up for humans is directed towards other people.

In such a spirit, this chapter assumes that the virtual space of our mind continues to structure itself because children, under the socio-communicative pressure of adults, become capable of turning on themselves a repertoire of socio-cognitive skills originally focused on others.[1] We will also suggest that the relevant skills involved in self-construction are mainly based on two neurocomputational systems: the first is the system underlying mindreading, and the second is the system underlying sociomoral thinking.

The mindreading system is the key construct in Peter Carruthers' theory of introspection, which belongs to a philosophical and psychological tradition that accounts for self-knowledge in terms of parity between the first- and third person. In contrast to inner sense approaches to self-knowledge, the parity tradition holds that the processes by which we acquire knowledge of our minds are the same processes by which we acquire knowledge of other people's minds.

In Carruthers' view, the parity thesis is restricted to a subset of mental states, namely, propositional-attitude states (henceforth 'thoughts'). More precisely: on the one hand, we have non-interpretative, direct access to sensory information; on the other hand, self-attribution of thoughts always occurs through a process of self-interpretation subserved by the mindreading faculty, which is turned upon ourselves. Still, as is characteristic of the parity thesis, first-person mindreading draws on the same sensory channels used to interpret the mental states of others.

Carruthers makes a strong case for the claim that knowledge of the mental states of other people has a functional and evolutionary priority over knowledge of one's mental states. He also gives third-person mentalistic knowledge an ontogenetic priority, but his theory says little about the mechanisms underlying the process of turning one's mindreading abilities on oneself; moreover, his analysis is restricted to the sphere of thought. Accordingly, it will require some additions, including the hypothesis on the development of emotional understanding which was the topic of Chapter 4.

1. Symmetrical or self/other parity accounts of introspective self-knowledge

During the 1980s and 1990s, most of the work in the theory of mind was concerned with the mechanisms that subserve the interpretation of other minds; since the beginning of the new millennium, the focus has broadened to first-person mentalization (henceforth 'introspection'). This required a synergy with other research traditions, most notably the studies on confabulation in cognitive neuropsychology and the research work on dissonance and self-attribution in social psychology (Nisbett and Wilson 1977; Nisbett and Ross 1980; Wilson 2002; Wegner 2017).

It is now well-known how easy it is to set up experimental settings that induce people to perform certain actions without having the slightest awareness that they are being manipulated. Consider, for example, the dichotic listening paradigm (Lackner 1973). If two different recordings are transmitted through two earphones, after a brief moment of confusion, people spontaneously focus their attention on one message, without retaining any explicit memory of the other. However, when confronted with a task in which they have the opportunity to use the instructions contained in both messages, at need they will take the latter into account (e.g. when the hidden message helps to disambiguate the content of the overt message). What is even more interesting is that if we ask people why they chose precisely that interpretation of the ambiguous message, they do not hesitate to provide an explanation in voluntary and rational terms, without any suspicion of making a false statement.

This is just one of many experimental results reviewed by Nisbett and Wilson (1977), findings that show a mismatch between the explanatory *motives* that people report to account for their behaviour and the *motivations* (i.e. the multiple real causes) of their behaviour.[2] In these social psychological experiments, participants' attitudes and behaviour are induced by motivational factors inaccessible to their consciousness – factors such as cognitive dissonance, numbers of bystanders in a public crisis, positional and 'halo' effects, subliminal cues in problem-solving and semantic disambiguation and so on. However, when explicitly asked about the motivations of their actions, participants engage in an activity of rationalization or confabulation, that is, they fabricate reasonable but imaginary explanations of the motivations of their attitudes and behaviour.

This is the kind of evidence that motivates a *symmetrical* or *self/other parity* account of self-knowledge (Schwitzgebel 2019): people enjoy no introspective self-knowledge of the causes of their behaviour; rather, they are engaged in an *interpretative* activity that depends on mechanisms capitalizing on explanatory theories that apply to the same extent to themselves and other people. Such mechanisms are triggered by information about mind-external states of affairs, that is, the person's behaviour and the situation in which it occurs – information, therefore, over which people enjoy no particular epistemic authority.

In social psychology, Bem's self-perception theory pioneered a self-other parity account of self-knowledge. Under Skinner's methodological guidance, but with a position that reveals affinities with symbolic interactionism, Bem held that 'individuals come to "know" their attitudes, emotions and other internal states partially by inferring them from observations of their overt behaviour and/or the circumstances in which this behaviour occurs' (1972, 5). This is reminiscent of Gilbert Ryle's passage from *The Concept of Mind*:

> The sort of things I can find out about myself are the same as the sorts of things I can find out about other people, and the methods of finding them out are much the same [. . .] in principle, as distinct from practice, John Doe's ways of finding out about John Doe are the same as John Doe's ways of finding out about Richard Roe. (Ryle 2009, 139)

Nisbett, Wilson and their co-authors (Nisbett and Bellows 1977; Nisbett and Wilson 1977; Nisbett and Ross 1980; Wilson 2002) developed Bem's approach, claiming that behavioural and contextual data are the input of mechanisms that exploit *theories* that apply to the same extent to ourselves and others.[3] Evidence of this effect comes from Nisbett and Bellows' (1977) utilization of the 'actor-observer' paradigm. In one experiment they compared the introspective reports of participants (actors) to the reports of a control group of observers who were given a general description of the situation and asked to predict how the actors would react. Observers' predictions were found to be statistically identical to – and as inaccurate as – the reports by the actors. This finding suggests that 'both groups produced these reports via the same route, namely by applying or generating similar causal theories' (Nisbett and Wilson 1977, 250–1; see also Schwitzgebel 2019, Sections 2.1.2, 4.2.2).

In this formulation, the symmetrical account of self-knowledge was welcomed by those developmental psychologists who, especially in the 1990s, had defended the *theory of theory of mind* (better known as 'theory theory').[4] For Alison Gopnik (1993), for example, there is good evidence of developmental synchronies: children's understanding of themselves proceeds in lockstep with their understanding of others. Since theory theory assumes that first-person and third-person mentalistic attributions are both subserved by the same theory of mind, it predicts that as long as the theory is not yet equipped to solve certain third-person false-belief problems, the child should also be unable to perform the parallel first-person task. In support of this parallelism, Wellman, Cross and Watson's (2001) meta-analytic findings show that performances on false-belief tasks for self and others are virtually identical at all ages.

Data from autism spectrum disorder have also been used to motivate the claim that first-person and third-person mentalistic attributions have a common basis. For example, a study by Williams and Happé (2010) investigated the ability to attribute intentions in both third- and first person. In a *Transparent Intentions* task, individuals with autism spectrum disorders and children with typical or atypical development were asked to complete a drawing on transparency (e.g. a boy singing in a choir and missing an ear). Unknown to the child, a second transparency with a different, unfinished drawing (e.g. of a cup with a missing handle) was laid in precise alignment on top of the first transparency. Therefore, participants ended up unintentionally finishing off the top drawing (of a handle on a cup) rather than the bottom drawing (of an ear on a boy). When their mistake was revealed, participants were asked both what they had *meant* to draw and what they had *thought* they were drawing throughout their action. These two types of test questions were designed to assess participants' awareness of their prior intentions and intentions-in-action, respectively. At a later stage, the children watched a video in which the same task was performed by another child; and the same test question was asked in the third person. It was found that as regards the ability to identify their own and others' intentions, people with autism spectrum disorders performed significantly worse than age- and ability-matched developmentally delayed participants; and in both groups, success was strongly correlated with success in some false-belief tasks. These findings show that people with autism spectrum disorders are impaired in their understanding of their own and others' intentions and that both deficits stem from the difficulties these patients have with mentalization in general (see also Nicholson et al. 2021).

Thus, evidence from social psychology, development psychology and cognitive psychopathology makes a case for a symmetrical account of self-knowledge. It should be pointed out, however, that no one advocates a thoroughly symmetrical conception, because some margin is always left for some sort of direct self-knowledge (Schwitzgebel 2019, Section 2.1.3). Nisbett and Wilson (1977), for example, draw a sharp distinction between cognitive processes (the causal processes underlying judgements, decisions, emotions and sensations) and mental content (those judgements, decisions, emotions and sensations themselves). In their view, people have 'direct access' to this mental content, and this allows them to know it 'with near certainty' (255). In contrast, they have no access to the processes that cause behaviour. However, insofar as Nisbett and Wilson do not make any hypothesis about this alleged direct self-knowledge, their theory is incomplete.

2. Sensory access and self-interpretation

To offer an account of this supposedly direct self-knowledge, some philosophers (Nichols and Stich 2003; Goldman 2006) made a more or less radical return to various forms of Cartesianism, construing introspection as a process that permits access to at least some mental phenomena in a relatively direct and non-interpretative way. From this perspective, introspective access does not appeal to theories that serve to interpret external information but rather exploits mechanisms that can receive information about inner life through a relatively direct channel – the *self-detection* account of self-knowledge in Schwitzgebel (2019); the *inner sense* account of self-knowledge in Carruthers (2011a).

However, against the inner sense account, Carruthers (2011a, 2015, 2019) set up a systematic defence of the symmetrical conception of introspection – the *Interpretive Sensory Access* (henceforth, ISA) theory of self-knowledge – which postulates both sensory access and self-interpretive processes.

2.1. The working memory system in the global neural workspace architecture

According to the ISA theory, one can have non-interpretive access only to a very limited range of sensory or sensory-involving states, which include seeing, hearing, feeling and so on, as well as imagistic versions of the same types of experience. Self-attribution of 'occurrent' thoughts – understood as propositional-attitude events that are both *episodic* (as opposed to persisting) and *amodal* in nature (having a non-sensory format)[5] – always occurs through unconscious processes of interpretation, drawing on the same sensory channels used to read the mental states of others.

To account for the possibility of conscious access to sensory or sensory-involving states, ISA theory adopts a functional architecture known as the *global workspace*. Initially proposed by Baars (1988) based on hypotheses made by Shallice and Posner, this architecture was later developed by Dehaene (2014) as the *Global Neural Workspace* (GNW) hypothesis.

The GNW model postulates two neurocomputational spaces, each characterized by a peculiar pattern of connectivity. The first space is a large network of parallel, distributed and functionally specialized processors or modular subsystems that are each attuned to the processing of a particular type of information. For instance, the occipito-temporal cortex is constituted of many such modular subsystems (e.g. movement processing in MT/V5 or face processing in the fusiform face area). They are implemented by cortical and subcortical regions, with highly specific local or medium-range connections that encapsulate information relevant to their function.

The specialized modules compete with each other to access the second computational space, a GNW with limited capacity, which is implemented by long-range cortico-cortical connections, mostly originating from the pyramidal cells of layers two and three that are particularly dense in prefrontal, parieto-temporal and cingulate associative cortices, together with their thalamo-cortical loops. Pyramidal neurons send and receive projections to many distant areas through long-range excitatory axons, thus breaking the modularity of the nervous system. When one of the modules accesses the GNW, its outputs (i.e. sensory information including perceptions of the world, the deliverances of somatosensory systems, imagery and inner speech) are broadcast to an array of specialized executive, conceptual and affective 'consumer' systems (e.g. systems that 'consume' the perceptual input to make inferences, construct memory traces, produce emotional responses, form judgements, plan actions, make decisions and generate verbal reports). The amplification of processing by top-down attention is the main way through which modules are mobilized and their outputs made available for the GNW.[6] This broadcasting creates a global availability of information that is what we experience as a conscious state: 'We call "conscious" whichever representation, at a given time, wins the competition for access to this mental arena and gets selected for global sharing' (Dehaene,

Lau and Kouider 2017, 488). The quotation makes it clear that the GNW hypothesis is representational and views access consciousness as an evolved neurocomputational system that enables the global sharing of representations.

Over the past fifteen years, abundant neurophysiological and neuroimaging studies in humans have provided evidence in support of the GNW model (Dehaene and Changeux 2011; Mashour et al. 2020). A much-cited example is an fMRI study by Dehaene et al. (2001) who used the masking priming paradigm to compare unconscious lexical processing with conscious processing. A word was projected onto a screen for a few tens of milliseconds, immediately followed by an image (the mask) that prevented awareness. The results were as follows: masked (unconscious) words induced local activity in the areas of the visual cortex deputed to word recognition, whereas visible (conscious) words generated intense activity also in the parietal, prefrontal and cingulate areas. Thus, as predicted by the GNW model, conscious information processing appears to recruit highly distributed brain resources, whereas unconscious processing is more localized.

Moreover, Kouider et al. (2013) applied the GNW model to the study of the infant mind. In an experiment, EEG recordings were made from five- to fifteen-month-old infants as they looked at photographs flashed briefly (for 17 to 300 ms), either of faces or of random patterns (as a control). These face/random images were preceded and followed by other random patterns. If the face photo is present for longer than 50 ms, adults can report that they briefly saw a face. The data revealed that the EEG recordings of one-year-old children resembled those considered the electrophysiological signature of conscious perception in adults – a late slow wave that exhibits the same nonlinear response profile as the adult P300 wave (so named because its latency is typically 300 ms or more) which strongly correlates with subjective reports of visibility.

Another feature of the GNW model of utmost importance to Carruthers is that it makes possible the development and subsequent benefits of a working memory system which exploits global broadcasting to subserve a wide variety of central-cognitive purposes.

Working memory (WM) is a theoretical construct which was originally proposed by Baddeley and Hitch (1974) and then underwent various reworkings over time. In its current form, the most accepted model of WM involves four interacting systems (Baddeley, Hitch and Allen 2021). Two of these are modality-specific storage systems: one verbal-acoustic (the *phonological loop*), and the other visuo-spatial (the *visuo-spatial scratchpad*).[7] The phonological loop deals with the maintenance and manipulation of verbal stimuli, as well as being responsible for the phonological recoding of visual stimuli. In turn, this subsystem consists of a phonological store and a system of articulatory control. The visuo-spatial scratchpad, on the other hand, is responsible for the maintenance and manipulation of visual mental images. It too is decomposed into two subsystems, closely analogous to the components of the phonological loop: a store that temporarily holds information about the shape or colour of an object (*visual cache*); and a mechanism that deals with spatial and movement information, rehearses information in the visual cache and transfers it to the central executive (*inner scribe*). Both subsystems are controlled by a third component, the *central executive*, which is a supervisory system with limited resources. The central executive is mainly responsible for inward-looking attentional control processes but also plays a role in the attentional selection of perceptual information. Information from these three components is coordinated with information from perception and long-term memory through an *episodic buffer*, that is, a limited-capacity system capable of storing information in a multimodal code. This component, capable of holding up to about four episodic chunks, is a valuable but passive storage system, controlled by the central executive and accessible to consciousness. It serves to integrate episodic and semantic conceptual information with the contents of the phonological loop and visuo-spatial sketchpad.

Building on this model, Carruthers (2015) defines WM as a virtual system that uses executive resources located in the frontal and parietal lobes to direct attention towards mid-level sensory areas, issuing imagistic representations that can then be sustained, transformed and manipulated in ways that are globally accessible. Thus WM takes the form of a sort of 'central arena of the mind' in which information can be made widely accessible, and within which representations can be endogenously generated and manipulated in the service of the organism's goals. But like attention, WM is a *sense-based* computational system: what figures within it are not propositional attitudes, but rather visual images, auditory images, imagined movements and so forth.[8]

In a nutshell, a global broadcast architecture arranges in parallel a wide range of conceptual and affective systems around the global broadcast of attended perceptual information and makes entry into a general-purpose WM system competitive.

2.2. Unconscious intuitive processes and conscious reflexive processes

The global broadcasting architecture provides Carruthers with a framework within which one can argue that occurrent thoughts are always unconscious and direct the stream of consciousness and reflection from behind the scene. Recall that the expression 'occurrent thoughts' refers to propositional attitude events that are episodic and amodal (see above, Section 2.1, note 5).

Carruthers' argument for the claim that only sensory or sensory-involving states can participate in consciousness and, *a fortiori*, reflection, while occurrent thoughts operate unconsciously in the background, consists of two steps (Carruthers 2017b).

First, occurrent thoughts cannot be first-order access-conscious. The GNW architecture makes it possible to explain the conscious accessibility of our sensory states. As said, when one of the modular subsystems accesses the global workspace, its outputs are broadcast to a wide range of executive, conceptual and emotional consumer systems. On the other hand, thoughts cannot be globally broadcast, and hence can never be consciously accessible. The reason is that global broadcasting depends upon a top-down attentional system that has an exclusively sensory focus insofar as its business end is the intraparietal sulcus, which projects both boosting and suppressing signals to targeted areas of mid-level sensory processing areas (Carruthers 2019, 102). Hence the anticipated conclusion: only mental events with a sensory-based format are capable of becoming first-order access-conscious.

Let us come to the second argumentative step: occurrent thoughts cannot be higher-order access-conscious either. The ISA theory predicts that non-interpretive access is limited to one's own perceptual and imagistic states; all knowledge of thoughts is a matter of interpretation. Let us look at the reasons for this prediction.

Among the consumer systems that form judgements (i.e. events of belief formation) is the multi-componential mindreading system which we investigated extensively in Chapter 5. This system was designed by evolution for reading other minds;[9] only at a later stage, the ancestral mindreaders started to apply this skill to themselves, forming beliefs about their mental states as they did about other people's. Since the mindreading system evolved for understanding other minds, it is *outward looking*: it has access only to information broadcast by our perceptual systems and must draw its conclusions from sensory information alone. But since it does not give us direct access to our thoughts, we must infer the latter from observations of our circumstances and behaviour, interpreting ourselves just as we interpret others. The only difference between self- and other- knowledge of thoughts is that in one's case, the mindreading system has more information upon which to base its interpretation. In addition to using overt behaviour, in one's case, it can also draw on a subject's affective, sensory and quasi-sensory states such as visual imagery or inner speech tokens that are globally broadcast in the mind. In brief, Carruthers' ISA theory restricts self-other parity to a particular subclass of mental states: propositional attitude events as opposed to mental events with a sensory-based format, which are introspectable.

The moral to be drawn is eliminativist. Since the distinctive feature of the global-broadcasting mechanism is that it is sensory-based, amodal propositional attitudes cannot broadcast themselves, though they might cause sensory-like events (e.g. sentences in inner speech) which are so broadcast. Outside of the broadly sensory domain (sensation, perception and affect), none of our mental states is ever conscious.

The disappearance of conscious thought still leaves room for a distinction between unconscious intuitive processes and conscious reflective processes. The latter are the forms of mental activity aimed, for example, at solving problems, making judgements or taking decisions: activities made possible by WM that, as we have seen, is the executive system responsible for directing attention, keeping images vivid and manipulating them in the GNW.

WM exploits attention to activate and maintain image-based representations in conscious form; there is therefore no room within it for amodal propositional attitudes. Since WM is the system underlying conscious reflexive processes, the latter must be imbued with sensory data. What is mistakenly conceptualized as conscious thoughts are in reality sensory images in WM (especially image-based utterances).

The distinction between unconscious intuitive systems and conscious reflection allows Carruthers (2015) to propose a specific version of the dual conception of human cognition different from the traditional distinction between System 1 (S1) and System 2 (S2) (see Chapter 5, Section 3.4).

First of all, Carruthers' distinction between unconscious intuitive processes and conscious reflective processes does not map onto the distinction between S1 and S2. It is difficult to see the evolutionary plausibility of two cognitive systems implemented in distinct neural subsystems: Why on earth would evolution start anew with S2 rather than modifying, expanding or integrating the architecture of the pre-existing S1? This sort of objection led Frankish (2009) to put forward the hypothesis that S2 is nested in S1, that is, that there are not two separate systems, but two levels or layers of cognitive processes, one dependent on the other. In this perspective, it is not necessary to suppose that evolution generated S2 by massively upgrading the architecture of S1; it may suffice to imagine that the subsystems underlying S1 have been orchestrated and used in new ways.

Moreover, we can admit the reality of the distinction between intuitive and reflective processes of reasoning. We can also accept Frankish's hypothesis that reflective reasoning is largely realized in cycles of operation of unconscious intuitive processes (including the subsystems that are typically associated with S1). This is not, however, a vindication of the S1/S2 distinction, since the properties typically used to distinguish S1 from S2 crosscut one another, and hence the distinction does not map onto the distinction between intuitive and reflective reasoning. Let us consider reflective reasoning: in some contexts, reflection does not improve, but rather impairs performance; there are some tasks where reliance on intuitive reasoning is best; reflective reasoning can also employ heuristics. As for intuitive systems, some can be slow, some can be controlled, and some can approach the highest normative standards. In brief, S1 and S2 are not natural kinds and the distinction should be abandoned (Carruthers 2014, 199).

As a result of this, Carruthers (2015) suggests a new two-system account, according to which there is an intuitive system and a reflective system. In this framework, sensory consciousness has causal efficacy, and for at least two reasons.

First, it performs an important coordination function. Only when information is broadcast globally does it become available to consumer systems, which draw inferences, form memories, make evaluations and so on. This allows all these systems (and thus the organism as a whole) to coordinate for a common goal.

Second, conscious reflexive processes emerge from cycles of unconscious intuitive processes. As we know, conscious reflexive processes require the construction and manipulation of mental images, among which the images of utterances play a special role. These processes are partly based on the capacity for mental rehearsal of action. When a motor command is sent from the centre to the periphery, an *efferent copy* of the motor instruction is normally created, thus generating a model that allows the sensory consequences of the movement to be predicted (i.e. a representation of the expected outcome). This predictive model is sent to a comparator mechanism, which receives sensory feedback from the ongoing action. When it detects discrepancies between the intended outcome and what is unfolding, the comparator activates a process that allows rapid corrections to be made to motor instructions (and, consequently, to muscle contractions in the periphery), to achieve a closer match.

This mechanism is probably evolutionarily ancient; but humans (perhaps along with other primates) have the more refined ability to activate action patterns offline, that is, to generate efferent copies without sending commands to the muscles. In this case, the sensory images generated allow us to mentally rehearse possible actions to assess whether or not to implement them. This occurs through the process of global broadcasting. The mental images generated by mental rehearsal (including articulatory and auditory images) are broadcast globally, and beliefs produced in this way are *conditional*, that is, they refer to 'what *would* happen if the rehearsed action were performed' (Frankish 2012, 43). This process can also elicit emotional and motivational responses to an imagined action, which may lead us to decide whether or not to perform it. In addition, global broadcasting may give rise to further mental rehearsals, generating cycles of mental images.

Thus, mental rehearsal provides a mechanism for hypothetical thinking, argument construction and problem-solving; it is therefore the basis for conscious reflection. The latter requires cycles of mental rehearsal, global transmission and unconscious processing, creating a virtual system that has no separate neural substrate but is based on intuitive processes.

2.3. Extending ISA theory to ontogenesis

Carruthers pursues his strategy of defending ISA theory by taking a position on the aforementioned studies on confabulation in cognitive neuropsychology and social psychology. One of the central predictions of ISA theory is that 'cases of confabulation should occur' (Carruthers 2011a, 365). Inner sense theories explain confabulation by postulating *two methods*, one introspective and one interpretative: it is true that in certain circumstances, individuals interpret themselves based on a theory (which may give rise to confabulatory discourses); but it is also true that on other occasions, they enjoy access to their mind that is direct and non-interpretive (Goldman 2006, 232). Yet, it is problematic for inner access theories to define exactly the circumstances in which one has direct access to one's propositional attitudes and those in which one resorts to self-directed mindreading. Conversely, assuming that knowledge of one's propositional attitudes is based on a theory-driven interpretative process fed by sensory and behavioural data, ISA theory enables one to predict confabulation effects whenever such data are misleading, or the theories used for interpretation are inadequate.

In its initial version, ISA theory gave third-person mindreading functional and phylogenetic priority over introspection, but Carruthers (2009, 167) felt there was insufficient data to pronounce on the possibility of a developmental priority. Carruthers (2020), however, points out that there is a case to be made that 'awareness of the mental states of other people emerges first in ontogeny [. . .]. Self-knowledge, on the other hand, results from turning one's mind-reading abilities on oneself' (9).

Insofar as Carruthers' theory gives third-person mindreading an ontogenetic priority, it is a natural complement to the hypothesis on the development of emotional introspection that was the topic of Chapter 4. However, Carruthers' theory does not go into the details of the process of turning the mindreading system on the self; moreover, the focus of his analysis is only on propositional-attitude states. Accordingly, we will strive to integrate his theory in two ways.

In the first place, since ISA theory views inner speech as providing the essential data for thought self-attribution, it can be profitably compared with Lev Vygotsky's theory of inner speech development.[10] In the next section, we will revisit the famous dispute between Vygotsky and Piaget, along with some recent experiments that attempt to detail the process of internalizing external language.

Second, the narrow focus on epistemic mindreading may have led Carruthers to underestimate the strong influence that the development of sociomoral thinking exerts on the process of turning our mindreading skills upon ourselves. Accordingly, in Section 4 we will explore the literature that investigates the connection between the construction of introspection and sociomoral knowledge.

3. Turning our mindreading skills upon ourselves I: Inner speech

In Vygotsky's psychosocial perspective, what fuels growth are discursive interactions with adults. Through their dialogical scaffolding, adults help and prompt children to pay attention to certain stimuli, guide them by commenting on and evaluating their actions and help them to remember events and concepts. Verbal communication, initially unidirectional by necessity, soon becomes interpersonal dialogue but also, from a certain point onwards, *inner speech*: a tool for talking to oneself and guiding decisions and actions; a thought without sound, but made of words. That is, something very close to what we know in contemporary literature to be an essential component of working memory: the phonological loop, namely, that subverbal stream of thought that feeds working memory, itself an essential component of executive function.

Actually, in Vygotsky's perspective, the path from public to inner speech passes through an intermediate stage: *private speech*. Although both private and inner speeches are self-directed, private speech is still a public act: the act of speaking to oneself in a loud or medium voice. The transition from private to inner speech is thus a gradual transition from a sound and potentially public act to an intimate action.[11] Not surprisingly, from the Vygotskian perspective inner speech is an arduous achievement (Fernyhough 2009).

On the interpretation to be given to private speech, the paths of the two great fathers of developmental psychology cross: it was Piaget (1959) who promoted the subject of what he called 'egocentric speech' (corresponding to private speech). Piaget noted the pervasiveness of loud speaking to oneself in childhood but reduced it to a mere side effect of the egocentrism characteristic (in his view) of earlier development. A mere verbal accompaniment to actions, then; it is nothing more than an impoverished version of the external discourse, destined to disappear soon and turn into mature social discourse. This analysis is perfectly consistent with the overall Piagetian theoretical framework, which conceives ontogenetic development as a pathway from the individual, egocentric mind, to full socialization – *via* private speech.

Collecting a significant amount of experimental data, Vygotsky (2012) made an interpretative inversion from the social to the private, thus marking a revolution in the history of scientific psychology. Children are immersed in communicative flows, first pre-linguistic and then linguistic, to which they pay full attention and from which they draw knowledge; and it is this dialogical structure that serves as a model as language becomes increasingly internalized, made up of almost imperceptible whispers, silent mouth movements and, finally, silent thoughts.

Far from being the mark of a progressive externalization, for Vygotsky private speech is the mark of a progressive internalization: it is by no means reduced to an expression that accompanies complex actions but is something that significantly contributes to making them possible. It is no coincidence – Vygotsky noted – that children talk to themselves especially when they have to face some obstacle in a planned action: if private speech were a mere side-effect as hypothesised by Piaget, this phenomenon would not be explained.

Private and inner speeches, while autonomous from interpersonal dialogue, inherit its distancing power: they provide children with tools to create the epistemic space that enables them to plan, control and evaluate their behaviour. They too, in fact, possess a dialogical structure that guarantees the comparison of alternative mental perspectives on reality (Fernyhough 2010). The only relevant difference is that the alternative perspectives are not held by two different persons, nor by the same person in a dissociative state, but by a single person who evaluates different states of affairs, in an imaginative act that is a necessary condition for planning and regulating behaviour, for creativity, but also for travelling through one's autobiographical time while keeping one's roots firmly in the present. We can therefore say that to gain conscious control over their behaviour, children must become able to address to themselves the words they exchanged with others and that others used to help them perform complex tasks and exercise self-regulating functions. It should be noted, in passing, that among the discourses in which children are immersed and which they will progressively internalise, a large part concerns norms, evaluations and moral and aesthetic judgements. We will deal with this later in this chapter.

For internal thought to take shape from external language, much time still has to pass: Vygotsky himself noted the 'inverted U-shaped' trajectory of private speech, which emerges before the age of four, consolidates and then declines after the age of eight (Winsler and Naglieri 2003). At this point, inner speech becomes dominant, although private speech continues to be useful in dealing with complex tasks throughout one's life (Fernyhough 2016).

This Vygotskian picture of the development and progressive internalization of language is corroborated by recent studies (e.g. Borghi and Fernyhough 2023; Langland-Hassan and Vicente 2018). Concerning private speech, observing forty-six children between the ages of five and six, Fernyhough and Fradley (2005) were able to positively correlate the frequency of non-communicative utterances (which arguably have a self-regulatory function) with success in the Tower of London task, namely, one of the main tests of executive functions.[12] Moreover, the amount of speech (as measured by two independent, trained judges) was correlated with more complex tower configurations, that is, it increased with more complex tasks. Even more interesting to us is another study, based on the dual-task paradigm and carried out with children aged between seven and ten years (Lidstone, Meins and Fernyhough 2010). To discriminate whether private and inner speeches play a genuine causal role and not, instead, one of mere accompaniment to action, two simultaneous tasks were assigned, and their possible interferences were observed. The first was a planning task: judging the minimum number of steps required to solve a problem (the Tower of London again); to answer this question, a series of successive moves had to be imagined and remembered. The second task concerned language used for non-communicative purposes: participants had to echo a few letters, words and so on. All this produces an effect of articulatory suppression: having to speak, children are prevented from helping themselves by talking to themselves about possible planning strategies – neither in public, nor in private speech, nor in inner speech. This was the result: in line with other studies (see, e.g., Al-Namlah, Fernyhough and Meins 2006), articulatory suppression affected the quality of planning.[13]

In contemporary research, the development of internal language has also been investigated in relation to the emergence of mindreading, understood as the interpretation of the mind of others. Admittedly, we have already expressed our scepticism towards those theories that see mindreading as causally issuing from interpersonal communication: the precocity of skills induces one to understand mentalization as a fact of nature, subject to a maturation much more linked to age than to social context and linguistic confrontation. (This does not exclude, of course, that interpersonal communication may foster an enrichment of the theory of mind, making it more sophisticated and conforming to the environmental-cultural context. And in the following pages we aim precisely to provide a significant example concerning the sociomoral sphere.) However, in the wake of Vygotskian thought, we focus on non-social discourses between self and self and reiterate the relevant question: What is the relationship between internal forms of language and mindreading?

If the data on early mindreading rule out the hypothesis of a causal role (as early mindreading precedes private and, a fortiori, inner speech by years), some interesting reflections on the later period of development remain to be made. For instance, Fernyhough and Meins (2009) investigated the possible correlation between private speech and theory of mind as found in the classic, verbal tests. In children aged three to four years, the authors found a positive correlation between the frequency of private speech and the level of mindreading. Probably due to a gradual transformation of private speech into inner speech, in later years the correlation becomes negative: children aged five to six who resort less to private speech (assuming that they, therefore, resort more to inner speech) perform best in mindreading (see the article for some *caveats*).

To conclude: Vygotsky's hypothesis on the nature and development of inner speech, a construct used in ISA theory as a basis for self-interpretation, has solid roots in psychosocial research. Viewing private speech as a product of the internalization of communicative language, Vygotsky regarded it as a fundamental tool for the self-regulation of behaviour, thus aligning perfectly with current research on working memory. And although, in the light of contemporary experimental data, one can exclude a constitutive role of language (in its dual public and private dimensions) in the development of naïve psychology, one cannot doubt its role as a factor of enrichment and – we believe – of progressive internalization.

4. Turning our mindreading skills upon ourselves II: Naïve ethics

In an attempt to explain why we have the self-deceptive intuition that there is introspection for our thoughts, Carruthers takes very seriously Gazzaniga's (2000) and Wilson's (2002) hypothesis that the self-transparency assumption 'may make it easier for subjects to engage in various kinds of adaptive self-deception, helping them build and maintain a positive self-image' (Carruthers 2009, 138, n. 5). Moreover, in examining the possibility that the emergence of introspection is a by-product of the evolution of mindreading, Carruthers considers such a possibility as compatible with the hypothesis that introspection 'might have come under secondary selection thereafter, perhaps by virtue of helping to build and maintain a positive self-image, as Wilson [. . .] suggests' (Carruthers 2009, 128).

Thus, a door is opened here to the topic of defence mechanisms, that is, the hypothesis that our activity of reappropriation of the products of the unconscious mind is ruled by a self-apologetic defensiveness; that is how it should be since the ISA theory draws heavily on the confabulation data from the huge cognitive dissonance and causal attribution literature, and such data can hardly be separated from the topic of the construction and maintenance of a positive self-image. In social psychology, the defence of self-image (closely linked to the defensive use of causal attribution), and the rationalising function of cognitive dissonance (as well as social attitudes in general, and stereotypes and prejudices in particular), are conceived as constitutive elements of an interpersonal and social reality which is rich in structures of self-deception, namely, defensive constructions resulting from mental processes in which cognitive aspects cannot be well separated from the affective ones.

There is a problem, however. Carruthers' focus is *not* on self-knowledge construed as 'awareness of oneself as an ongoing bearer of mental states and dispositions, who has both a past and a future' (Carruthers, Fletcher and Ritchie 2012, 14). As we know, his focus is on knowledge of one's current mental states, and this knowledge 'is arguably more fundamental than knowledge of oneself as *a self with an ongoing mental life*' (Carruthers, Fletcher and Ritchie 2012, 14; italics added). However, insofar as introspection is taken merely as a competence to self-attribute one's current mental states, Wilson's hypothesis of the self-defensive nature of introspection cannot be built into the ISA theory. The topic of psychological defences makes sense only in the context of the construction and protection of a self with an ongoing mental life. That is, Carruthers' focus is on a minimal sense of introspection as competence to self-attribute one's current mental states taken independently from any cognition of oneself as a self that builds itself as an introspective self-description. But it is precisely this broader sense of introspection that is relevant to the psychodynamic topic of defences: the turning of one's mindreading abilities upon oneself is to be conceived as part of the construction of a psychological self-awareness that occurs in the socio-communicative interaction with caregivers and other social partners investigated by attachment theory.

This interaction is made first of preverbal proto-communicative exchanges, and then of words, descriptions, designations and evaluations of the person. During verbal conversations, the evaluative descriptions are progressively internalized by children, becoming part of their subjective identity. At the heart of this internalization process is a primary need for *interpersonal validation* of one's subjective identity. As we shall see in the next chapter, children cannot ascribe concreteness and solidity to their self-awareness if it does not possess at its centre, and as its essence, a description of identity that must be clear and, indissolubly, 'good': one's mental equilibrium is based on one's feeling of solidly existing as a self that is *worthy of being loved*, which consequently constitutes for the subject what more than anything else must be defended.

This need for interpersonal validation of subjective identity leads us to consider the close link between the construction of interiority and ethics, to which Locke had already drawn attention: this is the theme to which we now turn, starting with a consideration of the data on the early development of sociomoral sense. Indeed, alongside the now decades-long investigation into children's naïve psychological competence, more recent investigations into the development of sociomoral reasoning have flourished (Baillargeon et al. 2014; Rochat 2015; Tomasello 2019; Grossmann, Missana and Vaish 2020), revealing an early and rapidly increasing tendency to judge individuals in positive or negative terms, and to evaluate actions as, from time to time, obligatory, permitted, forbidden. In a synergistic relationship, naïve psychology and sociomoral competence are likely to provide children with essential tools to prepare them for progressively more expert and effective social navigation (Banaji and Gelman 2013). We will now deal with these processes, once again taking the opportunity to appreciate how the interpersonal relationship provides a scaffold – and not only in the cognitive sense as understood by Vygotsky – essential for the introspective folding of skills that are partly natural, and partly socially acquired. A social acquisition that begins with infant-caregiver relationships and continues uninterruptedly after early childhood, within a wider community of adults and peers.

In exploring the cornerstones of research on children's sociomoral thinking, we will make extensive reference to two authors who have combined clarity of thought and experimental insight: Renée Baillargeon and Michael Tomasello.

4.1. Innate sociomoral competence

Along with innate sensitivity to others and the maturation of the ability to interpret behaviour in psychological terms, children show a significant ability to attribute moral value to actions from a very early age. The same children who see Massimo unsuccessfully looking for a bar of chocolate in the cupboard where it is usually found, and shortly afterwards see Cristina (who had always been next to Massimo) open a nearby drawer and take out a whole box of chocolates, not only attribute to Massimo the desire for chocolate and the mistaken belief that the chocolate is in the cupboard but also judge that Cristina should offer chocolate to her greedy friend. In other situations, children will evaluate other actions as permitted, prohibited and so on.

Against the constructivist approaches that since Piaget (1968b), have considered the moral sense as a product of explicit or implicit teaching by adults and peers (for a review, see Eisenberg, Fabes and Spinrad 2006; Turiel 2006), a recent consensus has been garnered by innatist positions that consider moral sense as an adaptive trait linked to those cooperative attitudes that fostered cohesion and (thus) the survival of early humans (see, e.g., Dupoux and Jacob 2007; Premack 2007; Sterelny and Fraser 2017). Not surprisingly, underlying this nativist hypothesis are considerations about the precocity of competence: as early as the second half-year of life, children show themselves capable of judging an action (even when the scene in which it takes place does not involve human beings, but only geometric shapes with eyes) along a valence dimension (positive vs. negative); they prefer the company of a helping person to that of a hindering one (and prefer a helping person to a neutral one, and a neutral person to a hindering one) (Hamlin, Wynn and Bloom 2007, with 6–10-month-old children). Furthermore, eight-month-olds favour people who act positively towards prosocial others and those who act negatively towards antisocial others. And they act consistently, behaving positively towards prosocial people and negatively towards antisocial people (they also show a preference for those who adopt this same attitude) (Hamlin et al. 2011; for a full meta-analysis, see Meristo, Strid and Surian 2016).

Apart from this basic agreement, however, the innatist party is significantly differentiated internally. In Haidt's (2012) socio-intuitionist model, moral judgement is likened to aesthetic judgement. The perception of emotional stimulus produces immediate feelings of approval or disapproval, highly affective intuitions that suddenly and effortlessly pop into consciousness without the person being aware of having sought and evaluated evidence or having drawn any conclusion. These intuitions have an innate basis and can be grouped into five categories of moral intuitions: harm/care, fairness/reciprocity/justice, ingroup/loyalty, authority/respect and purity/sanctity. The process often stops once the intuition gives rise to a judgement; but when the social situation requires the actors to justify their judgement, they will engage in moral reasoning to produce a justification. Moral reasoning is then nothing other than the capacity to explain one's actions *ex-post* – nothing more than "the rational tail of the emotional dog" (Haidt 2001).

In contrast, other authors (e.g. Premack 2007) support the hypothesis of innate and autonomous moral knowledge, whose connection with emotions would therefore not be constitutive. Among them, Renée Baillargeon (Baillargeon et al. 2014, 2015; Buyukozer Dawkins et al. 2020; Ting et al. 2020) has promoted extensive empirical research of innate sociomoral principles, which in its most recent outcomes (Buyukozer Dawkins et al. 2020) attests the existence of "at least four principles": fairness, harm avoidance, ingroup support, and authority. Let us briefly consider them in order.

Fairness (*ceteris paribus*, individuals endowed with sociomoral status are expected to treat others fairly, according to what they deserve). Children aged four, nine and nineteen months watched an experimenter divide two identical objects (e.g. two biscuits) between two identical animated puppets (e.g. two penguins). In one case, the experimenter gave one object to each puppet; in the other, she gave both objects to the same puppet. At all ages, the children watched the discriminatory event significantly longer than the egalitarian event (but, significantly, only if the two puppets were animate, i.e. they spoke and moved) (Buyukozer Dawkins, Sloane and Baillargeon 2019). Furthermore, infants appear to be early sensitive not only to the principle of *equality* but also to the more complex principle of *equity*: seventeen months-olds looked significantly longer when two puppets (a koala bear puppet and a kangaroo puppet, in an Australian experiment) shared a resource (a jar containing six sweets) in a manner inconsistent with the effort they respectively made to obtain it (Wang and Henderson 2018).

Harm avoidance (*ceteris paribus*, individuals belonging to the same sociomoral circle (e.g. humans) are expected not to harm each other significantly). When children observe interactions among individuals who belong to the same moral circle (e.g. humans, but also human-like puppets), but who show no evidence of belonging to the same group in a stricter sense (in that case, the *ingroup support* principle would intervene), they are not surprised when someone directs a relatively mild negative action towards another (e.g. someone who ignores requests for assistance, such as in seventeen-month-old children studied by Jin and Baillargeon 2017). However, they are surprised when someone's negative actions are more intense (Ting et al. 2020).

Ingroup support (*ceteris paribus*, people are expected to be particularly loyal to the group to which they belong). Suffice it to mention an experiment conducted on young children: after watching two groups of non-human characters (identified by their geometric shape and peculiar behaviour) perform distinct actions such as jumping and sliding, 7–12-month-old children looked longer when a member of one group imitated the characteristic action of the other group (Powell and Spelke 2013).

Authority (*ceteris paribus*, leaders are expected to exercise effective leadership and subordinates to obey; consequently, rights granted to leaders are matched by special duties for subordinates). Children as young as seventeen months attribute special authority to leaders and expect them to restore order in the group (Stavans and Baillargeon 2019). In the experiment, three bear toys were used, and one of them was identified as the leader based on size or ability to command. The leader brought two identical toys to share with the others, but one of the subordinates took them both. Children paid more attention when the leader refrained from intervening than when the leader took a toy from the offender and gave it to the victim. However, this effect was not observed if the leader was not distinguishable from the other bears.

In the early stages of development, sociomoral principles are most evident in third-person tasks, in which children just observe social interactions without taking part in them themselves (see, e.g., Baumard, Mascaro and Chevalier 2012). In first-person tasks, in which children are directly involved in interactions, conflicts between moral attitudes and self-interest are sometimes resolved in favour of the latter. But this is not always the case (Behne, Carpenter, Call and Tomasello 2005). Children aged between nine and eighteen months interacted with an experimenter who was sometimes unwilling and sometimes unable to give them a toy: sometimes the experimenter offered children a ball but withdrew it when they reached for it (teasing event), while sometimes she tried to give children a ball but clumsily dropped it. Even younger children reached more for the ball in teasing trials than in clumsiness trials, suggesting that from an early age, humans discriminate between unwilling and trying actions. Overall, therefore, the discrepancy between first- and third-person tasks may not be so significant and depend instead on the choice of experimental settings. Furthermore, it should be noted that the fact that children are involved in social actions in no way implies that they evaluate those actions morally (for other data on active helping in childhood, see also Hepach et al. 2023). However, what experimental results suggest overall is that socialization might play an important role in encouraging children to overcome immediate self-interest and pay attention to sociomoral rules (Baillargeon et al. 2015).

4.2. The cognitive bases of moral thinking: The limits of individual intentionality

Like Baillargeon, Tomasello also traces the origins of morality to cooperation, which he considers to be a uniquely human trait that evolved due to its adaptive value in ancient societies where individuals had to rely on group coordination and fair distribution of resources to survive in challenging environments. This natural propensity for collaboration would in turn be closely linked to a predisposition to non-egocentric forms of thinking (*intentionality*, in Tomasello's terminology).

To get a better understanding of the point, it is useful to look at other animals who, while excelling in various domains of expertise, never outgrow the individual perspective: our 'cousins' chimpanzees and bonobos, whose phyletic line separated from humans some six million years ago. Various experimental data, largely produced by Tomasello and his collaborators (Tomasello 2016, 2019), remove any doubts about their high level, strategic and abstract reasoning; and the same can be said for mindreading. Thus, non-human primates do possess an excellent cognitive basis for cooperation and frequently engage in group actions, which are necessary to face environmental challenges. Still, the social attitude of bonobos and chimps always remains instrumental and egocentric. They do not incline to cooperate and, if forced by the situation, use skills to their exclusive advantage, so as not to miss any opportunity to pocket the spoils for their enjoyment. They fail to understand the benefits of collaborating per se; they do not derive pleasure from merely sharing attention with others, nor do they appreciate the value of creativity for its own sake, independent of practical purposes. In an experiment that remains exemplary years later (Warneken, Chen and Tomasello 2006; see also Tomasello 2016), the interactive styles of human 18–24 month-old children and three young chimpanzees (raised, as every non-human primate in Tomasello' s studies, with humans and thus familiar with them) were compared. In each task, an experimenter first proposed a playful activity and suddenly stopped participating in it. Whereas all of the children produced at least one communicative attempt to reconnect, often manifesting that they were trying to restore a shared goal, chimpanzees were not interested in reconnecting to the social games.

In the human species, what Tomasello calls 'individual intentionality' characterizes early infancy but soon expands into a broader horizon of thought. From birth, children can perceive, feel and make choices, and they become increasingly independent as they develop, as revealed by the ability of two-month-olds to selectively smile at whomever they prefer. They also possess innate abilities that have been extensively studied in developmental psychology. Nonetheless, while younger children limit their social engagement to dyadic relationships with their caregivers or with external objects that attract their attention, they soon turn to a deeply social, communicative and cooperative dimension that is precluded to other animals: they enter into the dimension of *joint intentionality*, which will be progressively accompanied and strengthened by *collective intentionality*.

4.3. The emergence of joint intentionality

Joint intentionality – or, in a nutshell, the ability to share and coordinate one's mental perspective with another individual – emerges in humans around nine months of age. The fact that the phenomenon is both universal and present from an early stage suggests it has a natural origin. As we know, from the age of nine months onwards children actively seek to share attention regarding objects, and they find pleasure in this activity. They seek the gaze of adults to direct their attention to something, often pointing at it, because they have realized that only shared attention creates the common ground indispensable for true communication. Towards the end of the first year of life, they begin to imitate their caregivers, thereby reversing roles and assuming other's perspective (Carpenter, Tomasello and Striano 2005); towards fourteen months, children pay attention not only to the results of imitated actions but also to the way actions are performed (Gergely, Bekkering and Király 2002).

These new capacities related to reaching a new stage of cognitive development are the basis for truly understanding the benefits of collaboration, which go far beyond simply satisfying immediate needs. Indeed, joint intentionality creates a shared psychological dimension – the new *we-space* – in which people cooperate for a common purpose: our shared purpose. A shared cognitive terrain is the foundation for commitment, equality and collaboration.[14]

We are already familiar with some of the many experimental data, largely collected by Michael Tomasello himself, that attest to a uniquely human propensity for cooperation and helping behaviour from childhood onwards (see, e.g., Warneken, Chen and Tomasello 2006; for an extensive review, see Tomasello 2019). Unlike chimpanzees and other animals, who help each other only episodically and instrumentally, or are strictly bound to strict species-specific routines, humans derive pleasure from collaboration, often in the form of play.

In human beings, the commonality and intimacy made possible by joint intentionality generate the desire and even an intimate need (initially implicit, then progressively more explicit) to conform to jointly established sociomoral rules. The caregiver and the child – initially only the caregiver, in fact, but soon it will no longer be so – can establish rules for a game or collaborative and shared routines such as those concerning feeding or bedtime; and if one of the pair does not adhere to the rule, the other has the right to protest. The space of rules and sociomoral evaluations thus opens up new horizons, in which adults play an important role that children can grasp – and, let's reiterate, gradually make their own – thanks to the new skills.

Any description of joint intentionality would be incomplete, however, if its relation to language were not taken into account. The attentional alignment that joint intentionality makes possible is not only a precondition for all forms of (proto)communication but more specifically influences the formation of the lexicon, which begins at the end of the first year and bursts in the following months (Bloom 2000). The speed and precision of lexical development cannot be explained through simple associative mechanisms, but necessarily call into question the attentive relationship with the adult. In a celebrated experiment (Baldwin 1991), an adult presents children with an object *O1* to manipulate and play with. While the children are engaged with the object, the adult introduces a second object (*O2*) into a container. He then draws children's attention to *O2* in the container and labels it with a novel word, such as 'modi'. Despite their stronger association with *O1*, children associate the new word 'modi' with the object in the container (*O2*), as demonstrated by their ability to retrieve it from the container when prompted with the new word. It is clear how relevant this type of behaviour is for showing the role of joint attention in the development of lexical competence, as it highlights how deeply the <name, object> association is influenced by the joint attentional focus.

Ultimately, the notion of joint intentionality helps to account for a wide and heterogeneous range of actions that require attentional alignment and a shared perspective. Since these are natural skills, which mature in all young human beings provided that they are not severely deprived of social relationships or affected by specific disorders, we can conclude that children are born pre-programmed for sociality, cooperation and morality. But joint intentionality is also the initial condition for the construction of a broader social and shared knowledge that progressively incorporates the cultural heritage of the community. In that process, language will play a fundamental although not exclusive role, making communication less ambiguous and more capable of conveying abstract concepts such as the concepts of permission, obligation and prohibition, as well as precise moral judgements. For the full development of sociomoral sense, however, people must attain the final step: collective intentionality.

4.4. The emergence of collective intentionality

Around the age of three, children enter the dimension of collective intentionality. In previous months, joint reference to external objects had provided young children with extraordinary learning opportunities; but from now on the dimension of 'we' expands to include other individuals. The sharing of knowledge and goods now fully mediated by language, together with the ability to adopt the perspective of others, gives rise to a broad objective perspective in which the culture of the community is created, maintained and revised in a context of equity (*distributive justice*) and respect. For example, studies have found that by age three children protest when social norms are violated and others are harmed (Vaish, Missana and Tomasello 2011; Rossano, Rakoczy and Tomasello 2011), while by the age of five, they are aware that a fair distribution of goods (Kanngiesser et al. 2019) and respect for property is expected of them (Rossano, Fiedler and Tomasello 2015). At the same age, they are ready to make some sacrifices to punish dishonest partners (Robbins and Rochat 2011). To limit ourselves to the description of a recent experiment, Kanngiesser et al. (2019) conducted a comparative study to test whether individuals refrained from appropriating their partner's resources in a situation where the latter could not immediately access and control them. While apes failed to respect their partner's property and were inclined to predate the resources, human children of about 4.5 years of age not only respected others' property but also spontaneously referred to ownership.

This long and complex process of growth is based on natural and species-specific competencies. But in later years collective intentionality is refined, stimulated by the scaffolding of adults and (we shall see) the challenge of peers. Children must, first of all, understand that they are part of a society (or rather, of several societies: the family, schoolmates, the karate group and so on) characterised by shared peculiar knowledge and rules that must be known and respected; but they must also discover that they can (indeed, are expected to) contribute to building new knowledge and proposing new sociomoral rules. They will also have to understand that not all rules are equivalent, but that there are more and less important (or even constitutive ones – Searle 2010) rules and that there are special rules and statuses reserved for someone. The complexity of such a process, which will enable children to play a mature role in their social *milieu*, is evidenced by its long duration: it lasts throughout the preschool and school years, as evidenced by numerous data that contrast mercilessly with that of non-human primates (on the development of the sharing attitude in five-year-olds, see Hamann et al. 2011; on the propensity of 5–7-year-olds to create rules even when not required, see Hardecker, Schmidt and Tomasello 2017).

In the course of human development, a phenomenon also emerges that is well attested in the collective dimension of intentionality but rooted in joint intentionality, so much so that Baillargeon even considers it part of the innate sociomoral principles: the propensity to care for *ingroup* members to the detriment of *outgroup* members (Tajfel 1981; for the evolution of the ingroup sense in children, see Fehr, Bernhard and Rosenbach 2008; Jordan, Mcauliffe and Warneken 2014; Fiske and Taylor 2020). The group doesn't need to be formed on the basis of natural or otherwise uncontroversial categories in the culture to which it belongs; the protective attitude is also implemented when groups are created based on a shared language or idiom (Kinzler, Dupoux and Spelke 2007), or on *ad hoc* categories invented on the spot, such as the colour of a shirt or the use of a certain hat. As widely remarked by many scholars, ingroup phenomena are socially (and evolutionarily) useful for the protection of the community, and probably for this reason they have been selected by nature; but the other side of the propensity to ingroup protection is spontaneous and unreflective discriminatory behaviour to the expense of the outgroup members – Zimbardo's (2007) experiment, with its extreme outcome, is famous in the literature.

The emergence of the sense of guilt also requires collective intentionality, as it is related to the awareness of having personally violated shared rules and commitments and, therefore, to the internalization of the social dimension. In the collective dimension, the we-space is a shared space of cooperation, equality and mutual trust; to be part of it and enjoy the special attention given to the ingroup, it is important to take care of one's reputation. 'Losing face' entails the risk of being observed with suspicion and, in the long run, of being relegated to the outgroup (evidence on the evolution of epistemic vigilance, namely, the propensity to filter information and isolate those who prove unreliable, is eloquent in this regard, see Sperber et al. 2010). It is therefore significant that from the age of three, children begin to control the impression they make on group members and that by the age of five, they share more and subtract less when they know they are being observed by peers – needless to say, chimpanzees show nothing similar (Engelmann et al. 2013; Engelmann, Herrmann and Tomasello 2016). A recent study (Hepach et al. 2023) also shows that five-year-old children engaged in helping behaviour experience stronger positive emotions (measured through postural changes) when an audience was assisting. And shared knowledge that someone needs help increases helping behaviour in six-year-olds (Siposova et al. 2020). These are clear examples of social regulation of the individual (Tomasello 2019), a process directed towards others in which peers become increasingly important: the need for parental care and, more generally, for adult assistance, loses progressively importance as a condition to safeguard basic needs; and from late childhood and throughout adolescence, development is marked by a growing need for autonomy. Much more than adults, peers will be an increasingly important source of knowledge and models to conform to: peers transmit knowledge, practices and values that help adolescents to revise previous cultural representations (Piaget 1985; Karmiloff-Smith 1992) and thus contribute to the creation of an autonomous moral identity.

4.5. The social dimension of moral identity

In Locke's forensic conception of identity, the attribution of moral responsibility is secondary, the unity of memory being the constitutive element of personal identity. Although philosophically influential, this position differs from common sense, which tends to assign a primary role to the moral dimension within the overall framework of the sense of self. In particular, a series of questionnaires proposed to adults shows that moral traits are taken as the most genuinely constitutive of personal identity: more than memory (Nichols and Bruno 2010; Prinz and Nichols 2016), basic cognitive processes, and dispositional traits (Strohminger and Nichols 2014). Following common sense, then, personal identity would consist mainly of the identity of moral principles that characterize it over time: what makes a person the same person over time would be more a question of being good or bad, empathic or selfish, than of being clever or foolish, intuitive or not, or even capable of remembering many events.

However, nothing in what has been said so far suggests that in early childhood children, while being able to evaluate the actions of others and predisposed to respect people and behave prosocially, are also able to perceive themselves as moral agents. Significantly, two authors at the forefront of empirical research on the moral sense – Tomasello (2019) and Rochat (2015) – agree that something significant happens around eighteen months; no less significant for us, they refer to mirror self-recognition as a diriment novelty. Through this new competence, children show that they have acquired a bodily sense of self: they are now aware that they have a body, that is, an object on which one can lay a judgemental gaze. According to Tomasello and Rochat, therefore, the body constitutes the material basis on which to build a moral status, a self-image as a bearer of values and as an individual capable of actions that are judged (initially by others, then also by oneself) as good or bad.

Both the sense of guilt and the care of reputation are marks of an advanced structuration of moral identity; only agents who possess a self-image as a moral subject have reasons to reflect on how others see them. As seen in the previous section, 4–5-year-old children have fully realized that they are judged by others, just as they tend to judge others from an early age. By the age of seven, moral identity is further articulated, as evidenced by the effort and time children devote to justifying their actions to groups of peers and adults, into which they are now fully integrated.

But the social context is not only the arena in which people have to justify and explain their actions: more constitutively, it is at the origin of moral identity itself. Indeed, the self-images conveyed by the judgements of others play an essential role in structuring the sense of self as a moral subject. From an early age, when children perform some asocial or even antisocial action, adults – and later also peers – intervene to comment: 'You've been naughty! You made your little brother cry; she is now sad'. This kind of reconstructive judgement that the child is invited to internalize is daily and continuous: 'You naughty boy! The kitten didn't want to scratch you!' or 'He didn't want to hurt you, but he was scared and reacted like this'. It is through this kind of verbal stereotypes and rhetoric that children can slowly but surely recognize the moral agents they are. These dialogical interactions help children to name actions and states of mind they are in, teaching them that those things they have inside are scares, bad things and so on; thus they are powerful pedagogical tools for building one's subjective identity. This is another example of the social scaffolding that in our constructivist model is always inextricably linked with the maturation of the endogenous psychobiological system (here the innate skeletal framework of abstract principles that guides infants' sociomoral reasoning).

7

Construction and defence of narrative identity

With the emergence of autobiographical memory in early childhood and the development of autobiographical reasoning skills in late childhood through adolescence, psychological self-consciousness evolves in the ability to construct a self-narrative as a layer of personality.

For the establishment of an autobiographical memory system, children must be able to represent not only the *what*, *where*, and *when* of a past event, but also themselves as the subjects who experienced that event; in Tulving's terminology, they must evolve an *autonoetic consciousness*. This rests on breakthroughs in self-understanding. The child must understand that she is a *self* that is remembering; that what she is remembering is something that happened to *her* in the past; that it was 'the same me that experienced that event in the past that is remembering that event in the present' (Fivush 2022, 5). To establish a connection between *the self in the present* and *the self in the past* (to have a genuine autobiography), the child must move beyond linking the past to the present to create a *personal timeline*, 'a sense of the *me* traveling along a temporal pathway' (Fivush 2022, 5; see also Fivush 2010; Nelson and Fivush 2020).

This personal timeline is a *narrative identity*. This will be examined here in light of Dan McAdams' neo-Jamesian approach, whereby narrative identity is *a person's life story*, the broad narrative of the Me that the I composes, edits and never ceases to work on. This autobiographical narrative must give to the tangle of autobiographical memories some unity, purpose and meaning. In other words, individuals make sense of their lives by making the Me an *internalized text*, complete with a setting, scenes, characters, plot and recurring themes.

Importantly, McAdams' is a *personological* approach to narrative identity. Within his conceptual framework for conceptualizing the whole person across her life span, narrative identity is a *layer of personality* that hinges on two other cognitive layers: *dispositional traits* and *characteristic adaptations*. During personality development, people's internalized and evolving life stories are layered over characteristic adaptations, which are, in turn, layered over dispositional traits. And note: this process of layering may be *integrative*, which means that the process of selfing may succeed in bringing traits, skills, goals, values and experiences together into a meaningful life story.

In the last section of the chapter, we explore the *defensive* nature of narrative identity. We will see how the incessant construction and reconstruction of an acceptable and adaptively functioning identity is the process through which our intra- and inter-personal balances are produced, and hence the foundation of psychological well-being and mental health. This process corresponds to the continuous construction of a system of defences, the continuously renovated capacity to curb and cope with anxiety and disorder.

1. Identity and memory

Autobiographical memory, namely, the story of one's life from a subjective perspective, can be defined in terms of *episodic* memory (Tulving 1972, 1983). Autobiographical memories are recollections of perceptually salient and spatiotemporally connoted episodes that contain a reference to ourselves or are highly relevant to us. Examples are the stern face of the teacher on our first day of primary school, that time in a remote village we met the friend we hadn't seen for twenty years, but also the pleasant experience of tasting a madeleine with tea.

Initially, the notion of episodic memory was introduced by Tulving (1972) to account for the kind of knowledge acquired in lexical learning experiments, during which the recall of a list of words constitutes precisely an *episode*. The episodic system, therefore, did not originally have any intrinsic relationship with the self; it was only later that self-reference was built into the notion of episodic memory (Tulving 2002). From then on, therefore, Turing has associated episodic memory with *autonoetic consciousness*, which adds information about *self over time* to the episodic recollection of perceptually salient and spatiotemporally connoted events – it is no longer just an event that occurred at a particular time and place; it is now an event that happened *to me* (see Fivush 2022, 5).

Alongside the episodic component, *semantic* memory (Tulving 1972) completes the explicit memory system by gathering general and long-term knowledge about the world: the knowledge that Paris is the capital of France and that it is located north of Madrid, the meaning of the word 'cat', the knowledge that the word 'cat' has the same number of letters as the word 'rat' (but that cats and rats are not at all alike). The sharp initial distinction between semantic and episodic, however, soon seemed artificial. For example, in recalling the episode of the meeting in the remote village, we not only remember the event itself but also where the village is located. Moreover, even before that we activate conceptual knowledge during our recollection, such as the concepts 'friend', 'surprise', 'pleasure' and so on. As a result, the two memory systems have been reclassified based on the two types of consciousness associated with them: the autonoetic consciousness of episodic memory is complemented by the *noetic* consciousness characteristic of semantic memory; noetic consciousness refers to knowledge of various aspects of reality without any first-hand experience, but with a mere *feeling of knowing* (Tulving 1985).

Of course, semantic memory can also contain a reference to the self. This happens when memories are about knowledge that although concerning ourselves, lacks any experiential dimension – our autobiography as it is described from an objectifying perspective, as in a sort of encyclopaedia rather than a diary. Therefore, semantic self-continuity is a form of self-continuity that is not experiential but *knowledge-based* (knowing that the self exists over time), mediated by semantic autobiographical memory which enables us to construct life narratives. It is therefore only episodic memory that is intrinsically linked to the sense of self, as it is associated with the immediate, intimate, direct sensation of having experienced a certain event (Wheeler, Stuss and Tulving 1997). In Tulving's words,

> episodic memory differs from other forms of memory in that its operations require a self. It is the self that engages in the mental activity that is referred to as mental time travel: there can be no travel without a traveller. (2002, 14–15)

A traveller who – it is important to note – moves *à rebours* in the past, but who also prospectively outlines plans for the future. Neurophysiological and neuropsychological studies have amply shown how the same structures that enable the recall of past episodes are involved in the prospective planning of future actions (see Michaelian 2016).

It should be noted, however, that it is Tulving himself who warns that autobiographical memory is not available at birth. Although episodic memory for time and place emerges early in development (in the second year of life according to the study by Bauer and Leventon 2013; on the neural changes underlying the development of episodic memory during middle childhood, see Ghetti and Bunge 2012), it is not until the age of four that children show autonoetic consciousness projected forward or backwards in time (Tulving 2005; see also Suddendorf and Corballis 2007). This is a piece of ontogenetic evidence systematically underestimated by those who theorize on the nature of episodic memory making use of the notion of pre-reflective self-consciousness. For example, Prebble, Addis and Tippett (2013) – the article discussed at some length in Chapter 2 – refer to pre-reflective self-experience as 'an elegant solution' to the classical problem of self-continuity over time or diachronic unity. Pre-reflective self-consciousness – evocatively described as 'the phenomenological flavour of mineness through time' (2013, 829) – is a precondition of episodic autobiographical memory. This, in virtue of the properties of autonoetic consciousness and mental time travel, would, in turn, be a precondition for experiencing unity in our subjective experience of *phenomenological* continuity: the ability to remember episodically would solve the problem of diachronic unity insofar as it transmits 'the inherent "mineness" of the original experience into the present moment' (818–9). As we already know, the last step in their hierarchical model is to acquire a sense of *narrative* continuity based primarily on semantic autobiographical memory (see also Addis and Tippett 2008).

However, at least two objections can be raised to Prebble, Addis and Tippett's notion of pre-reflective self-consciousness as the key to solving the problem of self-continuity over time.

First objection: the precondition for the encoding and storage of autobiographical memories is bodily self-awareness, which we defined in Chapter 3 as a capacity that is not already given but must be constructed. Most theories of the development of autobiographical memory have been developed as explanations for childhood amnesia, the phenomenon whereby adults cannot remember most of their early childhood experiences. According to Howe and Courage (1993, 1997; see also Courage and Howe 2002; Howe, Courage and Rooksby 2009; Howe 2014), this is because, before the preschool period, children lack a cognitive or socio-cognitive frame of reference that allows them to encode and store memories in such a way that they can later be retrieved as relevant to themselves. This frame of reference is self-consciousness as commonly measured by the Mirror Self-Recognition (MSR) test. Bodily self-awareness is therefore responsible for 'kick-starting' autobiographical memory: having acquired recognizable features, the self 'can serve to organize and structure experiences in memory'. Before this,

> experiences were simply remembered as events that happened, events that were only loosely bound in relatively fragmented trace structures. With the advent of self-consciousness, the events that are now being experienced become

personalised, in the sense that they are now events that happened to this self, events that happened to 'me'. (Howe 2014, 552)

If self-awareness as measured by the MSR test is the most important factor in the development of autobiographical memory, the sense of self over time is rooted in the emergence of a physical form of self-descriptiveness. As we argued in Chapter 3, the representation of one's body taken as a whole, constructed in the second year of life, makes it possible to understand the sense of one's singularity as a subjective-objective, active-passive space with reference to the act of representing. This bodily self then serves as a fixed referent around which memories of personally experienced events begin to be organized. In James' terms, the Me to which the child begins to assign episodic memories is the material self.

We now come to the second objection to the use of the notion of pre-reflective self-consciousness as the key to solving the problem of self-continuity over time. Prebble, Addis and Tippett (2013, 819) claim that they can integrate their conception of episodic memory in terms of pre-reflective self-consciousness and the model of the interconnectedness of self and memory elaborated by Martin Conway into a single theoretical framework. But this integration is impossible; let us see why.

In Conway's cognitive-motivational model, autobiographical memories are generated, maintained and retrieved within a complex neurocognitive system, the *Self-Memory System* (SMS). The system has a hierarchical structure. At the macro level, the SMS is structured into two main components: the *working self* (WS) and the *autobiographical memory knowledge base.*

According to Conway and Pleydell-Pearce (2000), the WS is a complex set of control processes devoted to planning personal purposes active in the present moment and organized in hierarchies of generality and importance to the agent; borrowing terminology from Baddeley, it is a component of working memory that accesses autobiographical databases. Acting as a supervisory system (Norman and Shallice 1986; Shallice 1988), the WS establishes hierarchies of goals and monitors their achievement; it also controls the retrieval of information from the autobiographical memory knowledge base and the storage of new information. The WS promotes adaptive behaviour by working to reduce and accommodate discrepancies between the present state and states relative to the desired goal. The knowledge base of autobiographical memory, for its part, contains spatiotemporally contextualized autonoetic knowledge structures organised in a hierarchy of generalities.

In most recent versions of the model (Conway 2005; with some advances in Conway, Meares and Standart 2004 and Conway, Singer and Tagini 2004), in addition to the WS there is a second control system: a *conceptual self*. This contains abstract knowledge that one knows about one's self (non-temporally specified conceptual self-structures), such as personal scripts, possible selves, self-with-other units, conceptual aspects of Bowlby's internal working models, relational schemas, self-guides, attitudes, values and beliefs (Conway, Singer and Tagini 2004: 500). The current conceptual self influences the WS by shaping current goals, and thereby influencing the retrieval (i.e. construction at recall) of memories.[1]

So let us come to the point. The autobiographical memory knowledge base is organized in hierarchical knowledge structures; these range from highly abstract and conceptual knowledge (such as that contained in the conceptual self) to conceptual knowledge that is *event-specific* and *experience-near*. Autobiographical memory knowledge structures terminate in episodic memories, which are (mostly imagistic) representations that provide summary records of sensory-perceptual-conceptual-affective processing derived from WS. Now, these episodic memories are retained in a durable form only if they become linked to conceptual autobiographical knowledge; otherwise, they are rapidly forgotten. In the SMS, therefore, autobiographical memory is no longer defined in terms of episodic memory; it is now 'a store of information a person possesses about herself, of which episodic memory is only one possible aspect or instance' (Hoerl 2007, 637, n. 4). It is the conceptual organization of episodic memories within the SMS that transforms them into autobiographical memory and allows them to play a role in the construction and maintenance of a coherent and stable mental representation of self over time.

It follows from this that phenomenological continuity cannot be theoretically and empirically separated from narrative continuity, as Prebble, Addis and Tippett (2013, 818) claim. Our experience of selfhood across time *is* our feeling of being here as being here in a certain way, through representing to oneself one's own person as a person of a certain type.

2. The sense of self over time: From the physical-social to the psychological dimension

Howe (2014, 549) sees the MSR test as the litmus test for the emergence of the objective, categorical (i.e. cognitive) aspect of the self, described by James as the Me component of the duplex self. Based on our discussion of the MSR test in

Chapter 3 (Section 3.1), we added that the Me in question is the material self. In this perspective, the sense of self over time is rooted in the onset of a self-description of identity of a corporeal nature – a physical self-concept. A more *psychological* self is still a long way to come.

Moreover, this self is not yet in time. It is only around the age of 4–5 that children understand that the self that experienced events in the past is the same self that experiences events in the present (and will be the same self in the future). Before then, children are unable to integrate their lived experiences into coherent causal and temporal organizations, hinged on a concept of self extended in time. It is this concept that allows us to declare 'I am the same me as I was yesterday'.

Daniel Povinelli investigated the development of an extended sense of self over time through a variant of the MSR test: the *delayed video self-recognition* paradigm. An experimenter was filmed while applying, unbeknownst to them, a large sticker on the heads of two, three and four-year-old children during a play session (Povinelli, Landau and Perilloux 1996). Three minutes later, children were shown the video recording of one of the following three moments: (1) the children intent on playing; (2) the experimenter in the act of placing the sticker; (3) the period during which children held the sticker on their heads. The results were as follows: none of the two-year-olds and only 25 per cent of the three-year-olds brought their hand to their head to remove the sticker; however, when a mirror was substituted for the video, they immediately got rid of the sticker. In contrast, 75 per cent of the four-year-olds removed the sticker immediately after viewing the deferred videos, that is, they had no difficulty integrating past and present self in a temporally extended self-representation.

In a follow-up study (Povinelli and Simon 1998), eighty-eight children aged three, four and five years were called in twice, one week apart. During the first visit, children were videotaped playing a game, while an experimenter placed a sticker on their heads (just as had been done in the previous study); however, once the game was over, the experimenter removed the sticker without being noticed and without showing them any video recording. During the second visit, the same children were videotaped playing a different game, and the experimenter again covertly placed the sticker on their heads. Half the children in each age group were then shown the video from three minutes earlier, while the other half watched the video recorded the previous week. Four- and five-year-olds arguably appreciated the difference between the two recordings: the majority of those who watched the video with a short delay brought their hand to their head in search of the sticker, while those who watched the video with a long delay did not; probably, therefore, the latter (who, let us remember, were selected randomly) realized that the event that occurred the week before no longer had any causal power to their current state, while the event they saw a few minutes earlier did. In contrast, three-year-olds brought their hand to their head with equal frequency regardless of the length of the delay. Possibly, their behaviour was driven by chance; in any case, younger children seemed scarcely able to appreciate the different causal relevance of brief *vs.* long delays to transient representations of the self.

Let us frame these data in Povinelli's overall view of the development of self-representation. Povinelli's (1995, 2001) interpretation proceeds from the hypothesis that a concept of self as an enduring entity emerges around the age of four as a consequence of general domain changes in children's representational abilities. Drawing on Perner's (1991) theory of multiple models (see Chapter 3, Section 3.1), Povinelli argues that around the middle of the second year, children become able to form explicit relationships between events and objects in the world (on the one hand) and representations of various aspects of the self (on the other hand). It is precisely such competence that would underlie their ability to recognize themselves in the mirror: children can detect the equivalence between the representations of their bodies and movements (kinaesthetic states) and the image they see meanwhile in the mirror: 'Everything that is true of this (my body here) is also true of that (the image), and vice versa' (Povinelli 2001, 84). At this age, however, children are not yet able to construct higher-order self-concepts that would enable them to place past self-states in temporal and causal relation to present self-states. Only around the age of four, when they become capable of simultaneously examining a plurality of discordant representations of the same object or event, do children begin to integrate memories concerning (hitherto unrelated) states of the self into a coherent temporal and causal organization centred on a diachronic self-concept. The availability of a time-enduring self-concept enables 4–5-year-olds to assess the causal impact of their past states on their current states, and thus to make causal inferences such as the following: 'If a few minutes ago a sticker was placed on my head (as the video shows), and my present state is likely to be affected by that past event, then it is likely that the sticker is still on my head'; but also: 'If a sticker was placed on my head many days ago (as shown in the video), even though my current state is generally influenced by past events, the image of my artificially created self during the experiment was too transient to expect the sticker to still be on my head'.

The flaw in Povinelli's hypothesis is that it is proposed as a thesis on the development of a *psychological* self that is continuous over time. If the task of delayed video self-recognition were a valid measure of self-understanding as a psychological self, it should prove impassable, or at least highly problematic, for individuals with autism spectrum disorders. However, this is not the case: individuals with autism spectrum disorders recognize themselves in the delayed image on a par with typically developing 4–5-year-olds (see Lind et al. 2018, 75). This suggests that self-recognition in the delayed video is indeed indicative of the ability to make a causal connection between a past and a present state of self, but that the self in question is a physical self, and not a psychological self. The deficit in mindreading does not prevent persons with autism from constructing the kind of metarepresentation necessary to grasp themselves as a bodily self that is continuous over time.

The test of self-recognition in the delayed video could therefore measure not the possession of a continuous psychological identity over time, but rather the ability to understand causal links between one's past physical states and those in the present. It is around the age of 5–6 years, and in the context of conversational exchanges with the caregiver, that children become capable of understanding the causal connection between past psychological states and actions performed in the present; an acquisition that has been investigated by Lagattuta and Wellman (2001, 2002) in some studies on affective forecasting (i.e. people's capacity to predict their future emotions and desires) in early childhood. To set a baseline, the two researchers asked children between the ages of three and seven years to predict how another child would behave in a certain situation (e.g. how they would react to a dog they encountered in the park). They then presented the participants with a series of drawings that narrated some children's past experiences (e.g. one child was afraid of dogs, and another was sad because his dog had died). Finally, they asked the participants to associate these narratives with a prediction of how the protagonist of the story would behave in the present. Under the age of five, the children completely ignored the drawings telling about the past experiences of the protagonists of the stories and predicted that they would approach the dog with enthusiasm – which was the prediction they had made at the beginning of the experiment. Around the age of five, they began to connect past and present, predicting that the child would be afraid of the dog or be very sad (in the two examples just considered). Furthermore, they justified their predictions through the persistence of mental states over time.

Between the ages of five and eight, children improve their ability to distinguish between different kinds of negative (e.g. anger versus sadness) and positive (e.g. happiness versus pride) emotions, they recognize the potential for experiencing mixed emotions, and they increasingly understand that personal characteristics (e.g. an individual's past experiences or personality traits) and mental states (e.g. beliefs, thoughts) influence how people feel. Research on parent–child conversations suggests that talking about and reflecting on negative emotions may play an especially important role in the development of children's understanding of emotions (Lagattuta 2014).[2]

Therefore, it is not until the end of the preschool years that children become capable to comprehend that mental states endure over time and can exert a causal influence on current behaviour. It is at this point in the development that children begin to rationalise their subjective identity in autobiographical terms; they begin to use an 'abstract historical-causal self-concept' that integrates 'memories of previously unrelated states of the self into an organized, coherent, and unified autobiographical self representation' (Gergely 2002, 45). This autobiographical self-representation is *narrative identity*.

3. Narrative identity

3.1. Narrative identity as a layer of personality

Let us therefore come to the personological theory of narrative identity proposed by Dan McAdams. The first formulation of the theory is found in McAdams (1985). Situated at the intersection of developmental and personality psychology, the theory combines James' theory of the self with Erikson's studies on identity acquisition in adolescence and the Study of Lives tradition germinated from the works of Adler, Murray and Tompkins. In 1989 Katherine Nelson proposed a theory of the development of narrative capacity very close to McAdams'. Subsequently, McAdams' theory became a reference paradigm in personality development studies (McLean and Syed 2015).

In McAdams' interpretation of the Jamesian theory of self, the I/Me distinction allows self-consciousness to be defined based on the notion of identity (see Chapter 1, Section 4). This identity is 'an internalized and evolving life story' (McAdams and Olson 2010, 527); it is 'the broad narrative of the Me that the I composes, edits, and continues to work on' (McAdams and Cox 2010, 169; see also Giddens 1991). The life-story format infuses the tangle of autobiographical memories with 'some semblance of unity, purpose, and meaning' (McAdams and Olson 2010, 527). That is, individuals give meaning to their life through narrative structures (characters, roles, scenes, scripts, plots) that make the Me take the form of 'an internalized drama' (McAdams and Cox 2010, 169). This narration of the self is therefore a process that synthesises, integrates and unifies:

> With respect to the I, the self functions as a unifying process through which subjective experience is synthesised and appropriated as one's own. On the side of the me, the process of appropriating experience as one's own results in a reflexive conception of self (the me that the I constructs), and such a reflexive product may itself express unity and purpose. Identity in the me is the extent to which the me can be arranged (by the I) as a unifying and purpose-giving story. For contemporary adults, therefore, the synthesizing I-process creates unity in the me by fashioning a self-defining product that ideally assumes the form of an integrative life narrative. (McAdams 1997, 56)

Defining the construction of narrative identity as a unifying, integrative, synthesizing process, McAdams places himself in a tradition that runs through developmental psychology, dynamic psychology and personality psychology. Although differing in many respects, concepts such as Werner's orthogenetic principle, Piaget's organizational tendencies,[3] Loevinger's Ego development and Jung's individuation, share the idea that human experience tends towards a fundamental sense of unity in that human beings apprehend experience through an integrative selfing process (McAdams 1997, 57).

McAdams locates the unity produced by autobiographical narrative in a theoretical framework that allows for the conceptualization of the person as an entity in endless development towards unity throughout the entire life cycle.

Narrative identity here becomes a layer of a personality hinged on two further layers. The first is a set of *dispositional traits* that explain the regularities of behavioural styles in various situations and over time.[4] The second layer is made up of a large number of *characteristic adaptations* (goals, projects, values, interests, defence mechanisms, coping strategies, relational patterns) concerning aspects of psychological individuality that are motivational and more socially contextualized.

During personality development, the internalized and evolving life histories are layered over characteristic adaptations, which in turn are layered over dispositional traits. This layering process can be *integrative*: the selfing process can succeed in synthesizing traits, abilities, purposes, values and experiences into a life story with meaning:

Traits capture the actor's dramaturgical present; goals and values project the agent into the future. An autobiographical author enters the developmental picture, in adolescence and emerging adulthood, to integrate the reconstructed past with the experienced present and envisioned future. (McAdams 2015, 226)

The selfing process then takes the form of the Jungian concept of individuation: a search for the self that tends towards the synthesis of the various layers of the personality (see Section 5.1).

3.2. The unity of a person as the unity of an autobiographical narrative

The claim that the type of continuity that connects psychological states across time in an identity-constituting way is specifically narrative in character is typically associated with concerns about *practical* identity, which is personal identity considered in its connection to ethical concerns, as in the case of Locke's theory of personhood.[5] The claim is that we constitute ourselves as 'Lockean persons' (i.e. as morally responsible agents) by forming and using autobiographical narratives. The unity of a person is a particular kind of psychological unity: the unity of an autobiographical narrative.[6]

Narrative theories of personal identity were born in the 1980's, often contrasting the project to amend Locke's memory criterion that can be found in Neo-Lockean psychological continuity theorists such as David Lewis, Derek Parfit, Sydney Shoemaker and John Perry. There are at least two issues here. First, a *metaphysical* identity question: on what basis should we reidentify a person as numerically the same despite qualitative differences over time or under different descriptions? Answering such a reidentification question calls for a criterion of diachronic numerical identity, a criterion of what makes something the same thing as itself at different times. However, when the focus shifts from solely metaphysical puzzles about the persistence of complex objects to the relationship between identity and practical and evaluative concerns, the question becomes one of *characterization* (Schechtman 1996): what characteristics (character traits, motivations, values, mental and bodily capacities and dispositions, emotional attachments, commitments, memories and so on) make a person the particular person that she is? Such a question concerns identity in the sense of Erikson's (1968) 'identity crisis'; it is a psycho/social/ethical identity question.

Both Locke's original view and present-day neo-Lockean theories assume that metaphysical and practical questions about personhood and personal identity are inherently linked. However, neo-Lockean theories that draw such a link have been problematic, leading to an opposing view that metaphysical and practical questions about persons should be sharply distinguished (Schechtman 2010).

A narrativist attempt to overcome this tension between the metaphysical and practical dimensions of personal identity proceeds as follows. First, those activities of self-interpretation and self-creation that are central to our experience of being persons are built into the kind of continuity that connects person A and person B across time in an identity-constituting way (Korsgaard 1989). Second, what enables persons to be actively self-interpreting and self-creating agents is identified with the construction of self-narratives. In short, 'the metaphysical "glue" that binds person stages together into persons is narrative connectedness, not "mere" psychological connectedness' (Schroer and Schroer 2014, 460; see also Schroer 2013).

A full discussion of this argument goes beyond the scope of this chapter.[7] Therefore, we will restrict ourselves to the realm of practical identity even though we believe the latter is not separate from metaphysical identity (see Schechtman 2014). What we want to focus on instead is that the narrative view can take a naturalistic or anti-naturalistic stance.

Authors such as Bruner (1990), Macintyre (1984) and Taylor (1989) view the person as a self-interpreting being in a sense inspired by the hermeneutical tradition, namely a tradition that is largely foreign – or even hostile – to naturalistic commitments. An empirically informed narrativist account of personal identity requires a view of self-interpretation as an activity of narrative reappropriation of the products of the unconscious processing – an activity implemented by apparatuses such as Dennett's (1991) Joycean machine, or Gazzaniga's (2011) interpreter module, or Carruthers' (2011) mindreading system. In this perspective, persons are self-interpreting beings in a sense that is congenial to a view of personal identity in terms of psychological continuity, but fundamentally foreign to the hermeneutical tradition.[8] A hermeneutical notion of self-interpretation, insofar as it puts exclusive emphasis upon meaning (i.e. the intentional directing of consciousness) at the expense of the psychobiological theme of the unconscious, surreptitiously reintroduces the pre-psychoanalytic, pre-cognitivist, idealistic conception of the conscious subject as primary subject (Jervis 1989).

Ricœur's (1965) psychoanalytic hermeneutics proves similarly problematic from the perspective of the naturalist. Ricœur made a significant attempt to conciliate between Freud's metapsychology and hermeneutics by investigating how psychoanalysis allows for both the hermeneutical theme of meaning and intentionality and the objective and biological theme of drive causality. This attempt, however, remains within a pre-cognitivist conception of the unconscious.

According to Ricœur, Freud's methodological approach is 'une anti-phénoménologie, qui exige, non la réduction à la conscience, mais la réduction de la conscience' (1969, 137). Psychoanalysis thus becomes a *demystifying* hermeneutics; and this project of demystification – the systematic search for self-deception and the uncovering of the underlying truth – is at the core of the critical tradition to which Freud belongs: the 'unmasking trend' that has been part of European thought from La Rochefoucauld through Enlightenment philosophers, Marx, Nietzsche and Ibsen (Ellenberger 1970, 537).

As seen in Chapter 2 (Section 2.1), however, consciousness is taken as *given* by Freud, and this makes psychoanalysis a dialectical variant of phenomenology. In contrast, a dynamic psychology firmly embedded in behavioural sciences is not vulnerable to this objection: it aims to pick up the critical content of psychoanalysis – namely, its being a demystifying project – but within a framework where consciousness is at issue and the unconscious is understood in terms of a particular conception of the relationship between the subpersonal and personal levels of analysis in which the former is always in a dialectical relationship with the latter.[9]

It should be emphasized that the naturalistic characterization of self-interpretation as a reappropriation of the products of the neurocognitive unconscious does not commit us to psychobiological reductionism. As we shall see in Section 4, sociocultural factors condition psychological self-awareness: studies in cultural psychology and ethnopsychiatry have shown that individuals from pre-modern cultural contexts possess a self-awareness that is primarily physical and social rather than psychological. And yet, whereas narrativist hermeneutics considers the socially and historically situated autobiographical self as the foundational aspect of human selfhood, we see narrative identity as only one of the three dimensions of the Me, a dimension that moreover, is constituted from bodily subjectivity. In this perspective, corporeal identity and narrative identity are two different forms of experiential unity that arise from the process of selfing.[10]

3.3. Autobiographical reasoning

The selfing process begins to arrange the Me into a self-defining narrative during early adolescence. At that age, there is also an increasing demand by others to acquire an individual sociocultural identity and prepare for an adult role in society. The upshot is the Eriksonian identity crisis, and a need arises to play a more active role in self-definition and self-creation. Constructing and internalizing a life story provides an answer to Erikson's key identity questions – questions regarding who one is, how one came to be and where one is going in life.

As Shoemaker notes,

> telling this unifying story both requires a robust set of psychological capacities and incorporates just those actions and experiences I have had (or will have) while in possession of that robust set of psychological capacities, i.e., the story is just about my life as a *Lockean person*. (2021, sect. 2.4)

Among the psychological capacities that enable one to take one's life as an object of systematic reflection, and thus give one's subjective identity an autobiographical form, is the ability to operate at the formal level that develops in adolescence (Breger 1974; McAdams 1985, 1996).

Two clarifications are needed. First, talking about formal thinking does not commit us to Piaget's notion of a *stage* of formal-operational thought. As Carey, Zaitchik and Bascandziev (2015; but see also Karmiloff-Smith 1992) argue, the age-related evolutions that Piaget explained within his stage theory can be seen as domain-general changes nowadays accounted for by the development of executive functions. Second, Piaget's distinction between concrete and formal thinking can be fruitfully considered in the context of Sternberg's (1988) triarchic theory of intelligence. Practical intelligence is the most limited of Sternberg's three forms of intelligence and is linked to concrete thinking: it deals with repetitive tasks and basic empirical know-how, is very rarely engaged in hypotheses and plans, hardly makes predictions and goes beyond immediate material data. By contrast, the analytic and creative aspects of intelligence involve very complex mental operations involving abstraction and mental modelling.

Now, whereas in concrete thinking possibility remains an extension of reality, in formal thinking reality is subordinated to possibility (Inhelder and Piaget 1958). Adolescents are capable of hypothetico-deductive thought by drawing necessary conclusions from truths that are considered merely possible. They can ask themselves questions such as: What is my life really about? Who might I be in the future? What if I decide to reject my parents' religion? What would it mean to live a good life? According to McAdams (2015), this emerging interest in concerns about practical identity requires a narrative frame.[11]

Habermas and Bluck (2000) have described the social-cognitive changes that must take place for the adolescent to initiate the crafting of the life story that is at the heart of McAdams' theory. The life story is most completely manifested in entire life narratives as specific, but rare, linguistic products. A more frequent but only partial manifestation of the life story is *autobiographical reasoning*, which is

> a process of thinking or speaking that links distant elements of one's life to each other and the self in an attempt to relate the present self to one's personal past and future. (Habermas and Köber 2015b, 3; see also Habermas 2011, 2019)

The term 'reasoning' is employed to highlight three aspects: the constructive and interpretative nature of the activity, its cognitive as well as communicative nature, and the normative facet implied by its appeal to reason and logic. Some sociocognitive competencies underpin autobiographical reasoning: (i) the ability to put past biographically salient events in temporal order (temporal coherence);[12] (ii) the ability to think about the self in abstract terms (i.e. as embodying certain personality traits) and account for changes or developments in the self over time (causal-motivational coherence); (iii) the ability to summarize and interpret themes within stories and apply these to one's own life (thematic coherence); and (iv) the awareness of cultural norms regarding the major events one is expected to experience during the life course.

The term 'reasoning' also alludes to the Piagetian cognitive-developmental tradition, which Habermas and Bluck (2000) aim to wed to the narrative tradition. In full harmony with Piaget's constructivism, they describe the development of the life story in adolescence as the emergence of a new quality: the *global coherence* of the life story. To convey the development of the self, up to the present, life narratives not only require the inclusion of various life events and aspects of the self but also those interpretative connections between events and the self that create globally coherent stories. Global coherence is the narrative feature that differentiates life narratives from mere lists of unconnected life memories.

In an extensive study, Habermas and de Silveira (2008) have shown that life narratives begin to emerge in middle childhood, with coherence progressively increasing (in all its dimensions) during adolescence. Participants from ages eight through twenty were asked to narrate seven personally significant events and place them on a personal timeline. Although eight-year-olds scored above chance, it was only around age twelve that children began to link events causally, with the complexity and coherence of causal and biographical reasoning increasing with age.

Köber, Schmiedek and Habermas (2015) longitudinally extended this study to explore the development of global coherence in life narratives from childhood to adulthood. They found that measures of temporal and causal-motivational coherence increase substantially across adolescence up to early adulthood, as does thematic coherence, which continues to develop throughout middle adulthood (see also Köber and Habermas 2017a, 2017b).

Finally, Camia and Habermas (2020) investigated stability and change of life stories by conducting a study on 145 participants aged between sixteen and sixty-nine years, who had mentioned personal memories four years prior but had omitted them from their current life narratives. They discovered that memory age (i.e. the difference between the age at the time of telling and the age at the time of the event) predicts omission, whereas valence does not. Additionally, memory prompts helped to recall these omitted memories. Finally, the study found that strong motivation, such as personal relevance at the time of mentioning, was linked to remembering and incorporating personal memories into one's life narrative.

4. Dissociation of the Jamesian selves

The ability to construct life stories emerges in adolescence when individuals acquire the cognitive tools to represent the self in more abstract ways and form a coherent life story. Further evidence in favour of such a hypothesis comes from cultural psychology and ethnopsychiatry, which show that the predominant self-consciousness in semi-literate or illiterate people living in pre-industrial societies is primarily physical and social rather than psychological.

Indeed, semi-literate or illiterate adults in pre-industrial cultures manifest considerable difficulty in constructing a virtual inner space of the mind. In this psychological-cultural condition, dreams are not conceptualized as the product of one's mind, but rather as night visions originating from outside the body. Emotions and passions, being experienced as objective rather than subjective events, are directly ascribed to chance accidents of the body, or are perceived as the effect of 'being possessed' by some force or entity that comes from the outside; thinking is confused with speaking (here 'I think' essentially means 'I say' or 'I tell myself'); furthermore, plans and fantasies are only partially objectified, and hence are examined with difficulty. In any case, all these events are always discontinuous, that is, unrelated to each other, insofar as they are not causally integrated within a unitary inner space. The individual feels only partially responsible for them.

It is noteworthy that the same difficulty in conceiving dreams as mental events can be observed in children. Piaget (1997, Chapter 3) describes three stages in children's understanding of their dreams. In the first stage, they experience dreams as coming from outside of themselves and remaining external. In the second stage, children do not yet know how to objectify their dreams, even though they know they have produced them subjectively. They experience either the objectivity or the subjectivity of dreams, but not both: they are unable to account for them 'from the inside' while examining them 'from the outside'. Consequently, children generally refer to dreams as external objects, that is, as events 'sent from outside' during the night, which they have witnessed without grasping them as subjective production. Or, on the contrary, they speak of them as things they have done ('Masha ate all the cherries'): they subjectivize the dream action, but without objectifying the dream. In the third stage, children experience dreams as internal and of internal origin, as part of their thoughts, feelings and ideas.

Early evidence concerning the difficulties of illiterate people in representing an inner experiential space was uncovered by Luria (1976) in his famous survey about the Kashgars in Uzbekistan in 1932 and 1933. Along with Vygotsky, Luria proposed a cultural-historical psychology, in which the construction of self-awareness requires that our species' neurocognitive mechanisms be accompanied by a repertoire of conceptual and (indissolubly) lexical tools, of an abstract kind. Where these tools are deficient and concrete thinking predominates,[13] great difficulty in reflexively and objectively representing the virtual inner space of the mind may be observed.[14]

The exclusive appeal to practical intelligence skills gives rise to a subjective sphere that fosters somatic-pragmatic rather than psychological conceptions of the individual. Consequently, agents conceive of themselves essentially in terms of physical identity, and it is the physical identity that forges social identity. Agents then consider themselves responsible insofar as they are held *socially* responsible for their actions, whether they be past, present or future. By contrast, agents are never fully able to responsibly and self-critically appropriate the products of their mind, given their difficulty in constructing an inner experiential space. In James' idiom, these persons possess a material self and a social self but lack a spiritual self. All acts (including linguistic ones) are certainly 'produced', and agents consider themselves as the owner of these acts, as the body identifies their origin and continuity; yet dreams, fantasies, plans, passions, anxieties, frenzies and sorrows, can be identified and conceptualized only with difficulty because their origin and phenomenological place are unclear. Nor, consequently, can we find a full conceptualization of intentionality, as it is expressed not only in emotions but also in fantasies and plans. In such cases, therefore, fantasies (understood as compensatory and unrealistic scenarios arising from emotional needs) and plans (understood as models arising from realistic examinations of one's possibilities) are confused with each other, since their respective origins can never be traced. This leads to a series of important and serious limitations both in planning the subject's future activities and in evaluating past ones.

In these psychological-cultural circumstances, it is quite consequent that agents evince a *hysterical splitting* tendency, which is psychological, but also ethical. Persons 'disclaim' their action (which consists of the body's moving or paralysing), and the mental state, being experienced as an objective rather than a subjective event (i.e. something that is not produced by the mind but which 'happens') is ascribed to chance accidents of the body.

Thus, cultural psychology and ethnopsychiatry provide us with data that seem to legitimize the hypothesis that the intelligence of adult illiterates living in pre-industrial societies is entirely focused on immediate practical experience,[15] and therefore lacks the necessary resources to make the complete shift from a physical to a psychological form of self-consciousness – the self-consciousness of ourselves as schooled members of large-scale industrialized societies, equipped with analytic and creative forms of intelligence.

This by no means implies that the distinction between illiterate and educated people is always clear-cut. It is easy to note that even our assumption of responsibility for passions or moods that we ourselves produce is often incomplete. For it is not unusual that in the face of responsibility for committing a serious offence with full lucidity, even schooled members of large-scale industrialized societies take refuge in splitting mechanisms. The ordinary verbalization 'I was out of my mind' (as one may say, conforming to a sort of rhetoric, 'I was out of my mind because I was blinded by rage' or 'by passion') easily turns into 'I was not myself', and even into 'Something inside me acted' – from here it is but a short step to hysteria.

Despite these failures of our psychological self-awareness, one cannot fail to take into account Anthony Giddens' socio-historical analysis according to which the post-traditional order emerging from the macrocontext of late modernity has contributed to mould persons characterized by a heightened level of self-reflection:

> Modernity is a post-traditional order, in which the question, 'How shall I live?' has to be answered in day-to-day decisions about how to behave, what to wear

and what to eat – and many other things – as well as interpreted within the temporal unfolding of self-identity. (Giddens 1991, 14)

In late modernity, the self is 'a reflexive project – a more or less continuous interrogation of past, present and future' (Giddens 1992, 30); it is a critical project, always open to risk.

This risk exposure – which is intrinsic to the construction of the self 'as reflexively understood by the person in terms of her or his biography' (Giddens 1991, 53) – brings us back to Ernesto De Martino's topic of the *precariousness* of identity self-construction (Chapter 1, Section 3). Contemporaneity is not only an objective reality full of social changes, but also a phantasmatic psychological world crowded with desires, disappointments, frustrations and consoling illusions; a world poised between psychological suffering and outright pathology.[16] Persons no longer easily know who they are because they can no longer refer to their social status of birth, but they may not know how to become something different.

Against this backdrop, anyone who proposes to address the issue of the construction and defence of subjective identity must distance itself from the illusory theme of 'self-invention' and focus instead on the process of 'self-realisation', with its two aspects of *autonomy* and *individuation*. We will discuss this in the next section.

5. The defensive nature of narrative identity

We have seen that with the emergence of autobiographical memory in early childhood and the development of autobiographical reasoning skills in late childhood through adolescence, psychological self-awareness evolves in the ability to construct a self-narrative as a layer of personality.

What we must now focus on is that autobiographical reasoning is a *defence mechanism*, a mechanism to compensate for threats of self-discontinuity (Habermas and Köber 2015a, 2015b). It embeds personal memories in a culturally, temporally, causally and thematically coherent life story; thus, in situations of biographical disruption (e.g. in the case of a serious bereavement), autobiographical reasoning can re-establish the diachronic continuity of the self through the use of arguments that bridge change by embedding it in a larger life story context.[17]

Another mechanism that can create self-continuity is postulated in the SMS framework (see Section 1). Here self-continuity may be established by the mechanism whereby 'the remembered self is systematically distorted by automatically assimilating it to the present self-concept, increasing the similarity between the present and remembered reflected self, to maintain conceptual self-sameness' (Habermas and Köber 2015b, 2).[18] In circumstances of relative stability, assimilating memories to a current self-concept may be sufficient to establish personal sameness in time or personal stability. However, insofar as such a mechanism bridges personal change 'simply by reducing the perception of change', it cannot 'create self-continuity when change is acknowledged' (Habermas and Köber 2015a, 155). In situations of biographical upheaval, disruptive effects on the sense of self-continuity can be compensated by the use of autobiographical arguments in life narratives.

The inherently psychodynamic character of these constructs introduces us to the matter of the defensive nature of narrative identity.

At the end of the preschool period, children feverishly ask adults things about themselves: what gender they are, what their attitudes are, whether they are good or bad; they want to be told – and they tell themselves – episodes and stories in which they can recognize themselves, in which they can perceive, objectify, distinguish and accept their characteristics. In this way, identity is placed in memory and rationalized as autobiography; and here – breaking with a long philosophical tradition that has viewed psychological self-consciousness as a purely cognitive phenomenon – the indissoluble link between identity and affectivity must be emphasized.

Attachment theory and infant research have shown that the self-description that children pursue is an *accepting* description, namely, an indissolubly cognitive description (as a *definition* of self) and emotional-affectional (as an *acceptance* of self). Hence, affective growth and identity construction cannot be separated. Children need a clear and consistent capacity to describe themselves in a manner that is fully legitimized by caregivers, socially valid, capable of attracting attention and serving as a base for ceaselessly renewed affectional transactions.

Thus, the construction of affectional life, throughout infancy and, subsequently, throughout one's entire life, is closely linked to the construction of a subjective identity that is well-defined and accepted as valid.

5.1. Autonomy, individuation and eudaimonia

During early childhood, the development of subjective identity exhibits a paradoxical feature. While each of us, with increasing clarity, constructs and recognizes the singularity of our being ourselves – a singularity that cannot be confused with others – at the same time and in a contradictory way, everyone 'plays' with identifications, introjections and projections, intermingling their own personality characteristics, more or less temporarily, with those of others. In the first place, children's construction of their own identity occurs through an introjective appropriation of parts of the identity of others – first and foremost, the idealized characteristics of the parent of the same gender. There is more to it than that, however; for the pretend play, so evident from the third year of life, makes explicit children's propensity to temporarily feel themselves different from what they are, to go through fictitious identities, to enhance themselves or explore their being and borders, mingling themselves with identities that are not theirs.

During adolescence, the process of construction/self-acceptance of one's identity is linked to one of the two main aspects of the process of self-realization: *autonomy* (the other aspect is *individuation*).

Adolescent crisis and together with it the process of social autonomization in post-adolescence are largely a problem of identity. The most widely referenced model of identity development is still Erikson's psychosocial theory, where indeed identity formation represents the main task of the developmental stage of adolescence.[19] More precisely, the adolescent faces the problem of sustaining and managing the end of the heteronomy of identity, whereby one's 'being this way' was hitherto a function of the definitions offered by caregivers; and this is the problem of how to move, in a risky leap, towards acquiring an autonomous self-definition: an identity unencumbered by any protective 'recognition', mediated by identifications with transactional figures and hinged on extra-familial life. In Jamesian terms, the various parts of the material, social and spiritual selves must be organized into 'a new pattern that confers upon the Me a unifying and purposeful sense of identity' (McAdams and Cox 2010, 164). The optimal outcome of this process is a kind of dialectic balance in which the so-called 'syntonic' pole of identity integration is predominant over the 'dystonic' pole of identity diffusion.

Regarding clinical themes that will be developed in the next section, it is to be noted that Erikson views identity diffusion as consisting of insufficient integration of self-images originating from a weakness of the ego.[20] Moreover, in a revision of Erikson's developmental theory, Crawford et al. (2004) suggest that young individuals who experience identity diffusion may use cluster B symptoms (borderline, histrionic and narcissistic symptoms) as a form of maladaptive defence against distress, which typically arises from a poorly consolidated identity. Intimacy and engagement imply a constant threat of fusion and consequent loss of a fragile identity, both of which can be defended against by the symptoms and disturbed behaviour seen in borderline patients. Finally, psychotic crisis or decompensation, a dramatic and common risk between sixteen and eighteen years of age, can be interpreted to a significant extent as a failure in achieving the autonomy of identity.

In the transition from emerging adulthood to young adulthood, problems with identity have an almost equally prominent role. Individuals who approach their late twenties carrying the burden of mental disorders, disturbed behaviour and unresolved social drifts, often begin to suffer acutely from having failed to build an identity that is adult, self-determined, socially recognizable and acceptable; in such an extremely painful crisis, the pre-existing psychological problems can easily worsen. A typical task of psychotherapeutic and psychoanalytic work is the maturational clearing up of infantile remains within the personality; that is, remnants of a psychological lack of autonomy in individuals in their late twenties and, often, early thirties.

Over the entire developmental lifespan, public sociality and private affectional bonds will jointly constitute the continuation of a quest for identity which cannot be separated from the search for recognition. Each of us, perhaps without clearly acknowledging it, will devote not a small part of our resources to creating situations that guarantee not only material protection, but also a positive self-image, and together with it appropriate supplies of self-esteem. In so doing, we seek confirmation of the solidity of our self-image. The competition for a social status aimed at providing a suitable public self-image which can guarantee characteristics of an objective dignity for one's image is connected with the search for more strictly affectional reassurances, namely, with the negotiation of forms of unconditional acceptance from a small number of individuals belonging to the intimate sphere.

Here, though, some possibilities of conflict arise. For example, the conflict between a competitive (and possibly also aggressive) attitude, aimed at securing a high social status, and a cooperative (and possibly submissive) attitude to secure acceptance and affectional protection. More generally, the contrast between the need for a relevant perception of one's identity and the necessity of preserving self-esteem through a 'high' – and possibly unrealistic – model of ideal identity. An incongruity between one's idealized self-concept and one's self-image (the self as it appears in behaviour) is inevitable and managed by the individual through particular defensive manoeuvres.[21]

Other more contingent or more strictly individual mechanisms suitable for producing self-esteem and security originate from the ways of self-presentation and the techniques of ongoing management of one's identity in the activities and banal conversations of everyday life. Here Goffman's work (1958) constitutes the essential reference point. Within the context of the conversation, the subject's true purpose in many explanatory or persuasive discourses, rather than explaining facts or convincing an audience of the soundness of a specific practical solution, is that of favourably presenting herself (Antaki 1985). Similarly, in the context of self-presentation, the analysis of the ordinary, folk-psychological descriptions and explanations of our own and other people's behaviour shows how self-image is closely linked to the self-defensive use of causal attributions (Weary and Arkin 1981). (As we shall see shortly, narcissistic defences, too, are ordinary strategies aimed at preserving a positive self-image.)

In the fourth and fifth decades, the existence of many people is dominated by the discovery of their real personality characteristics, and thus their basic inclinations. This is the second of the two main aspects of the self-realization process: individuation.

As we know, in McAdams' personological theory of narrative identity, the unity produced by the autobiographical narrative is situated in a theoretical framework that allows the person to be conceptualized in its entirety and throughout the life cycle. During the development of the personality, the layering of life stories on characteristic adaptations, and of the latter on dispositional traits, is a process that can be integrative: the process of selfing then operates a synthesis of traits, capacities, purposes, values and experiences into a life story with meaning. This is Jungian individuation: a self-seeking that aspires to the synthesis of the layers of personality.

Picking up on a cultural theme that was already alive in the nineteenth century, Jung (1976) argues that each person has a task towards himself or herself that, while continuing throughout life, most typically concerns the period of maturity. In Jung, individuation is a synthesis of several things at once: it is the maturation of the personality, and thereby actualization and self-realization in one's aptitudes; it is a process of integration, that is, consistent unification of one's psychological characteristics (including, says Jung, those that had remained 'in the shadows' until then); and it is a spiritual journey in search of awareness and wisdom.

Individuation has an ethical dimension that is linked to the ancient ideal of *eudaimonia*. The term means 'to live in harmony with one's potential' – and well, considering this a goal that is not already vicious but socially virtuous. Eudaimonia is also referred to as 'ethical perfectionism', 'self-actualisation ethics' and 'normative individualism' (Norton 1976); and it is approached as the 'ethics of authenticity' by Ferrara (1998).

Ferrara convincingly argues that one may 'interpret *eudaimonia* or well-being in terms of a philosophical theory of the identity of the human self' (1998, 31). In other words, one can follow Aristotle when he defines the concept of the good life as the telos towards which the best human action tends; but unlike the Greek philosopher, one can consider that this end does not transcend the individual, nor is it external to him, but is instead immanent to the vicissitudes of his mental life. That is to say, acting according to virtue is not to be understood as performing well that task which is proper to the human being in general; it is rather to be understood as performing well the task, which varies concretely from individual to individual, 'of maintaining the integrity of one's own identity in the plurality of situations and of inscribing the salient features in an unrepeatable biography' (1998, 31). In this perspective, the good life or *eudaimonia* is

> a life-course in which one is able to enrich the main plot of one's life-narrative with the largest possible amount of episodes and sub-plots compatible with the preservation of a sense of overall unity. The ability to unify one's biography into a coherent narrative is a good which plays a similar role to *eudaimonia* for Aristotle. (1998, 31)

According to Ferrara, this reinterpretation of eudaimonia in terms of identity allows for the reformulation of the normative ideal of *authenticity*: according to which individuals are called in their own life to fulfil themselves, that is, to follow their vocation, to listen to their inner voice, to be faithful to their innermost nature (Varga and Guignon 2020).

5.2. Ontological insecurity and attachment psychopathology

We can summarize the content of the last section by stating that identity self-construction, in the course of childhood and beyond, changes its procedures and characteristics according to the stages of life: but always its importance is such that we can consider it the cornerstone of the development of the entire existence of the individual.

This lays the ground for cautiously advancing a hypothesis about human nature. Human life does not respond only to elementary biological needs, such as surviving and reproducing; nor can our motivations be traced back only to universal forms of social competition which can be observed in the rivalry among animals. Rather, our everyday life takes shape in conformity with 'a specifically human necessity', namely, the 'maintenance of identity' (Lichtenstein 1977, 77), an identity that must fulfil a fundamental requirement, that is, it must be 'a self-image endowed with at least a minimal solidity, and that is, solid enough to confirm to ourselves that *we exist without dissolving ourselves*' (Jervis 2019, 102; italics in the text; our translation).

This anthropological hypothesis is reinforced by considering the clinical dimension of the inextricable link between identity self-description and self-consciousness. One cannot ascribe concreteness and solidity to one's self-consciousness if it does not possess at its centre, and as its essence, a description of identity that must be clear and, inextricably, 'good', in the sense of being worthy of love (Balint 1985). If the self-description becomes uncertain, the subject soon loses the feeling of being present. So, let us reiterate: as in De Martino's theory of presence, identity self-construction is not a Kantian unifying process. Unlike Kant's originally unitary subject, the psychodynamic subject is primarily non-unitary and incessantly works to gain its unity (or illusion of unity) in the act of mobilizing resources against the threat of disgregation.

The idea that the selfing process imposes a teleology of self-defence on the human psychobiological system finds illustration in the theories of object relations and attachment, whose theoretical focus is on problems arising from a weakness, fragility, scarce cohesion or insufficient integration of those structures of the mind that Freud calls '*das Ich*' (essentially, the system of defences). This structural condition of fragility is experienced by the subject as a chronic feeling of insecurity, lack of self-esteem and lack of confidence in oneself.

Drawing on Ronald Laing's *The Divided Self* (1960), we can describe the experiences originating from the fragility of the ego as symptoms of *ontological insecurity*. The individual with a firm core of ontological security, Laing affirms, owns a sense of the self as a cohesive and well-demarcated entity, as well as a consistent feeling of biographical continuity. By contrast, the ontologically insecure individual is liable to the collapse of subjectivity described as an experience of disintegration, psychic deadness or numbness and a sense of moral emptiness: 'He may not possess an overriding sense of personal consistency or cohesiveness. He may feel more insubstantial than substantial, and unable to assume that the stuff he is made of is genuine, good, valuable' (Laing 1960, 42). In the ordinary circumstances of living such an individual is plagued by a feeling that the living spontaneity of the self has become something dead and lifeless: '[he] may feel more unreal than real; in a literal sense, more dead than alive; precariously differentiated from the rest of the world so that his identity and autonomy are always in question' (Laing 1960, 42). Discontinuity in temporal experience is a basic feature of such a condition: 'He may lack the experience of his own temporal continuity' (Laing 1960, 42). Time may be understood here as 'a series of discrete moments, each of which severs prior experiences from subsequent ones in such a way that no continuous narrative can be sustained' (Giddens 1991, 53).

In the context of attachment theory, Laing's symptoms of ontological insecurity can be conceptualized as the last traces of a remote 'basic fault' (Balint 1992), which is to be traced back mainly to early deficiencies in the infant-caregiver relationship. In this context, the idea of an ego that is fragile, or the idea of a self that lacks 'cohesion', identifies a condition that predisposes individuals to a broad and varied pathology including psychoses and personality disorders. Narcissistic personality disorder offers an incisive exemplification of this.

In contemporary psychoanalysis, narcissism is regarded as one of the tenets of the dynamic structure of personality. All the premises for the modern development of this topic are already found in Freud (1957). First, this work puts forward the idea that narcissism is a necessary phenomenon for establishing a healthy mental life. It is self-love (or self-cathexis), and as such, governs the constitution of the ego; it is the starting point for the subsequent construction of one's identity; it is what prevents the ego from breaking apart. Not only in very early infancy, but all through life, self-love constantly restores self-esteem and grounds the capacity to love. Thus, only individuals who have a good relationship with themselves, accept themselves, love themselves and take care of themselves with affection, possess the security and wealth of affectional bonds that will spontaneously pour out in work and enthusiasm, in acceptance and willingness.

The most important revision of Freud's theory of narcissism is that of Federn (1952), who argues that schizophrenia is due not to a withdrawal of libido into the ego, as Freud maintained in his theory of 'narcissistic neurosis', but, to the contrary, to a dissolution of ego boundaries because of a *deficiency* of ego cathexis. The more endowed the ego is with narcissistic libido, the more capable it is of holding out against the already-mentioned process of psychotic disgregation.

According to Federn, that type of personality that (also without being affected by schizophrenia) appears to us as narcissistic, that is, retreated into its world, mirroring itself in a grandiose image of its self-sufficiency, is, in reality, *deficient* in narcissism. Narcissists, contrary to appearances, suffer from a chronic deficit of self-love. And it is precisely because they are insecure, do not love themselves and believe that they are not worthy of love, that they anxiously watch themselves and constantly strive to reassure themselves and strengthen their image – an image that is perceived as fragile, poor and perpetually deficient – with ornaments and illusions. Briefly, narcissism is a normal phenomenon but becomes pathological when it is exploited to compensate for a condition of insecurity and insufficient self-esteem. Here the fundamental anxiety is *the dread of not existing*.

In the very early infancy, there may have been an insufficiency of that narcissistic investment that is normally mediated by a good relationship with the caregiver, and in subsequent years no remediation of this insufficiency. The individual is left with what may be termed 'a narcissistic credit': the consequent fragility of the ego manifests itself at the simplest level in the development of a personality characterized by insecurity, a deficit of primary self-esteem, low tolerance for frustrations and a continuous need to supply himself (albeit never sufficiently) with self-appreciation and confirmation. The original deficit of self-love and self-esteem, and hence the inner affectional misery, give rise to a difficulty in loving and being loved, come to be connected to poorly managed aggression and produce deep self-destructive unhappiness that conceals itself, typically, through complacent, evanescent and grandiose self-illusions, identifications with persons, things or movements provided with the chrism of power and interpersonal relationships which may at times be handled skilfully but are nevertheless characterized by egocentricity, avidity and instrumentality.

In this context, narcissistic defences are the ways in which patients' dramatic struggle to keep themselves alive – brought on by ontological insecurity – seek containment. In other terms, narcissistic defences are the attempts, often sorrowful and at times desperate, to care for and defend one's image as protection for an identity felt as excessively fragile. This theme was explored in depth by Heinz Kohut, who presented afresh the Freudian metaphor of the solidity of the ego in terms of the cohesion and self-legitimation of identity.

Note that a narcissistic defence consists not only in the more or less anxious safeguarding of the image that we want to have of ourselves but also in a certain kind of relationship with the external world; in this case, we are dealing with an object relation of a narcissistic type, namely, a link with situations, things or persons that serve as symbols to help reassure ourselves about our identity. In narcissistic personality disorders, the feeling of identity is so precarious (the self is so scarcely cohesive, Kohut would say) that patients find it difficult to feel existent and are afraid of completely losing contact with themselves if deprived of such reassurances. These include what Kohut calls 'self-objects', namely, objects of a narcissistic type that are experienced as neither internal nor external to the bounds of a person's identity. He writes about a patient (Mr W.):

It was at such times, when his unsupported childhood self began to feel frighteningly strange to him and began to crumble, that he had in fact surrounded himself with his possessions – sitting on the floor, looking at them, checking that they were there: his toys and his clothes. And he had at that time a particular drawer that contained his things, a drawer he thought about sometimes at night when he could not fall asleep, in order to reassure himself. (Kohut 1977, 167–8)

In a category of clinical cases less serious than full-blown narcissistic personality, individuals who suffer from an insufficient sense of identity, while not being forced to adopt a defensive style that can give rise to pathological problems, can lead a normal life only by placing themselves within a situation of dependence, and hence by eschewing positions of affiliation and responsibility. This is an indication that narcissistic problems, in attenuated forms, are ubiquitous, and thus, in addition to the theme of narcissistic personalities, there is that of the more or less effective ways in which each of us comes to deal with the thorny problem of our narcissistic equilibria.

Let us now consider another personality disorder: borderline personality disorder. This pathology is of great interest to us here since it has been described as a disorder of attachment, with symptoms of fear of abandonment, and intense, unstable relationships; as a disorder of self, with symptoms of identity disturbance, chronic feelings of emptiness and dissociative states under stress; and as a disorder of self-regulation, with symptoms of impulsivity, suicidal behaviour, self-mutilation, affective instability and difficulty controlling anger.

As to etiopathogenesis, the presence of impairments in mindreading and autobiographical memory is a key to understanding the broad spectrum of dysfunctions related to the self, including disturbances in self-narratives, commonly observed in borderline patients.

First, disruptions of early attachment experiences can derail the development of first-person mentalization. The hypothesis has been made that the absence of empathic affect-regulative-mirroring interactions may prevent children from creating the necessary mappings between the emerging causal representations of emotional states in others and emerging distinct emotional states in themselves; this may in turn give rise to a compromised representational system for internal self-states (Hernik, Fearon and Fonagy 2009).

Second, the presence of impairments in first-person mentalization may hamper the forming of self-concept as an organized, coherent and unified autobiographical self-representation. Building on Erikson's work, Otto Kernberg observed that borderline patients often vacillate between extremely positive and negative representations of self and others. In terms of the earlier-discussed self-memory system, borderline patients may be able to cluster their episodic information in the slots of the autobiographical knowledge base, but they fail to integrate this information into a distinct self-concept, unifying both positive and negative aspects. As a result, they have a fragmented self-concept, consisting of different, mostly poorly elaborated current self-concepts, which are activated in turn, depending on the situation one is in, or on the people, one is with (Kernberg et al. 1989). The borderline patient's self-image or sense of self, therefore, is 'markedly and persistently unstable' (APA 2013, 664), incoherent and discontinuous. In this perspective, switching self-concepts is a strategy to preserve the present fragile structure, because it is a potentially adaptive response to self-discrepant information (van den Broeck 2014, 199).

Finally, it should be noted that a diminishing of the feeling of existing, to the point of a 'conversion of ourselves to nothingness' (James 1981, 281), may be the result not only of a psychopathological process. An analogous outcome can arise from a sudden breakdown of self-esteem, from unexpected emotional upheavals, or when the continuity of the tissue of our sociality is broken, as can happen when one is suddenly thrown into a dehumanizing total institution.[22]

A brief overview

This book drew on the psychological sciences to put forward a conception of the constitution of ourselves as persons in terms of the establishment of a process of self-description that is a unifying, integrative, synthesizing selfing process. This is a (non-Kantian) psychobiological synthetic function that has as its most advanced product the subject's narrative identity, which is the key ingredient in a developmental account of the identity of the person as a continuity across time and space, interpreted reflectively by the agent.

After outlining, in the first two chapters, the bottom-up, systemic-relational and naturalistic approach within which we have built on the Jamesian theory of the self, we began to investigate the process of construction of subjective identity.

In Chapter 3, we delved into the question of how, between the ages of fifteen and twenty-four months, human psychobiological systems build representations of themselves as acting physical units, namely as 'particular' bodily spaces: the location of one's own identity. Self-awareness in its simplest form, that is, the awareness of existing, is the perception of physical identity.

Then, we have come to grips with the question of how children become able to recognize, introspectively, the presence of the inner virtual space of mind – in other words, how children become able to know that they are considering, *objectively*, the various aspects of their *subjectivity*. The construction of this *psychological* self-consciousness occurs in two steps. The first is the internalization of basic emotions hinging on bodily self-awareness (Chapter 4). The second is the act of exercising on oneself some of one's socio-cognitive capacities directed towards others, based on neurocomputational mechanisms and concerning the domains of naïve psychology and ethics (Chapters 5 and 6).

Thereafter, with the development of autobiographical memory and autobiographical reasoning, children track their own continuous identity as persons through time and space. This diachronic dimension of self-consciousness – the ability to identify in one's inner universe a unity persisting in time – requires subjects to have the capacity to organise their own experiences in a *personal history*. This is the *narrative* identity, that is, the Jamesian *Me* as a history internalized by the individual through the process of selfing (Chapter 7).

Lastly, we argued that this narration of oneself is not an epiphenomenon, but rather a layer of personality working as a *causal* centre of gravity in the history of a psychobiological system. This is a point often underestimated in the debate on the nature of the self. According to Dennett, for example, the 'I' that claims to be the subject of experience, thought and action, does not exist; and the continuously self-rewriting autobiographies of the Joycean machine turn out to be a confabulatory by-product of the brain's decentralized activity, which is what governs behaviour. And yet, when he is not in his radically eliminative mood, Dennett recognizes that the self that is 'the center of narrative gravity' is 'a causally efficacious part of the whole system' (Flanagan 1992, 195). For example, in responding to a critique addressed to him by Lynne Rudder Baker, Dennett speaks of 'an emergent, virtual self' whose function is 'to solve the myriad little problems of interpersonal activity we encounter every day, from the moment of our birth' (Dennett 2016, 16). In our book, however, this observation on the function of the self – whose primary theoretical reference is Erving Goffman's concept of self-presentation – expanded out of all proportion, until it assumed the dimensions of a hypothesis on human nature. Indeed, we have argued that an enormous amount of systematic research in developmental psychology, infant research, social psychology and personality psychology leads to the hypothesis that human life is conditioned by a need that is no less important than elementary biological needs or universal forms of social competition: the need to build and, indeed, defend a subjective identity whose solidity and clarity is the foundation of our intra- and inter-personal equilibrium, and therefore of psychological well-being and mental health.

Notes

Chapter 1

1 On the history of the personal identity debate in philosophy and psychology, we consulted Barresi and Martin (2000), Izenberg (2016), Lecaldano (2021), Martin and Barresi (2006), Seigel (2005), Sorabji (2006), Thiel (2011).
2 A few years later, Jonathan Swift does not ignore this issue, which is only apparently paradoxical, when he writes his masterpiece: he imagines, among other things, that Gulliver lands on an island where horses are intelligent and extremely civilized persons, while human beings are not. Today we might imagine being visited by the inhabitants of highly evolved civilizations from other worlds: such aliens might not have anything human, while being persons.
3 '["Person"] is a Forensick Term appropriating Actions and their Merit; and so belongs only to intelligent Agents capable of a Law, and Happiness and Misery' (Locke 1975, 346).
4 The author also mentions other names by which this dissociative state is designated: 'irkunii' by the Yukagires, 'amurak' by the Yakuts, 'menkeiti' by the Koriaks and 'imu' by the Ainus.
5 *Ecopraxia* is the automatic repetition by imitation of the movements of others, typically found in catatonic-type schizophrenia. It was first described by the psychiatrist Emil Kraepelin at the end of the nineteenth century, as a particular form of echo phenomenon. *Echolalia* is the unsolicited repetition of vocalizations made by another person.
6 Specifically, a reduction in the self-referential awareness that defines normal waking consciousness has been reported with all classical psychedelic drugs (5-HT2A receptor agonists), including psilocybin, lysergic acid diethylamide (LSD) and dimethyltryptamine (DMT), as well as with other psychoactive substances such as nitrous oxide and ketamine.
7 Ginzburg sees here the influence of those passages of the second volume of *Philosophie der Symbolischen Formen* where Ernst Cassirer speaks of 'the limited validity of the "unity of the feeling of self" in mythic thought and of the relationship between the I and external reality conceived as a process rather than as a given' (1991, 45).
8 In a passage of the *Analytic of Concepts*, Kant envisages the possibility of the loss of the original synthetic unity of apperception; but this possibility is taken

into account not as a real risk, but only as an absurd consequence of failing to recognize the necessity of that unity. In such a case, Kant writes, 'I would have as multicoloured, diverse a self as I have representations of which I am conscious' (1998, 147–8). In opposition to Kant De Martino 'interprets as a real existential risk what in Kant's criticism is only controversial argument' (2021, 21; translation ours).

9 'The entire history of madness stems from the weakness of actual synthetic power, which is itself moral weakness and psychological misery' (Janet cit. in De Martino 2012, 437).

10 '[T]here are some philosophers, who imagine we are every moment intimately conscious of what we call our self [. . .]. For my part when I enter most intimately into what I call *myself*, I always stumble on some particular perception or other, of heat or cold, light or shade, love or hatred, pain or pleasure. I never can catch *myself* at any time without a perception, and never can observe anything but the perception' (Hume 1739–40: bk. 1, ch. 4, §6).

11 Psychology concerning these issues is for James 'a psychology without a soul' (1981, 15), dating back to Hume, J. S. Mill, A. Bain and J. F. Herbart and making it possible to deem the *ego* of the individual not as 'the pre-existing source of the representations, but rather as their last and most complicated fruit' (16).

12 'Since Descartes, idealistic philosophers and psychologists have maintained that self-awareness is a primary and irreducible property of mental life, with no history in and of itself. The conviction that self-awareness is primary underlay Descartes' maxim, *cogito ergo sum*, and was one source of idealistic psychology' (Luria 1976, 144).

13 There are multiple representational theories of consciousness, corresponding to different uses of the term 'conscious', each attempting to explain the corresponding phenomenon in terms of *intentionality* (see as follows) and assumes that intentionality is *representation*: 'The aim of a representationalist theory of consciousness is to extend the treatment of intentionality to that of consciousness, showing that if intentionality is well understood in representational terms, then so can be the phenomena of consciousness in whichever sense of that fraught term' (Lycan 2019). See also Chapter 2, Section 2.1.

14 'Look at a tree and try to turn your attention to intrinsic features of your visual experience. I predict you will find that the only features there to turn your attention to will be features of the presented tree, including relational features of the tree "from here"' (Harman 1990, 39; see also Martin 2002). Thus, if in introspection the experience itself is not glimpsed but only the objects of the experience, conscious experience does not include the consciousness of experience. But as we shall see later (Chapter 3, Section 2.2), this argument is contested by those philosophers who claim that it is a phenomenal fact or self-evident that 'pre-reflective self-consciousness' exists (see Giustina 2022; Lang 2022).

Chapter 2

1. James' naturalistic theory of mental processes is the primary inspiration of the Chicago school of functional psychology (see Shook 2001).
2. On this, see Ben-Menahem (2016, 67).
3. Darwin wrote this in 1838; the biologist Dorothy Cheney and the psychologist Robert Seyfarth take it very seriously in *Baboon Metaphysics* (2007).
4. 'What is meant by consciousness we need not to discuss; it is beyond all doubt' (Freud 1964, 70).
5. It should be noted that contrary to the simplifying stereotype, very young children, even just a few months old, are normally able to develop relationships not only with the mother but also with the father and other family members, and even with strangers.
6. Bowlby was strongly influenced by the study of behaviours as *signals* (rather than instinctual energies) carried out by the British ethological school. Another fundamental clue came from the experiments by Harry Harlow, who underlined that in rhesus monkey cubs the need for affectionate care prevails over the search for food: they prefer to seek protection from a soft surrogate-mother unable to provide food, rather than from a surrogate mother able to provide milk but made of iron wire, a material offering little comfort.
7. Attachment is an *autonomous* behavioural system since 'the infant's attachment to the caregiver is not reducible to or secondarily derived from other experiences and gratification of presumably more primary instinctual systems such as the hunger drive' (Eagle 2013, 8).
8. For this, see Oyama (2000). For an introduction to the Developmental Systems Theory, see Griffiths and Tabery (2013).
9. A distinction should be made between the concepts of *innate* and *precocious*. A biological system is innate if it is inscribed in the heritage of the individual, even without manifesting precociously. Consider, for instance, secondary sexual characteristics or permanent teeth.
10. A case in point is Mehler and Bever's (1967) criticism of Piaget's (1952) test to investigate the understanding of number conservation in children.
11. See also Graffi (2019), who discusses Piattelli Palmarini's assessment of the Royaumont debate together with the – opposite – one by Boeckx (2014).
12. Historically, work by Robert Fantz in the 1950s and 1960s has been credited with sparking interest in the habituation methodology for use in examining infant perception and cognition (see Tsang 2012).
13. One thing, indeed, is to argue that some competences are innate or domain-specific, another thing is to argue that processes are.
14. Actually, beyond the evident affinity, there are important distinctions. Where Vygotsky mainly observes processes within small groups, often dyads, according

to Mead (as already in James, whose ideas and terminology are used by Mead to further emphasize the importance of sociocultural determinants in the definition of individual identity) personality constitutes itself in the relationship with society understood more globally, and especially through the characteristics that others attribute to us through linguistic-symbolic communication.

Chapter 3

1. The interpersonal dimension of the ontogenesis of bodily self-awareness is well captured by Wallon (1959), who argues that it is through the consciousness of the other that the concept of bodily self develops; very young children, in interaction with their microsocial environments, gradually become self-aware of their own bodies.
2. See Gillihan and Farah (2005) who propose a taxonomy of self-awareness that clearly distinguishes between physical and psychological aspects of self.
3. We will return to these important aspects in the next chapter when we examine the notion of *vitality form* proposed by Daniel Stern.
4. It is in this sense that numerous concepts, often found in the interdisciplinary areas between personality theory, dynamic psychology and social psychology, are currently used: concepts such as 'self-image', 'real self' and 'ideal self', 'accepted self' and 'rejected self', 'self-judgement', 'self-assessment', 'working self' and so on. Winnicott's 'false self' and 'true self' or Kohut's concept of object-self are also concepts of an experiential nature.
5. Note that at some points, Neisser clearly understands the ecological self in the objective sense: 'The ecological self is not to be thought of in phenomenological terms' (personal communication cited in Shontz 1994, 89).
6. In this regard, Musholt draws a distinction between 'self-representationalist' and 'non-self-representationalist' accounts of non-conceptual self-consciousness (2015, chs. 3–4).
7. Gallagher (2017) frames Di Francesco, Marraffa and Paternoster's (2016) criticism in the context of the 'deflationary' and 'eliminativist' critiques of his and Zahavi's notion of a pre-reflective, minimal sense of self or sense of ownership. These critiques were also made by Barry Dainton, Jesse Prinz, Jay Garfield and José Luis Bermúdez; however, Gallagher's (2017) reply focuses on 'the eliminativist views expressed in Bermúdez [2011, 2018] and defended by Di Francesco and colleagues' (note 1).
8. In Chapter 6, we will see how this awareness also acquires a diachronic dimension.
9. The default mode network overlaps considerably with the social brain network and is composed of the medial prefrontal cortex, the precuneus, the posterior and

anterior cingulate cortex, the inferior parietal lobe, the medial temporal lobe and the temporoparietal junction.

10 Many studies have shown that our brain displays correlations between spontaneous fluctuations in activation in the low-frequency range (<0.1 Hz) while we are not engaged in any specific task. Resting-state recording refers to the acquisition of this intrinsic brain activity during quiet wakefulness, in the absence of any cognitive, sensory or social stimulation.

11 See Kristen-Antonow et al. (2015) who purport to show that contingency detection in social interactions at nine months predicts mirror self-recognition at twenty-four months.

12 One's representation of oneself is a secondary representation because it is not a perceptual reality; instead, it is a constructed mental image of oneself that can be manipulated in imagination.

13 Mental states (beliefs, desires, etc.) are often referred to as 'propositional attitudes' because in ascribing them to a subject S we use utterances of the form 'S believes (or desires/intends/hopes, etc.) that p', where proposition p expresses the content of S's mental state.

Chapter 4

1 Thus, whereas the phenomenality of emotions suggests that emotions are similar to sensations, their intentionality seems to place them into the same class of mental states as beliefs and desires, the two basic kinds of intentional mental states.

2 It is worth noting that social interaction is also the key to the developments of Jamesian functionalist psychology in the work of John Dewey and George H. Mead (see Chapter 2, Section 3.2).

3 These are understood as 'pre-wired, stimulus-driven, procedural physiological and motor automatisms that are initially not accessible to conscious awareness and over which the baby has no voluntary control at first' (Gergely and Unoka 2008b, 61–2).

4 The terms 'referential decoupling' and 'referential anchoring' have originally been introduced by Leslie (1987) to characterize the representational properties of communicative expressions produced in pretend play. These terms are applied here to suggest a potential developmental and functional relationship between the markedness of affect-reflective expressions, on the one hand, and the markedness of expressions in the 'pretend' mode of communication, on the other.

5 The claim that first-person access to the emotional state is made possible by second-level representations places the social biofeedback hypothesis in the realm of the higher-order representational theory of consciousness. These metarepresentations are seen here, originally, as the result of a social mediation.

6 Griffiths has particularly insisted on the plasticity of affect programs on the input side, going so far as to argue that 'most emotion-eliciting stimuli are learned' (1997, 89), but stressing how this kind of 'learning' should be understood as a kind of Pavlovian associative process with an innate bias towards certain kinds of biologically salient stimuli.
7 But note the contrast with LeDoux (2015a, 2015b, 2017) discussed as follows, in Section 5.
8 However, this did not put an end to the debate on facial expressions of emotions, since a subsequent meta-analytic study by Barrett et al. (2019) claims to drastically scale back the results of the 2002 study.
9 On the role of multimodal stimuli in enhancing emotional competence, see Walker-Andrews (2008).
10 A substantial part of the confusion in the debate about the nature of emotions arguably comes from having interpreted the theories about emotional behaviour as explanations of emotional experience (for a lucid analysis and self-criticism, see LeDoux 2014).
11 '[V]alence is best thought of as a neural signal that makes whatever is at the locus of attention at that moment seem good or bad, welcome or unwelcome (without employing the concepts of goodness or badness, of course; it isn't the same as judging – albeit unconsciously – that the attended-to object is good or bad). [It] should be thought of as *a nonconceptual indicator of value*' (Carruthers 2011a, 128; italics ours). See also Carruthers (2018).
12 Barrett endorses Barsalou's (1999) theory of concepts, according to which concepts are not abstract, amodal entities, but rather situated and related to the goals of the individual. They are collections of memory traces resulting from the various encounters with an object or an event and represent a heterogeneous set of experiences: motoric, perceptual, emotional and so on.
13 The purported role of concepts, and consequently the influence of language, explains why the non-specificity of causal mechanisms underlying emotion components does not imply a complete lack of correlation; indeed, the emotion components associated with basic emotions correlate 'to some extent'. Whether a discrete emotion episode is instantiated depends on the extent to which such components correlate. If they correlate sufficiently to match the mental prototype for some folk emotion category E, an episode of E is instantiated (whether or not anyone categorizes the episode as E) (Fehr and Russell 1984).
14 Other promising candidates for determining category formation are appraisal configurations, core relational themes and action tendencies (see Scherer 2009, 1323).
15 Damasio, in turn, acknowledges that his notion of background feeling 'is similar to the notion of vitality affects presented by the developmental psychologist Daniel Stern' (1999, 287).

16 Damasio notoriously distinguishes between *emotions* – which are bodily states – and *feelings* – which are mental representations of emotions. With this distinction, he puts himself beyond one of his main reference authors, James, who takes emotions to issue from the perception of bodily states.
17 It is also worth noting that the extensive, empirical research carried on by Damasio strengthens a construct – that of vitality forms – which otherwise risks being elusive (see Køppe et al. 2008). Actually, we are persuaded that our analysis can help to give further support to this direction of research to the extent that it is alternative to the received view which sees Stern (and, for this point, also Damasio) as providing empirical evidence for pre-reflective self-consciousness (see Section 1).
18 The representations generated by ID and EDD (or even only by one of the two, as it happens forcibly in blind people) flow into two further modules, SAM (Shared Attention Mechanism) and ToMM (Theory of Mind Mechanism) that respectively reveal situations of shared attention and, finally, interpret behaviour mentalistically.

Chapter 5

1 Meins (2011) proposes a more elaborate hypothesis: both attachment and mindreading (understood in all its forms, whether directed towards others or directed at oneself) can be predicted on the basis of caregivers' mind-mindedness, that is, adults' tendency to treat children as naïve psychologists. Therefore, there would not be a linear influence of one mechanism on the other, but both systems would be influenced by a mentality-focused relational style.
2 Theory of Mind is the branch of cognitive science that investigates mindreading abilities. These abilities are often called 'folk psychology' by philosophers, and 'naïve psychology' or 'intuitive psychology' by cognitive scientists.
3 Notice that, from a purely perceptual point of view, the parabolic trajectory is a stimulus much closer to the one proposed in the habituation phase: the only thing missing is the obstacle, which, however, is removed under all conditions. Therefore, the greater recovery of attention in this condition rather reveals early sensitivity to a more abstract difference, a sensitivity that is arguably related to the rationality of the action.
4 These results contradict Woodward (1998), who, following an earlier experiment with five- to nine-month-old children, suggested that goal allocation is conditioned by the perception of human-like forms. Moreover, the extension of goal attribution to biomechanically impossible actions indicates that the notion of goal is unlikely to be derived directly from infants' experience.

5 For an accurate reflection on the relationship between teleology and mindreading, see Loria (2020).
6 For a comprehensive review of the philosophical and experimental literature, see Tomasello (2019).
7 Although aligning ourselves with the received terminology, we cannot but point out that strictly speaking, beliefs are not false, but rather mistaken, erroneous. Thus, *erroneous belief task* would be a more precise formula.
8 We will not complicate the description of this and the other experiments by also illustrating the habituation phases and control conditions; however, we would like to emphasize once and for all that all the experiments mentioned meet the highest epistemological standards.
9 It is worth emphasizing that special precautions have been taken to dispel the suspicion that their behaviour stems simply from noticing the violation of a typical behavioural pattern.
10 See also the video of the experiment: <https://www.science.org/doi/10.1126/science.1190792#supplementary-materials>.
11 See also Song and Baillargeon (2008) for a study of fourteen-month-old children; for a comprehensive review, Carruthers (2013) and Jacob (2019b).
12 A puppet has a false belief about the position of some bananas. Children, who know the real location, are asked: 'What happens next? You can take the girl yourself if you want. What is she going to do now?' Most three-year-old children arguably consider the content of the puppet's false belief, as they move it to the empty location.
13 Interestingly, this point of Southgate's hypothesis reminds of Bob Gordon's (1995) radical simulation theory, an influential voice in the theory theory *vs* simulation theory debate on the nature of adult mindreading (see Chapter 6, Section 1).

Chapter 6

1 As Gergely and Unoka put it, to the extent that these mentalistic activities get turned towards the self, 'the proper domain of the human mindreading becomes ontogenetically extended to include in its actual domain the mind of one's own self as well' (2008, 74).
2 The language of social psychology and sociology clearly distinguishes motivations from motives. The term 'motive', as a technical term, has come into use to designate what people claim to be the motives for their actions, irrespective of their causes. Motives are 'prevailing' and 'acceptable' interpretations of conduct according to the conventions of a given culture. The critical study of motives dates back to Charles Wright Mills and was mainly developed in sociology, in the context of symbolic interactionism and ethnomethodology. This topic has also had an important

development in social psychology and general psychology, where is related to the topic of causal attribution.

3 See also Johansson et al. (2006), where Nisbett and Wilson's legacy is developed through a new experimental paradigm to study introspection, the *choice blindness* paradigm.

4 *Theory theory* is the view that mindreading depends on the deployment of a theory of the mental domain, analogous to the theories of the physical world (naïve physics). More precisely, it is a family of theories. According to the 'child as little scientist' theory, the body of internally represented knowledge that drives the exercise of mentalistic abilities has much the same structure as a scientific theory, and it is acquired, stored and used in much the same way that scientific theories are. By contrast, the modularist version of theory theory holds that the body of knowledge underlying mindreading lacks the structure of a scientific theory, being stored in one or more innate modules, which gradually become functional during infant development.

5 Thoughts thus include events of wondering whether something is the case, judging something to be the case, recalling that something is the case, deciding to do something, actively intending to do something, adopting something as a goal and so forth. Unlike these episodic attitudes, the 'standing' attitudes are stored and remain in existence even when we sleep.

6 Attention can be bottom-up, caused by highly salient stimuli, sudden changes in the environment or stimuli of innate or learnt emotional significance; or it can be top-down, driven by the subject's high-level goals and interests in the circumstances.

7 Suppose someone tells you a telephone number: the number, through the sound of the words used to pronounce it, enters the phonological storehouse. If you do not want to forget the number in the time it takes to reach the telephone, you must rehearse it (mentally, under your breath or aloud) to reactivate the memory trace.

8 The hypothesis that WM emerges and depends constitutively on sensory systems was advanced – among others – by Postle (2006), and contrasts with previous conceptualizations of WM as an abstract process (see, e.g., Goldman-Rakic 1995, 76).

9 More precisely, to the extent that mindreading is an essential element of human social intelligence, it can be assumed that it evolved to provide an adaptive advantage in pursuit of the goals of the two motivational systems discussed earlier: the first one dedicated to self-assertion and competition, the second aimed at pro-sociality and cooperation (Chapter 2, Section 2.2).

10 In doing so, we do not disagree with Carruthers when he writes that only a restricted version of Vygotsky's 'conception of the mind as being to an important extent socially constructed, developing in plastic ways in interactions with elements of the surrounding culture, guided and supported by adult members of that culture'

may be plausible from the perspective of contemporary cognitive psychology (2011b, 387–8).
11 Compared to public speech, self-directed speech presents – as noted by Vygotsky himself – certain peculiarities. In particular, private speech (and this is even more likely to be the case with inner speech) is visibly and progressively simplified in its syntax (new information remains, while the background is often taken for granted) and semantics (utterances are condensed into one or a few contextually significant terms.).
12 See also Al-Namlah, Fernyhough and Meins (2006), with children aged between four and eight years from Great Britain and the United Arab Emirates, to appreciate the role of language in general rather than a specific language or culture.
13 The reduction in performance did not depend on a more general cognitive overload due to the concomitance of two demanding tasks: as a control condition, children had to perform a body tapping exercise (e.g. tapping to the rhythm of a metronome as a control on who had to pronounce certain letters); but in this condition, there was no significant reduction in performance.
14 As attested by a recent study by Vasil and Tomasello (2022), a normative sense of 'we' capable of creating commitment and a sense of obligation can be induced purely verbally. Children aged three and four years interacted with a puppet sitting at a table; depending on the experimental condition, the puppet repeatedly framed linguistic interaction as 'we' or 'you' (e.g. 'We/You are going to sit at the table'). At each age, children turned out to be more committed after the we-framing than after the you-framing.

Chapter 7

1 See Demiray and Bluck (2011) for references to a growing body of empirical research that suggests that specific aspects of the current conceptual self influence the themes found in retrieved autobiographical memories.
2 It should be noted, however, that despite advances in causal reasoning about emotions, considerable research work shows that several errors in emotion forecasting persist throughout the lifespan (see, e.g., Gilbert and Wilson 2003).
3 'Piaget [. . .] assumes that the organizational tendencies observed in biology extend to cognitive development. He postulated an *organizational schema* that encompasses assimilation and integration, the latter taking the form of ongoing reciprocal assimilation between schemas, such that there tends to be an internal consistency and equilibration among varied functions and structures' (Ryan 1995, 400).
4 These traits include, for example, the so-called 'Big Five': extraversion, neuroticism, agreeableness, conscientiousness and openness to experience.

5 'It was not until John Locke that there was an explicit attempt to connect personal identity with broader ethical concerns' (Shoemaker 2021, section 1).
6 Metzinger (2003) and Strawson (2004, 2020) profess a radical scepticism about the relevance of narrative selves for theories on the self. Schechtman (2007, 2014) amends and expands Schechtman's (1996) narrative account in response to – inter alia – some of Strawson's challenges. See also Dings and Newen (2023) who reject Strawson's view that we can fully understand cognitive systems without invoking narrative selves by clarifying how the narrative self modulates our memory in everyday cases.
7 Mainly because it would engage us in a discussion of the opposition between *reductionist* and *non-reductionist* narrative identity theories. See Corcuera (2021).
8 This is not a new complaint, of course: it is presumably 'what Habermas was getting at when he remarked that Dreyfus treats *Being and Time* as if it had just washed up as flotsam on the shores of some Californian beach' (Christensen 1998, 84).
9 For a discussion of this approach to the mark of the mental issue, see Di Francesco, Marraffa and Paternoster (2016, 43–6).
10 This connects our approach with the so-called 'multifactorial pattern theory of the self', which construes the self as multidimensional and integrative, with the narrative self as one of those dimensions (see Gallagher 2013; Newen 2018).
11 Earliest drafts of narrative identity may take the form of 'the personal fable', a construct proposed to conceptualize a manifestation of the Piagetian adolescent egocentrism, that is, the adolescents' belief that they are special and unique, omnipotent and invulnerable, which gives rise to a propensity for behavioural risk-taking (Elkind 1967). Later drafts of narrative identity become more realistic and tempered, as reality testing improves, and narrative skills become further refined.
12 As seen in Section 2, the ability to order one's own experiences on a personal timeline is a gradual process based on advances in abstract thinking.
13 For example, Luria reports that in two (concrete vs abstract) categorization tasks, '[o]nly classification based on practical experience struck them [the unsophisticated group of subjects] as proper or important' (1976, 71).
14 Luria's data were replicated in West Africa by Michael Cole, Sylvia Scribner and their collaborators. See Cole et al. (1971); Scribner and Cole (1981).
15 'In particular it is quite possible (and it is the impression given by the known ethnographic literature) that in numerous cultures adult thinking does not proceed beyond the level of concrete operations, and does not reach that of propositional [formal] operations, elaborated between 12 and 15 years of age' (Piaget 1974, 309). On the Piagetian cross-cultural psychology, see Hallpike (1979); Oesterdiekhoff (2013).
16 See, for example, Giddens (1991, 1992), who sees addictions as incidents in the individuals' need to create and maintain their own separate subjective identity.

17 These arguments may help to bridge personal discontinuity by learning a lesson ('After that I told myself, when I fall in love the next time, I must take care that school doesn't suffer') or abstracting a general insight from a specific event that may also cover other events ('I was missing him for many months. Probably it's always like that when it's the first kiss'), or by localizing an event in a larger concept of normal development ('At the time I wasn't aware of any of that, after all, I was still too young for that').

18 Once again, note the radical difference from Tulving's model. Whereas for the latter remembering past events establishes a sense of self-continuity in time through a specific phenomenal quality (i.e. the immediate feeling that I experienced the remembered event), Conway reverses the approach: it is the present self-concept that selects and even distorts personal memories to enhance the sense of personal continuity. Consequently, the continuity of the self over time is not determined by 'the identity of the remembering I, but by the perceived similarity of the present and past Me' (Habermas and Köber 2015a, 153).

19 Since Marcia's (1966) elaboration of the identity statuses, Erikson (1968) has represented, with some important variants, the dominant approach to the study of identity development (McLean and Syed 2015, 2).

20 It is to be noticed that in this context Freud's *das Ich* is taken as a synthetic function, a synthesizing process, and thus coinciding with selfing. See McAdams (1997, 57).

21 The mechanisms to manage real- and ideal-self discrepancies were first investigated by Duval and Wicklund (1972).

22 Two classic books on this topic are *The Informed Heart* by Bruno Bettelheim (1960) and Erving Goffman's *Asylums* (1961).

References

Adamson, L. B., and J. E. Frick (2003), 'The Still Face: A History of a Shared Experimental Paradigm', *Infancy*, 4 (4): 451–73.
Addis, D. R., and L. J. Tippett (2008), 'The Contributions of Autobiographical Memory to the Content and Continuity of Identity', in F. Sani (ed), *Self-Continuity: Individual and Collective Perspectives*, 71–84, New York: Psychology Press.
Ainsworth, M. D. S., M. C. Blehar, E. Waters, and S. N. Wall (2015), *Patterns of Attachment*, New York: Psychology Press.
Al-Namlah, A. S., C. Fernyhough, and E. Meins (2006), 'Sociocultural Influences on the Development of Verbal Mediation: Private Speech and Phonological Recoding in Saudi Arabian and British Samples', *Developmental Psychology*, 42 (1): 117–31.
Amsterdam, B. (1972), 'Mirror Self-Image Reactions before Age Two', *Developmental Psychobiology*, 5 (4): 297–305.
Antaki, C. (1985), 'Ordinary Explanation in Conversation: Causal Structures and Their Defence', *European Journal of Social Psychology*, 15 (2): 213–30.
APA (American Psychiatric Association) (2013), *Diagnostic and Statistical Manual of Mental Disorders*, 5th edn, Arlington: American Psychiatric Publications.
Apperly, I. A., and S. A. Butterfill (2009), 'Do Humans Have Two Systems to Track Beliefs and Belief-Like States?', *Psychological Review*, 116 (4): 953–70.
Arnold, M. B. (1960), *Emotion and Personality*, New York: Columbia University Press.
Asendorpf, J. B. (2002), 'Self-Awareness, Other-Awareness, and Secondary Representation', in A. N. Meltzoff, and W. Prinz (eds), *The Imitative Mind*, 63–73, Cambridge: Cambridge University Press.
Averill, J. R. (1980), 'A Constructivist View on Emotions', in R. Plutchik, and H. Kellerman (eds), *Theories of Emotion*, 305–39, New York: Academic Press.
Baars, B. J. (1988), *A Cognitive Theory of Consciousness*, Cambridge: Cambridge University Press.
Baddeley, A. D., and G. J. Hitch (1974), 'Working Memory', in G. A. Bower (ed), *The Psychology of Learning and Motivation: Advances in Research and Theory*, 47–89, New York: Academic Press.
Baddeley, A. D., G. J. Hitch, and R. Allen (2021), 'A Multicomponent Model of Working Memory', in R. Logie, V. Camos, and N. Cowan (eds), *Working Memory: State of the Science*, 10–43, Oxford: Oxford University Press.
Bahrick, L. E., and J. S. Watson (1985), 'Detection of Intermodal Proprioceptive-Visual Contingency as a Potential Basis of Self-Perception in Infancy', *Developmental Psychology*, 21 (6): 963–73.

Baillargeon, R., R. M. Scott, and Z. He (2010), 'False-Belief Understanding in Infants', *Trends in Cognitive Sciences*, 14 (3): 110–18.

Baillargeon, R., Z. He, P. Setoh, R. M. Scott, S. Sloane, and D. Y.-J. Yang (2013), 'False-Belief Understanding and Why It Matters: The Social-Acting Hypothesis', in M. R. Banaji, and S. A. Gelman (eds), *Navigating the Social World*, 88–95, New York: Oxford University Press.

Baillargeon, R., P. Setoh, S. Sloane, K. Jin, and L. Bian (2014), 'Infant Social Cognition: Psychological and Sociomoral Reasoning', in M. S. Gazzaniga, and G. R. Mangun (eds), *The Cognitive Neurosciences*, 5th edn, 7–14, Cambridge: MIT Press.

Baillargeon, R., R. M. Scott, Z. He, S. Sloane, P. Setoh, K.-S. Jin, D. Wu, and L. Bian (2015), 'Psychological and Sociomoral Reasoning in Infancy', in M. Mikulincer, P. R. Shaver, E. Borgida, and J. A. Bargh (eds), *APA Handbook of Personality and Social Psychology: Vol. 1. Attitudes and Social Cognition*, 79–150, Washington: American Psychological Association.

Baldwin, D. A. (1991), 'Infant's Contribution to the Achievement of Joint Reference', *Child Development*, 62 (5): 875–90.

Balint, M. (1985), *Primary Love and Psychoanalytic Technique*, London: Routledge.

Balint, M. (1992), *The Basic Fault*, Evanston: Northwestern University Press (orig. ed. 1968).

Banaji, M. R., and S. A. Gelman, eds. (2013), *Navigating the Social World*, New York: Cambridge University Press.

Baron-Cohen, S. (1995), *Mindblindness*, Cambridge: MIT Press.

Baron-Cohen, S., A. M. Leslie, and U. Frith (1985), 'Does the Autistic Child Have a "Theory of Mind"?', *Cognition*, 21 (1): 37–46.

Barresi, J., and R. Martin (2000), *Naturalization of the Soul: Self and Personal Identity in the Eighteenth Century*, London: Routledge.

Barrett, L. F. (2006a), 'Are Emotions Natural Kinds?', *Perspectives on Psychological Science: A Journal of the Association for Psychological Science*, 1 (1): 28–58.

Barrett, L. F. (2006b), 'Solving the Emotion Paradox; Categorization and the Experience of Emotion', *Personality and Social Psychology Review: An Official Journal of the Society for Personality and Social Psychology, Inc*, 10 (1): 20–46.

Barrett, L. F. (2015), 'Ten Common Misconceptions about the Psychological Construction of Emotion', in Barrett, and Russell (eds), 45–79.

Barrett, L. F. (2017), *How Emotions Are Made*, New York: Houghton-Mifflin-Harcourt.

Barrett, L. F., R. Adolphs, S. Marsella, A. M. Martinez, and S. D. Pollak (2019), 'Emotional Expressions Reconsidered: Challenges to Inferring Emotion from Human Facial Movements', *Psychological Science in the Public Interest: A Journal of the American Psychological Society*, 20 (1): 1–68.

Barrett, L. F., B. Mesquita, K. N. Ochsner, and J. J. Gross (2007), 'The Experience of Emotion', *Annual Review of Psychology*, 58: 373–403.

Barrett, L. F., and J. A. Russell, eds. (2015), *The Psychological Construction of Emotion*, New York: Guilford Press.

Barsalou, L. W. (1999), 'Perceptual Symbol Systems', *Behavioral and Brain Sciences*, 22 (4): 577–609; discussion 610.
Bates, E., L. Camaioni, and V. Volterra (1975), 'The Acquisition of Performatives Prior to Speech', *Merrill-Palmer Quarterly*, 21 (3): 205–26.
Bauer, P. J., and J. S. Leventon (2013), 'Memory for One-Time Experiences in the Second Year of Life: Implications for the Status of Episodic Memory', *Infancy*, 18 (5): 755–81.
Baumard, N., O. Mascaro, and C. Chevallier (2012), 'Preschoolers Are Able to Take Merit into Account When Distributing Goods', *Developmental Psychology*, 48 (2): 492–8.
Bechtel, W. (2008), *Mental Mechanisms*, London: Routledge.
Bechtel, W., and A. Abrahamsen (2010), 'Dynamic Mechanistic Explanation: Computational Modelling of Circadian Rhythms as an Exemplar for Cognitive Science', *Studies in History and Philosophy of Science Part A*, 41 (3): 321–33.
Bechtel, W., and R. C. Richardson (2010), *Discovering Complexity: Decomposition and Localization as Strategies in Scientific Research*, Cambridge: MIT Press/Bradford Books.
Behne, T., M. Carpenter, J. Call, and M. Tomasello (2005), 'Unwilling versus Unable: Infants' Understanding of Intentional Action', *Developmental Psychology*, 41 (2): 328–37.
Bem, D. J. (1972), 'Self-Perception Theory', in L. Berkowitz (ed), *Advances in Experimental Social Psychology*, 1–62, New York: Academic Press.
Ben-Menahem, Y. (2016), 'The Web and the Tree: Quine and James on the Growth of Knowledge', in F. Janssen-Lauret, and G. Kemp (eds), *Quine and His Place in History*, 59–75, Berlin: Springer.
Bermúdez, J. L. (1998), *The Paradox of Self-Consciousness*, Cambridge: MIT Press.
Bermúdez, J. L. (2011), 'Bodily Awareness and Self-Consciousness', in S. Gallagher (ed), *The Oxford Handbook of the Self*, 156–79, Oxford: Oxford University Press (Reprint 2018, in Bermúdez).
Bermúdez, J. L. (2018), *The Bodily Self: Selected Essays*, Cambridge: MIT Press.
Bertenthal, B. I., and K. W. Fischer (1978), 'Development of Self-Recognition in the Infant', *Developmental Psychology*, 14 (1): 44–50.
Bettelheim, B. (1960), *The Informed Heart*, Glencoe: The Free Press.
Bischof-Köhler, D. (2012), 'Empathy and Self-Recognition in Phylogenetic and Ontogenetic Perspective', *Emotion Review*, 4 (1): 40–8.
Bjorklund, D. F. (2015), 'Developing Adaptations', *Developmental Review*, 38: 13–35.
Bloom, P. (2000), *How Children Learn the Meanings of Words*, Cambridge: MIT Press.
Bodei, R. (2002), *Destini personali*, Milano: Feltrinelli.
Bodei, R. (2011), 'Memory and the Construction of Personality', *Iris*, 3 (5): 87–98.
Boeckx, C. (2014), 'The Roots of Current Biolinguistic Thought: Revisiting the "Chomsky-Piaget Debate" in the Context of the Revival of Biolinguistics', *Teorema*, 33 (1): 83–94.

Borghi, A. M., and C. Fernyhough (2023), 'Concepts, Abstractness and Inner Speech', *Philosophical Transactions of the Royal Society of London. Series B, Biological Sciences*, 378 (1870): article ID:20210351. https://doi.org/10.1098/rstb.2021.0371.

Bowlby, J. (1969–80), *Attachment, Separation, Loss*, 3 vols, New York: Basic Books.

Boyd, R. (1991), 'Realism, Anti-Foundationalism and the Enthusiasm for Natural Kinds', *Philosophical Studies*, 61 (1–2): 127–48.

Breger, L. (1974), *From Instinct to Identity: The Development of Personality*, Englewood Cliffs: Prentice-Hall.

Bremner, A. J. (2022), 'Developmental Origins of Bodily Awareness', in A. J. T. Alsmith, and M. R. Longo (eds), *The Routledge Handbook of Bodily Awareness*, 279–97, London: Routledge.

Brentano, F. (1874), *Psychologie vom Empirischen Standpunkt*, Leipzig: Duncker & Humblot (2nd enl. ed. by O. Kraus, 1924, Leipzig: Meiner); Engl. transl. *Psychology from an Empirical Standpoint*, London: Routledge, 1973.

Brooks-Gunn, J., and M. Lewis (1984), 'The Development of Early Visual Self-Recognition', *Developmental Review*, 4 (3): 215–39.

Brownell, C. A., M. Svetlova, and S. R. Nichols (2012), 'Emergence and Early Development of the Body Image', in V. Slaughter, and C. E. Browner (eds), *Early Development of Body Representations*, 37–58, Cambridge: Cambridge University Press.

Brownell, C. A., S. Zerwas, and G. B. Ramani (2007), '"So big": The Development of Body Self-Awareness in Toddlers', *Child Development*, 78 (5): 1426–40.

Bruner, J. S. (1962), 'Introduction', in L. S. Vygotsky (ed), *Thought and Language*, v–x, Cambridge: MIT Press.

Bruner, J. S. (1990), *Acts of Meaning*, Cambridge: Harvard University Press.

Bulgarelli, C., A. Blasi, C. C. J. M. de Klerk, J. E. Richards, A. Hamilton, and V. Southgate (2019), 'Fronto-Temporoparietal Connectivity and Self-Awareness in 18-Month-Olds: A Resting State fNIRS Study', *Developmental Cognitive Neuroscience*, 38: 100676.

Bulgarelli, C., C. C. J. M. de Klerk, J. E. Richards, V. Southgate, A. Hamilton, and A. Blasi (2020), 'The Developmental Trajectory of Fronto-Temporoparietal Connectivity as a Proxy of the Default Mode Network: A Longitudinal fNIRS Investigation', *Human Brain Mapping*, 41 (10): 2717–40.

Buttelmann, D., M. Carpenter, and M. Tomasello (2009), 'Eighteen-Month-Old Infants Show False Belief Understanding in an Active Helping Paradigm', *Cognition*, 112 (2): 337–42.

Buttelmann, F., J. Suhrke, and D. Buttelmann (2015), 'What You Get Is What You Believe: Eighteen-Month-Olds Demonstrate Belief Understanding in an Unexpected-Identity Task', *Journal of Experimental Child Psychology*, 131: 94–103.

Butterfill, S. A., and I. A. Apperly (2013), 'How to Construct a Minimal Theory of Mind', *Mind and Language*, 28 (5): 606–37.

Butterworth, G. (1995), 'An Ecological Perspective on the Origins of Self', in P. Rochat (ed), *The Self in Infancy*, 35–51, Amsterdam: Elsevier.

Buyukozer Dawkins, M., F. Ting, M. Stavans, and R. Baillargeon (2020), 'Early Moral Cognition: A Principle-Based Approach', in V. D. Poeppel, G. R. Mangun, and M. S. Gazzaniga (eds), *The Cognitive Neurosciences*, 7–16, Cambridge: MIT Press.

Buyukozer Dawkins, M., S. Sloane, and R. Baillargeon (2019), 'Do Infants in the First Year of Life Expect Equal Resource Allocations?', *Frontiers in Psychology*, 10: 116. https://doi.org/10.3389/fpsyg.2019.00116.

Camia, C., and T. Habermas (2020), 'Explaining Change in Content of Life Narratives over Time', *Memory*, 28 (5): 655–68.

Byrne, R. W., and A. Whiten (eds.) (1988), *Machiavellian Intelligence: Social Expertise and the Evolution of Intellect in Monkeys, Apes, and Humans*, Oxford: Clarendon Press/Oxford University Press.

Campanella, S. (2019), 'Understanding Bio-Cognitive Change: Jean Piaget and the Path to Epigenetic Innovation', *Paradigmi*, 37 (1): 7–22.

Camras, L. A., and M. M. Shuster (2013), 'Current Emotion Research in Developmental Psychology', *Emotion Review*, 5 (3): 321–9.

Carey, S., D. Zaitchik, and I. Bascandziev (2015), 'Theories of Development: In Dialog with Jean Piaget', *Developmental Review*, 38: 36–54.

Carlson, E. A. (1998), 'A Prospective Longitudinal Study of Disorganized/Disoriented Attachment', *Child Development*, 69: 1970–9.

Carpenter, M., M. Tomasello, and T. Striano (2005), 'Role Reversal Imitation and Language in Typically Developing Infants and Children with Autism', *Infancy*, 8 (3): 253–78.

Carruthers, P. (2009), 'How We Know Our Own Minds: The Relationship between Mindreading and Metacognition', *Behavioral and Brain Sciences*, 32 (2): 121–38; discussion 138.

Carruthers, P. (2011a), *The Opacity of Mind*, Oxford: Oxford University Press.

Carruthers, P. (2011b), 'Language in Cognition', in E. Margolis, R. Samuels, and S. Stich (eds), *The Oxford Handbook of Philosophy of Cognitive Science*, 382–401, Oxford: Oxford University Press.

Carruthers, P. (2013), 'Mindreading in Infancy', *Mind and Language*, 28 (2): 141–72.

Carruthers, P. (2014), 'The Fragmentation of Reasoning', in P. Quintanilla, C. Mantilla, and P. Cépeda (eds), *Cognición Social y Lenguaje*, 181–204, Lima: Fondo Editorial de la Pontificia Universidad Católica del Perú.

Carruthers, P. (2015), *The Centered Mind*, Oxford: Oxford University Press.

Carruthers, P. (2017a), 'Mindreading in Adults: Evaluating Two-Systems Views', *Synthese*, 194 (3): 673–88.

Carruthers, P. (2017b), 'The illusion of conscious thought', *Journal of Consciousness Studies*, 24 (9–10): 228–52.

Carruthers, P. (2018), 'Valence and Value', *Philosophy and Phenomenological Research*, 97 (3): 658–80.

Carruthers, P. (2019), *Human and Animal Minds*, Oxford: Oxford University Press.

Carruthers, P. (2020), 'Questions in Development', in L. Butler, S. Ronfard, and K. Corriveau (eds), *The Questioning Child: Insights from Psychology and Education*, 6–28, Cambridge: Cambridge University Press.

Carruthers, P., L. Fletcher, and J. B. Ritchie (2012), 'The Evolution of Self-Knowledge', *Philosophical Topics*, 40 (2): 13–37.

Chemero, A. (2009), *Radical Embodied Cognitive Science*, Cambridge: MIT Press.

Chemero, A., and M. Silberstein (2008), 'After the Philosophy of Mind: Replacing Scholasticism with Science', *Philosophy of Science*, 75 (1): 1–27.

Cheney, D. L., and R. M. Seyfarth (2007), *Baboon Metaphysics: The Evolution of a Social Mind*, Chicago: University of Chicago Press.

Chevalier-Skolnikoff, S. (1973), 'Facial Expression of Emotion in Nonhuman Primates', in P. Ekman (ed), *Darwin and Facial Expression*, 11–90, New York: Academic Press.

Christensen, C. B. (1998), 'Getting Heidegger off the West Coast', *Inquiry*, 41 (1): 65–87.

Clark, A. C. (1997), *Being There*, Cambridge: MIT Press.

Cole, M., J. Gay, J. A. Glick, and D. W. Sharp (1971), *The Cultural Context of Learning and Thinking*, New York: Basic Books.

Conway, M. A. (2005), 'Memory and the Self☆', *Journal of Memory and Language*, 53 (4): 594–628.

Conway, M. A., and C. W. Pleydell-Pearce (2000), 'The Construction of Autobiographical Memories in the Self-Memory System', *Psychological Review*, 107 (2): 261–88.

Conway, M. A., K. Meares, and S. Standart (2004), 'Images and Goals', *Memory*, 12 (4): 525–31.

Conway, M. A., J. A. Singer, and A. Tagini (2004), 'The Self and Autobiographical Memory: Correspondence and Coherence', *Social Cognition*, 22 (5): 491–529.

Corcuera, A. M. (2021), 'Narrativism, Reductionism and Four-Dimensionalism', *Ágora: Papeles de Filosofía*, 40 (2): 63–86.

Courage, M. L., and M. L. Howe (2002), 'From Infant to Child: The Dynamics of Cognitive Change in the Second Year of Life', *Psychological Bulletin*, 128 (2): 250–77.

Craik, K. (1943), *The Nature of Explanation*, Cambridge: Cambridge University Press.

Crawford, T. N., P. Cohen, J. G. Johnson, J. R. Sneed, and J. S. Brook (2004), 'The Course and Psychosocial Correlates of Personality Disorder Symptoms in Adolescence: Erikson's Developmental Theory Revisited', *Journal of Youth and Adolescence*, 33 (5): 373–87.

Csibra, G. (2008), 'Goal Attribution to Inanimate Agents by 6.5 Month-Old Infants', *Cognition*, 107 (2): 705–17.

Csibra, G., and G. Gergely (2007), 'Obsessed with Goals: Functions and Mechanisms of Teleological Interpretation of Actions in Humans', *Acta Psychologica*, 124 (1): 60–78.

Csibra, G., and G. Gergely (2009), 'Natural Pedagogy', *Trends in Cognitive Sciences*, 13 (4): 148–53.

Csibra, G., and V. Southgate (2006), 'Evidence for Infants' Understanding of False Beliefs Should Not Be Dismissed. Response to Ruffman and Perner', *Trends in Cognitive Sciences*, 10 (1): 4–5.

Damasio, A. (1994), *Descartes' Error: Emotion, Reason, and the Human Brain*, New York: Penguin Book.

Damasio, A. (1999), *The Feeling of What Happens*, New York: Pantheon.
D'Arms, J., and D. Jacobson (2003), 'The Significance of Recalcitrant Emotion (or, Anti-Quasi Judgmentalism)', *Royal Institute of Philosophy Supplement*, 52: 27–45.
Darwin, C. (1872/1998), '*The Expression of the Emotions in Man and Animals*', Introduction, Notes and Commentaries by P. Ekman, London: Harper Collins.
Dehaene, S. (2014), *Consciousness and the Brain*, London: Viking Penguin.
Dehaene, S., and J. P. Changeux (2011), 'Experimental and Theoretical Approaches to Conscious Processing', *Neuron*, 70 (2): 200–27.
Dehaene, S., L. Naccache, L. Cohen, D. L. Bihan, J. F. Mangin, J. B. Poline, and D. Rivière (2001), 'Cerebral Mechanisms of Word Masking and Unconscious Repetition Priming', *Nature Neuroscience*, 4 (7): 752–8.
Dehaene, S., H. Lau, and S. Kouider (2017), 'What Is Consciousness, and Could Machines Have It?', *Science*, 358 (6362): 486–92.
Deigh, J. (2014), 'William James and the Rise of the Scientific Study of Emotion', *Emotion Review*, 6 (1): 4–12.
De Martino, E. (2012), 'Crisis of Presence and Religious Reintegration', *HAU: Journal of Ethnographic Theory*, 2 (2): 434–50 (orig. ed. 1956).
De Martino, E. (2021), *Morte e pianto rituale*, Torino: Einaudi (orig. ed. 1958).
De Martino, E. (2022), *Il mondo magico*, Torino: Einaudi (orig. ed. 1948).
Demiray, B., and S. Bluck (2011), 'The Relation of the Conceptual Self to Recent and Distant Autobiographical Memories', *Memory*, 19 (8): 975–92.
Dennett, D. C. (1991), *Consciousness Explained*, Boston: Little Brown and Co.
Dennett, D. C. (1993), 'Review of J. Searle, The Rediscovery of the Mind', *Journal of Philosophy*, 60 (4): 193–205.
Dennett, D. C. (2016), 'Artifactual Selves: A Response to Lynne Rudder Baker', *Phenomenology and the Cognitive Sciences*, 15 (1): 17–20.
Flanagan, O. (1992), *Consciousness Reconsidered*, Cambridge: MIT Press.
D'Entremont, B., and D. Muir (1999), 'Infant Responses to Adult Happy and Sad Vocal and Facial Expressions during Face-to-Face Interactions', *Infant Behavior and Development*, 22 (4): 527–39.
Di Francesco, M., M. Marraffa, and A. Paternoster (2016), *The Self and Its Defences*, London: Palgrave.
Dings, R., and A. Newen (2023), 'Constructing the past: The Relevance of the Narrative Self in Modulating Episodic Memory', *Review of Philosophy and Psychology*, 14 (1): 87–112.
Dretske, F. (1988), *Explaining Behavior*, Cambridge: MIT Press.
Dretske, F. (1995), *Naturalizing the Mind*, Cambridge: MIT Press.
Dunn, J. (1996), 'Family Conversations and the Development of Social Understanding', in B. Bernstein, and J. Brannen (eds), *Children, Research and Policy: Essays for Barbara Tizard*, 81–95, Washington: Taylor and Francis.
Dupoux, E., and P. Jacob (2007), 'Universal Moral Grammar: A Critical Appraisal', *Trends in Cognitive Sciences*, 11 (9): 373–8.

Duval, S., and R. A. Wicklund (1972), *A Theory of Objective Self-Awareness*, New York: Academic Press.
Eagle, M. N. (2011), *From Classical to Contemporary Psychoanalysis: A Critique and Integration*, New York: Routledge.
Eagle, M. N. (2013). *Attachment and Psychoanalysis: Theory, Research, and Clinical Implications*, New York: Guilford Press.
Egyed, K., I. Király, and G. Gergely (2013), 'Communicating Shared Knowledge in Infancy', *Psychological Science*, 24 (7): 1348–53.
Ekman, P. (1999), 'Basic Emotions', in T. Dalgleish, and M. Power (eds), *Handbook of Cognition and Emotion*, 45–60, Chichester: Wiley.
Ekman, P., and W. V. Friesen (1971), 'Constants across Cultures in the Face and Emotion', *Journal of Personality and Social Psychology*, 17 (2): 124–9.
Ekman, P., E. R. Sorenson, and W. V. Friesen (1969), 'Pan-Cultural Elements in Facial Displays of Emotion', *Science*, 164 (3875): 86–8.
Eibl-Eibesfeldt, I. (1973), 'Expressive Behaviour of the Deaf and Blind Born', in M. von Cranach, and I. Vine (eds), *Social Communication and Movement*, 163–94, London and New York: Academic Press.
Eisenberg, N., R. A. Fabes, and T. L. Spinrad (2006), 'Prosocial Development', in W. Damon, R. M. Lerner, and N. Eisenberg (eds), *Handbook of Child Psychology, 6th Ed., Vol. 3. Social, Emotional, and Personality Development*, 646–718, New York: Wiley.
Elfenbein, H. A., and N. Ambady (2002), 'On the Universality and Cultural Specificity of Emotion Recognition: A Meta-Analysis', *Psychological Bulletin*, 128 (2): 203–35.
Elkind, D. (1967), 'Egocentrism in Adolescence', *Child Development*, 38 (4): 1025–34.
Ellenberger, H. F. (1970), *The Discovery of the Unconscious*, New York: Basic Books.
Engelmann, J. M., H. Over, E. Herrmann, and M. Tomasello (2013), 'Young Children Care More about Their Reputations with Ingroup Members and Potential Reciprocators', *Developmental Science*, 16 (6): 952–8.
Engelmann, J. M., E. Herrmann, and M. Tomasello (2016), 'The Effects of Being Watched on Resource Acquisition in Chimpanzees and Human Children', *Animal Cognition*, 19 (1): 147–51.
Erikson, E. H. (1968), *Identity, Youth and Crisis*, New York: Norton.
Evans, J. S. B., and K. E. Frankish, eds. (2009), *In Two Minds: Dual Processes and Beyond*, Oxford and New York: Oxford University Press.
Evans, J. S. B., and K. E. Stanovich (2013a), 'Dual-Process Theories of Higher Cognition: Advancing the Debate', *Perspectives on Psychological Science: A Journal of the Association for Psychological Science*, 8 (3): 223–41.
Evans, J. S. B., and K. E. Stanovich (2013b), 'Theory and Metatheory in the Study of Dual Processing: Reply to Comments', *Perspectives on Psychological Science: A Journal of the Association for Psychological Science*, 8 (3): 263–71.
Federn, P. (1952), *Ego Psychology and the Psychoses*, New York: Basic Books.
Fehr, E., H. Bernhard, and B. Rockenbach (2008), 'Egalitarianism in Young Children', *Nature*, 454 (7208): 1079–83.

Fehr, B., and J. A. Russell (1984), 'Concept of Emotion Viewed from a Prototype Perspective', *Journal of Experimental Psychology: General*, 113 (3): 464–86.

Fernyhough, C. (2009), 'What Can We Say about the Inner Experience of the Young Child?', *Behavioral and Brain Sciences*, 32 (2): 143–4.

Fernyhough, C. (2010), 'Vygotsky, Luria, and the Social Brain', in B. Sokol, U. Müller, J. Carpendale, A. Young, and G. Iarocci (eds), *Self- and Social-Regulation: Social Interaction, and the Development of Social Understanding and Executive Functions*, 56–79, Oxford: Oxford University Press.

Fernyhough, C. (2016), *The Voices Within*, London: Profile Books.

Fernyhough, C., and E. Fradley (2005), 'Private Speech on an Executive Task: Relations with Task Difficulty and Task Performance', *Cognitive Development*, 20 (1): 103–20.

Fernyhough, C., and E. Meins (2009), 'Private Speech and Theory of Mind: Evidence for Developing Interfunctional Relations', in A. Winsler, C. Fernyhough, and I. Montero (eds), *Private Speech, Executive Functioning, and the Development of Self-Regulation*, 95–104, Cambridge: Cambridge University Press.

Ferrara, A. (1998), *Reflective Authenticity*, London: Routledge.

Fischman, L. G. (1983), 'Dreams, Hallucinogenic Drug States and Schizophrenia: A Psychological and Biological Comparison', *Schizophrenia Bulletin*, 9 (1): 73-94.

Fiske, S. T., and S. E. Taylor (2020), 'Social Cognition Evolves: Illustrations from Our Work on Intergroup Bias and on Healthy Adaptation', *Psicothema*, 32 (3): 291–7.

Fivush, R. (2010), 'The Development of Autobiographical Memory', *Annual Review of Psychology*, 62: 559–82.

Fivush, R. (2022), *Autobiographical Memory and Narrative in Childhood*, Cambridge and New York: Cambridge University Press.

Fodor, J. A. (1983), *The Modularity of Mind*, Cambridge: MIT Press.

Fodor, J. A. (1992), 'A Theory of the Child's Theory of Mind', *Cognition*, 44 (3): 283–96.

Fonagy, P., G. Gergely, E. Jurist, and M. Target (2002), *Affect Regulation, Mentalization, and the Development of the Self*, London: Other Press.

Frankenhuis, W. E., G. Gergely, and J. S. Watson (2013), 'Infants May Use Contingency Analysis to Estimate Environmental States: An Evolutionary, Life-History Perspective', *Child Development Perspectives*, 7 (2): 115–20.

Frankish, K. (2009), 'Systems and Levels: Dual-System Theories and the Personal-Subpersonal Distinction', in J. S. B. Evans, and K. E. Frankish (eds), *Two Minds*, 89–107, New York: Oxford University Press.

Frankish, K. (2012), 'Dual Systems and Dual Attitudes', *Mind and Society*, 11 (1): 41–51.

Franzese, S. (2008), *The Ethics of Energy: William James's Moral Philosophy in Focus*, Frankfurt: Ontos Verlag.

Freud, S. (1957), 'On Narcissism: An Introduction', in J. Strachey (ed), *The Standard Edition of the Complete Psychological Works of Sigmund Freud, Vol. 14*, 67–102, London: Hogarth Press (orig. ed. 1914).

Freud, S. (1964), 'New Introductory Lectures on Psycho-Analysis', in J. Strachey (ed), *The Standard Edition of the Complete Psychological Works of Sigmund Freud, Vol. 22*, 1–267, London: Hogarth Press (orig. ed. 1933).

Freundlieb, M., Á. M. Kovács, and N. Sebanz (2018), 'Reading Your Mind While You Are Reading – Evidence for Spontaneous Visuospatial Perspective Taking during a Semantic Categorization Task', *Psychological Science*, 29 (4): 614–22.

Gallagher, S. (2013), 'A Pattern Theory of Self', *Frontiers in Human Neuroscience*, 7: 443. https://doi.org/10.3389/fnhum.2013.00443.

Gallagher, S. (2017), 'Self-Defense: Deflecting Deflationary and Eliminativist Critiques of the Sense of Ownership', *Frontiers in Psychology*, 8. https://doi.org/10.3389/fpsyg.2017.01612.

Gallagher, S., and D. Zahavi (2019), 'Phenomenological Approaches to Self-Consciousness', in E. N. Zalta (ed), *The Stanford Encyclopedia of Philosophy*. https://plato.stanford.edu/archives/sum2019/entries/self-consciousness-phenomenological/.

Gallagher, S., and D. Zahavi (2020), *The Phenomenological Mind*, 3rd edn, London: Routledge.

Gallop, G. G. (1970), 'Chimpanzees: Self-Recognition', *Science*, 167 (3914): 86–7.

Gazzaniga, M. S. (2000), 'Cerebral Specialisation and Inter-Hemispheric Communication: Does the Corpus Callosum Enable the Human Condition?', *Brain*, 123 (7): 1293–326.

Gazzaniga, M. S. (2011), *Who's in Charge? Free Will and the Science of the Brain*, New York: HarperCollins.

Gendron, M., and L. F. Barrett (2009), 'Reconstructing the past: A Century of Ideas about Emotion in Psychology', *Emotion Review: Journal of the International Society for Research on Emotion*, 1 (4): 316–39.

Gergely, G. (1992), 'Developmental Reconstructions: Infancy from the Point of View of Psychoanalysis and Developmental Psychology', *Psychoanalysis and Contemporary Thought*, 15 (1): 3–55.

Gergely, G. (1994), 'From Self-Recognition to Theory of Mind', in S. Parker, R. Mitchell, and M. Boccia (eds), *Self-Awareness in Animals and Humans: Developmental Perspectives*, 51–61, Cambridge: Cambridge University Press.

Gergely, G. (2002), 'The Development of Understanding Self and Agency', in U. Goswami (ed), *Blackwell Handbook of Childhood Cognitive Development*, 26–46, Oxford: Blackwell.

Gergely, G. (2004), 'The Social Construction of the Subjective Self: The Role of Affect-Mirroring, Markedness, and Ostensive Communication in Self Development', in L. Mayes, P. Fonagy, and M. Target (eds), *Developmental Science and Psychoanalysis*, 45–82, London: Karnac.

Gergely, G. (2007), 'The Social Construction of the Subjective Self: The Role of Affect-Mirroring, Markedness, and Ostensive Communication in Self-Development', in L. Mayes, P. Fonagy, and M. Target (eds), *Developmental Science and Psychoanalysis: Integration and Innovation*, 45–82, London: Karnac.

Gergely, G. (2011), 'Kinds of Agents', in U. Goswami (ed), *Wiley-Blackwell Handbook of Childhood Cognitive Development*, 76–105, Oxford: Blackwell.

Gergely, G., H. Bekkering, and I. Király (2002), 'Rational Imitation in Preverbal Infants', *Nature*, 415 (6873): 755.

Gergely, G., and G. Csibra (2013), 'Natural Pedagogy', in M. R. Banaji, and S. A. Gelman (eds), *Navigating the Social World*, 127–32, Cambridge: Cambridge University Press.

Gergely, G., and I. Király (2019), 'Natural Pedagogy of Social Emotions', in D. Dukes, and F. Clément (eds), *Foundations of Affective Social Learning*, 87–114, Cambridge: Cambridge University press.

Gergely, G., O. Koós, and J. S. Watson (2010), 'Contingency Perception and the Role of Contingent Parental Reactivity in Early Socio-Emotional Development', in T. Fuchs, H. C. Sattel, and P. Henningsen (eds), *The Embodied Self*, 141–69, Stuttgart: Schattauer.

Gergely, G., Z. Nádasdy, G. Csibra, and S. Bíró (1995), 'Taking the Intentional Stance at 12 Months of Age', *Cognition*, 56 (2): 165–93.

Gergely, G., and Z. Unoka (2008a), 'The Development of the Unreflective Self', in F. N. Busch (ed), *Mentalization*, 57–102, London: Routledge.

Gergely, G., and Z. Unoka (2008b), 'Attachment and Mentalization in Humans: The Development of the Affective Self', in E. L. Jurist, A. Slade, and S. Bergner (eds), *Mind to Mind*, 305–42, Oxford: Oxford University Press.

Gergely, G., and J. S. Watson (1996), 'The Social Biofeedback Theory of Parental Affect-Mirroring: The Development of Emotional Self-Awareness and Self-Control in Infancy', *International Journal of Psycho-Analysis*, 77 (6): 1181–212.

Gergely, G., and J. S. Watson (1999), 'Early Social-Emotional Development: Contingency Perception and the Social Biofeedback Model', in P. Rochat (ed), *Early Social Cognition*, 101–37, Hillsdale: Erlbaum.

Gerrans, P. (2004), 'Individualism and Cognitive Development', *Behavioral and Brain Sciences*, 27 (1): 107–8.

Ghetti, S., and S. A. Bunge (2012), 'Neural Changes Underlying the Development of Episodic Memory during Middle Childhood', *Developmental Cognitive Neuroscience*, 2 (4): 381–95.

Giddens, A. (1991), *Modernity and Self-Identity*, Cambridge: Polity Press.

Giddens, A. (1992), *The Transformation of Intimacy*, Stanford: Stanford University Press.

Gilbert, D. T., and T. D. Wilson (2003), 'Affective Forecasting', in M. Zanna (ed), *Advances in Experimental Social Psychology*, 345–411, New York: Elsevier.

Gillihan, S. J., and M. J. Farah (2005), 'Is Self Special? A Critical Review of Evidence from Experimental Psychology and Cognitive Neuroscience', *Psychological Bulletin*, 131 (1): 76–97.

Ginzburg, C. (1991), 'Momigliano and de Martino', *History and Theory*, 30 (4): 37–48.

Giustina, A. (2022), 'A Defense of Inner Awareness: The Memory Argument Revisited', *Review of Philosophy and Psychology*, 13 (2): 341–63.

Goffman, E. (1958), *The Presentation of Self in Everyday Life*, New York: Dubleday.

Goffman, E. (1961), *Asylums: Essays on the Social Situation of Mental Patients and Other Inmates*, New York: Doubleday.
Goldman, A. (2006), *Simulating Minds*, Oxford: Oxford University Press.
Goldman-Rakic, P. S. (1995), 'Cellular Basis of Working Memory', *Neuron*, 14 (3): 477–85.
Gopnik, A. (1993), 'How We Know Our Minds: The Illusion of First-Person Knowledge of Intentionality', *Behavioral and Brain Sciences*, 16 (1): 1–14.
Gordon, R. M. (1995), 'Simulation Without Introspection or Inference from Me to You', in M. Davies, and T. Stone (eds), *Mental Simulation*, 60–73, Oxford: Blackwell.
Graffi, G. (2019), 'The Piaget-Chomsky Debate, Forty Years Later. A Retrospective Evaluation and Some Open Issues', *Paradigmi*, 37 (1): 53–72.
Greenwood, J. (2015), *Becoming Human: The Ontogenesis, Metaphysics, and Expression of Human Emotionality*, Cambridge: MIT Press.
Griffiths, P. E. (1997), *What Emotions Really Are: The Problem of Psychological Categories*, Chicago: University of Chicago Press.
Griffiths, P. E. (2004), 'Is Emotion a Natural Kind?', in R. C. Solomon (ed), *Philosophers on Emotion*, 233–49, Oxford: Oxford University Press.
Griffiths, P. E. (2007), 'Ethology, Sociobiology, and Evolutionary Psychology', in S. Sahotra, and A. Plutynski (eds), *A Companion to the Philosophy of Biology*, 393–414, Oxford: Blackwell.
Griffiths, P. E. (2017), 'Mechanisms Can Be Complex', *Metascience*, 26 (3): 387–91.
Griffiths, P. E., and A. Scarantino (2009), 'Emotions in the Wild: The Situated Perspective on Emotion', in P. Robbins, and M. Aydede (eds), *The Cambridge Handbook of Situated Cognition*, 437–53, Cambridge: Cambridge University Press.
Griffiths, P. E., and J. Tabery (2013), 'Developmental Systems Theory: What Does It Explain, and How Does It Explain It?', *Advances in Child Development and Behavior*, 44: 65–94.
Grosse Wiesmann, C., and V. Southgate (2021), 'Early Theory of Mind Development: Are Infants Inherently Altercentric?', in M. Gilead, and K. N. Ochsner (eds), *The Neural Basis of Mentalizing*, 49–66, Berlin: Springer.
Grossmann, T., and M. H. Johnson (2007), 'The Development of the Social Brain in Human Infancy', *European Journal of Neuroscience*, 25 (4): 909–19.
Grossmann, T., M. Missana, and A. Vaish (2020), 'Helping, Fast and Slow: Exploring Intuitive Cooperation in Early Ontogeny', *Cognition*, 196: 104144.
Guidorizzi, G. (1997), 'The Laughter of the Suitors: A Case of Collective Madness in the *Odyssey*', in L. Edmunds, and R. W. Wallace (eds), *Poet and Public, and Performance in Ancient Greece*, 1–7, Baltimore and London: John Hopkins University Press.
Habermas, T. (2011), 'Autobiographical Reasoning: Arguing and Narrating from a Biographical Perspective', *New Directions for Child and Adolescent Development*, 131: 1–17.
Habermas, T. (2019), *Emotion and Narrative: Perspectives in Autobiographical Storytelling*, Cambridge: Cambridge University Press.

Habermas, T., and S. Bluck (2000), 'Getting a Life: The Emergence of the Life Story in Adolescence', *Psychological Bulletin*, 126 (5): 748–69.

Habermas, T., and C. de Silveira (2008), 'The Development of Global Coherence in Life Narratives across Adolescence: Temporal, Causal, and Thematic Aspects', *Developmental Psychology*, 44 (3): 707–21.

Habermas, T., and N. Kemper (2021), 'Psychoanalytic Perspectives on Identity: From Ego to Life Narrative', in M. Bamberg, C. Demuth, and M. Watzlawik (eds), *The Cambridge Handbook of Identity*, 193–214, Cambridge: Cambridge University Press.

Habermas, T., and C. Köber (2015a), 'Autobiographical Reasoning Is Constitutive for Narrative Identity: The Role of the Life Story for Personal Continuity', in K. C. McLean, and M. Syed (eds), *The Oxford Handbook of Identity Development*, 149–65, Oxford: Oxford University Press.

Habermas, T., and C. Köber (2015b), 'Autobiographical Reasoning in Life Narratives Buffers the Effect of Biographical Disruptions on the Sense of Self-Continuity', *Memory*, 23 (5): 664–74.

Haidt, J. (2001), 'The Emotional Dog and Its Rational Tail: A Social Intuitionist Approach to Moral Judgment', *Psychological Review*, 108 (4): 814–34.

Haidt, J. (2012), *The Righteous Mind*, New York: Penguin.

Hallpike, C. R. (1979), *The Foundations of Primitive Thought*, Oxford: Oxford University Press.

Hamann, K., F. Warneken, J. R. Greenberg, and M. Tomasello (2011), 'Collaboration Encourages Equal Sharing in Children but Not in Chimpanzees', *Nature*, 476 (7360): 328–31.

Hamlin, J. K., K. Wynn, and P. Bloom (2007), 'Social Evaluation by Preverbal Infants', *Nature*, 450 (7169): 557–9.

Hamlin, J. K., K. Wynn, P. Bloom, and N. Mahajan (2011), 'How Infants and Toddlers React to Antisocial Others', *Proceedings of the National Academy of Sciences of the United States of America*, 108 (50): 19931–6.

Hardecker, S., M. F. H. Schmidt, and M. Tomasello (2017), 'Children's Developing Understanding of the Conventionality of Rules', *Journal of Cognition and Development*, 18 (2): 163–88.

Harman, G. (1978), 'Studying the Chimpanzee's Theory of Mind', *Behavioral and Brain Sciences*, 1 (4): 576–7.

Harman, G. (1990), 'The Intrinsic Quality of Experience', in J. E. Tomberlin (ed), *Action Theory and Philosophy of Mind (Philosophical Perspectives, Vol. 4)*, 31–51, Atascadero: Ridgeview.

Harré, R. (1987), 'The Social Construction of Selves', in K. Yardley, and T. Honess (eds), *Self and Identity*, 41–52, New York: Wiley.

Heyes, C. M., and C. D. Frith (2014), 'The Cultural Evolution of Mind Reading', *Science*, 344 (6190): 1243091.

Helming, K. A., B. Strickland, and P. Jacob (2014), 'Making Sense of Early False-Belief Understanding', *Trends in Cognitive Sciences*, 18 (4): 167–70.

Helming, K. A., B. Strickland, and P. Jacob (2016), 'Solving the Puzzle about Early Belief-Ascription', *Mind and Language*, 31 (4): 438–69.

Hepach, R., J. M. Engelmann, E. Herrmann, S. C. Gerdemann, and M. Tomasello (2023), 'Evidence for a Developmental Shift in the Motivation Underlying Helping in Early Childhood', *Developmental Science*, 26 (1): e13253.

Hernik, M., P. Fearon, and P. Fonagy (2009), 'There Must Be More to Development of Mindreading and Metacognition than Passing False Belief Tasks', *Behavioral and Brain Sciences*, 32 (2): 147–8.

Hinde, R. A. (1985), 'Expression and Negotiation', in G. Zivin (ed), *The Development of Expressive Behavior*, 103–16, New York: Academic Press.

Hoemann, K., F. Xu, and L. F. Barrett (2019), 'Emotion Words, Emotion Concepts, and Emotional Development in Children: A Constructionist Hypothesis', *Developmental Psychology*, 55 (9): 1830–49.

Hoerl, C. (2007), 'Episodic Memory, Autobiographical Memory, Narrative: On Three Key Notions in Current Approaches to Memory Development', *Philosophical Psychology*, 20 (5): 621–40.

Howard, L. H., and A. L. Woodward (2019), 'Human Actions Support Infant Memory', *Journal of Cognition and Development: Official Journal of the Cognitive Development Society*, 20 (5): 772–89.

Howe, M. L. (2014), 'The Co-Emergence of the Self and Autobiographical Memory', in P. J. Bauer, and R. Fivush (eds), *The Wiley Handbook on the Development of Children's Memory*, 545–67, Hoboken: Wiley-Blackwell.

Howe, M. L., and M. L. Courage (1993), 'On Resolving the Enigma of Infantile Amnesia', *Psychological Bulletin*, 113 (2): 305–26.

Howe, M. L., and M. L. Courage (1997), 'The Emergence and Early Development of Autobiographical Memory', *Psychological Review*, 104 (3): 499–523.

Howe, M., M. Courage, and M. Rooksby (2009), 'The Genesis and Development of Autobiographical Memory', in M. L. Courage, and N. Cowan (eds), *The Development of Memory in Infancy and Childhood*, 2nd edn, 177–96, Hove: Psychology Press.

Hrdy, S. B. (2009), *Mothers and Others: The Evolutionary Origins of Mutual Understanding*, Cambridge: Harvard University Press.

Hume, D. (1739–40), *A Treatise of Human Nature*, edited by L. A. Selby-Bigge, 2nd edn, revised by P. H. Nidditch, Oxford: Clarendon Press, 1975.

Inhelder, B., and J. Piaget (1958), *The Growth of Logical Thinking from Childhood to Adolescence*, New York: Basic Books.

Izenberg, G. (2016), *Identity: The Necessity of a Modern Idea*, Philadelphia: University of Pennsylvania.

Jacob, P. (2019a), 'Intentionality', in E. N. Zalta (ed), *The Stanford Encyclopedia of Philosophy*. https://plato.stanford.edu/archives/win2019/entries/intentionality/.

Jacob, P. (2019b), 'Challenging the Two-Systems Model of Mindreading', in A. Avramides, and M. Parrott (eds), *Knowing Other Minds*, 79–106, Oxford: Oxford University Press.

James, W. (1884), 'What Is an Emotion?', *Mind*, 9: 188–205.
James, W. (1894), 'Discussion: The Physical Basis of Emotion', *Psychological Review*, 1 (5): 516–29.
James, W. (1981), *The Principles of Psychology*, 3 vols, Cambridge: Harvard University Press (orig. ed. 1890).
James, W. (1992–2004), *The Correspondence of William James*, edited by I. K. Skrupskelis, and E. M. Berkeley, 12 vols, Charlottesville: University Press of Virginia.
Jervis, G. (1989), *La psicoanalisi come esercizio critico*, Milano: Garzanti.
Jervis, G. (1993), *Fondamenti di psicologia dinamica*, Milano: Feltrinelli.
Jervis, G. (2011), *Il mito dell'interiorità*, edited by G. Corbellini, and M. Marraffa, Torino: Bollati Boringhieri.
Jervis, G. (2019), *La conquista dell'identità*, edited by M. Marraffa, Reggio Emilia: Dot Company.
Jin, K. S., and R. Baillargeon (2017), 'Infants Possess an Abstract Expectation of Ingroup Support', *Proceedings of the National Academy of Sciences of the United States of America*, 114 (31): 8199–204.
Johansson, P., L. Hall, S. Sikström, B. Tärning, and A. Lind (2006), 'How Something Can Be Said about Telling More than We Can Know: On Choice Blindness and Introspection', *Consciousness and Cognition*, 15 (4): 673–92; discussion 693.
Jordan, J. J., K. McAuliffe, and F. Warneken (2014), 'Development of in-Group Favouritism in Children's Third-Party Punishment of Selfishness', *Proceedings of the National Academy of Sciences of the United States of America*, 111 (35): 12710–15.
Jung, C. G. (1976), 'Psychological Types', in *Collected Works of C.G. Jung, Vol. 6*, Princeton: Princeton University Press (orig. ed. 1921).
Kampis, D., E. Parise, G. Csibra, and Á. M. Kovács (2015), 'Neural Signature for Sustaining Objects Representations Attributed to Others in Preverbal Human Infants', *Proceedings Biological Sciences*, 282 (1819): 20151683.
Kampis, D., D. Fogd, and Á. M. Kovács (2017), 'Nonverbal Components of Theory of Mind in Typical and Atypical Development', *Infant Behavior and Development*, 48 (A): 54–62.
Kampis, D., and V. Southgate (2020), 'Altercentric Cognition. How Others Influence Our Cognitive Processing', *Trends in Cognitive Sciences*, 24 (11): 945–59.
Kanngiesser, P., F. Rossano, R. Frickel, A. Tomm, and M. Tomasello (2019), 'Children, but not Great Apes, Respect Ownership', *Developmental Science*, 23: e12842.
Kant, I. (1998), *Critique of Pure Reason*, Cambridge: Cambridge University Press (orig. ed. 1781–87).
Kaplan, D. M., and W. Bechtel (2011), 'Dynamical Models: An Alternative or Complement to Mechanistic Explanations?', *Topics in Cognitive Science*, 3 (2): 438–44.
Kaplan, D. M., and C. F. Craver (2011), 'The Explanatory Force of Dynamical and Mathematical Models in Neuroscience: A Mechanistic Perspective', *Philosophy of Science*, 78 (4): 601–27.
Karmiloff-Smith, A. (1992), *Beyond Modularity*, Cambridge: MIT Press.

Keenan, J. P., G. G. Gallup, and D. Falk (2003), *The Face in the Mirror: The Search for the Origins of Consciousness*, London: HarperCollins.

Kenny, A. (1963), *Action, Emotion and Will*, New York: Humanities Press.

Kernberg, O., M. A. Selzer, H. W. Koenigsberg, A. C. Carr, and A. H. Appelbaum (1989), *Psychodynamic Psychotherapy of Borderline Patients*, New York: Basic Books.

Kinzler, K. D., E. Dupoux, and E. S. Spelke (2007), 'The Native Language of Social Cognition', *Proceedings of the National Academy of Sciences of the United States of America*, 104 (30): 12577–80.

Köber, C., and T. Habermas (2017a), 'Development of Temporal Macrostructure in Life Narratives across the Lifespan', *Discourse Processes*, 54 (2): 143–62.

Köber, C., and T. Habermas (2017b), 'How Stable Is the Personal Past? Stability of Most Important Autobiographical Memories and Life Narratives across Eight Years in a Life Span Sample', *Journal of Personality and Social Psychology*, 113 (4): 608–26.

Köber, C., F. Schmiedek, and T. Habermas (2015), 'Characterizing Lifespan Development of Three Aspects of Coherence in Life Narratives: A Cohort-Sequential Study', *Developmental Psychology*, 51 (2): 260–75.

Kohut, H. (1977), *The Restoration of the Self*, New York: International Universities Press.

Køppe, S., S. Harder, and M. S. Væver (2008), 'Vitality Affects', *International Forum of Psychoanalysis*, 17 (3): 169–79.

Korsgaard, C. M. (1989), 'Personal Identity and the Unity of Agency: A Kantian Response to Parfit', *Philosophy and Public Affairs*, 18 (2): 101–32.

Kouider, S., C. Stahlhut, S. V. Gelskov, L. S. Barbosa, M. Dutat, V. de Gardelle, A. Christophe, S. Dehaene, and G. Dehaene-Lambertz (2013), 'A Neural Marker of Perceptual Consciousness in Infants', *Science*, 340 (6130): 376–80.

Kovács, Á. M., E. Téglás, and A. D. Endress (2010), 'The Social Sense: Susceptibility to Others' Beliefs in Human Infants and Adults', *Science*, 330 (6012): 1830–34.

Kristen-Antonow, S., B. Sodian, H. Perst, and M. Licata (2015), 'A Longitudinal Study of the Emerging Self from 9 Months to the Age of 4 Years', *Frontiers in Psychology*, 6: 789. https://doi.org/10.3389/fpsyg.2015.00789.

Lackner, J. R. (1973), 'Resolving Ambiguity: Effect of Biasing Context in the Unattended Ear', *Cognition*, 1: 359–72.

Lagattuta, K. H. (2014), 'Linking past, Present, and Future: Children's Ability to Connect Mental States and Emotions across Time', *Child Development Perspectives*, 8 (2): 90–5.

Lagattuta, K. H., and H. M. Wellman (2001), 'Thinking about the past: Early Knowledge about Links between Prior Experience, Thinking, and Emotion', *Child Development*, 72 (1): 82–102.

Lagattuta, K. H., and H. M. Wellman (2002), 'Differences in Early Parent-Child Conversations about Negative versus Positive Emotions: Implications for the Development of Psychological Understanding', *Developmental Psychology*, 38 (4): 564–80.

Laing, R. D. (1960), *The Divided Self*, London: Tavistock.

Lang, S. (2022), 'A Methodological Objection to a Phenomenological Justification of the Ubiquity of Inner Awareness', *ProtoSociology*, 38: 59–73.
Langland-Hassan, P., and A. Vicente, eds. (2018), *Inner Speech: New Voices*, Oxford: Oxford University Press.
Lazarus, R. (1991), *Emotion and Adaptation*, Oxford: Oxford University Press.
Leary, M. R., and J. P. Tangney (2012), *Handbook of Self and Identity*, 2nd edn, New York: Guilford.
Lecaldano, E. (2021), *Identità personale. Storia e critica di un'idea*, Roma: Carocci.
LeDoux, J. E. (1996), *The Emotional Brain*, New York: Simon and Schuster.
LeDoux, J. E. (2014), 'Coming to Terms with Fear', *Proceedings of the National Academy of Sciences of the United States of America*, 111 (8): 2871–8.
LeDoux, J. E. (2015a), 'Afterword: The Psychological Construction in the Brain', in Barrett, and Russell (eds), 459–63.
LeDoux, J. E. (2015b), *Anxious*, New York: Viking.
LeDoux, J. E. (2017), 'Semantics, Surplus Meaning, and the Science of Fear', *Trends in Cognitive Sciences*, 21 (5): 303–6.
Leslie, A. M. (1987), 'Pretense and Representation: The Origins of "Theory of Mind"', *Psychological Review*, 94 (4): 412–26.
Leslie, A. M., O. Friedman, and T. P. German (2004), 'Core Mechanisms in "Theory of Mind"', *Trends in Cognitive Sciences*, 8 (12): 528–33.
Letheby, C. (2021), *Philosophy of Psychedelics*, Oxford: Oxford University Press.
Letheby, C., and P. Gerrans (2017), 'Self Unbound: Ego Dissolution in Psychedelic Experience', *Neuroscience of Consciousness*, 2017 (1): nix016. https://doi.org/10.1093/nc/nix016.
Lewis, M. (1986), 'Origins of Self-Knowledge and Individual Differences in Early Self-Recognition', in A. G. Greenwald, and J. Suls (eds), *Psychological Perspectives on the Self*, 55–78, Hillsdale: Erlbaum.
Lewis, M. (2014), *The Rise of Consciousness and the Development of Emotional Life*, New York and London: Guilford Press.
Lewis, M., and J. Brooks-Gunn (1979), *Social Cognition and the Acquisition of the Self*, New York: Plenum Press.
Lichtenberg, J. D. (1989), *Psychoanalysis and Motivation*, Hillsdale: Analytic Press.
Lichtenstein, H. (1977), *The Dilemma of Human Identity*, New York: Jason Aronson.
Lidstone, S. M., E. Meins, and C. Fernyhough (2010), 'The Roles of Private Speech and Inner Speech in Planning in Middle Childhood: Evidence from a Dual Task Paradigm', *Journal of Experimental Child Psychology*, 107: 438–51.
Liljenfors, R., and L. G. Lundh (2015), 'Mentalization and Intersubjectivity: Towards a Theoretical Integration', *Psychoanalytic Psychology*, 32 (1): 36–60.
Lind, S. E., D. M. Williams, C. Grainger, and J. Landsiedel (2018), 'The Self in Autism and Its Relation to Memory', in J. L. Johnson, G. S. Goodman, and P. C. Mundy (eds), *The Wiley Handbook of Memory, Autism Spectrum Disorder, and the Law*, 70–91, New York: Wiley.

Liotti, G. (1992), 'Disorganized/Disoriented Attachment in the Etiology of the Dissociative Disorders', *Dissociation*, 4: 196–204.

Locke, J. (1975), 'An Essay Concerning Human Understanding', in P. H. Nidditch (ed), *The Clarendon Edition of the Works of John Locke*, Oxford: Oxford University Press (orig. ed. 1689/1694).

Loria, E. (2020), *Learning Through Others: Natural Pedagogy and Mindreading: A Possible Cooperation*, Turin: Accademia University Press.

Low, J., I. A. Apperly, S. A. Butterfill, and H. Rakoczy (2016), 'Cognitive Architecture of Belief Reasoning in Children and Adults: A Primer on the Two-Systems Account', *Child Development Perspectives*, 10 (3): 184–9.

Luo, Y., and R. Baillargeon (2007), 'Do 12.5-Month-Old Infants Consider What Objects Others Can See When Interpreting Their Actions?', *Cognition*, 105 (3): 489–512.

Luria, A. R. (1976), *Cognitive Development: Its Cultural and Social Foundations*, Cambridge: Harvard University Press.

Lycan, W. (2019), 'Representational Theories of Consciousness', in E. N. Zalta (ed), *The Stanford Encyclopedia of Philosophy Edition*. https://plato.stanford.edu/archives/fall2019/entries/consciousness-representational/.

Lyyra, P. (2009), 'Two Senses for "Givenness of Consciousness"', *Phenomenology and the Cognitive Sciences*, 8 (1): 67–87.

Macintyre, A. (1984), *After Virtue*, Notre Dame: University of Notre Dame Press.

Maddy, P. (2001), 'Naturalism: Friends and Foes', in J. Tomberlin (ed), *Philosophical Perspectives, Vol. 15, Metaphysics*, 37–67, Oxford: Blackwell.

Marcia, J. E. (1966), 'Development and Validation of Ego-Identity Status', *Journal of Personality and Social Psychology*, 3 (5): 551–8.

Marraffa, M., and A. Paternoster (2012), 'Functions, Levels, and Mechanisms: Explanation in Cognitive Science and Its Problems', *Theory and Psychology*, 23 (1): 22–45.

Marraffa, M., and A. Paternoster (2016), 'Disentangling the Self. An Outline of a General Theory of Self-Consciousness', *New Ideas in Psychology*, 40: 115–22.

Martin, M. G. F. (2002), 'The Transparency of Experience', *Mind and Language*, 17 (4): 376–425.

Martin, R., and J. Barresi (2006), *The Rise and Fall of Soul and Self: An Intellectual History of Personal Identity*, New York: Columbia University Press.

Mashour, G. A., P. R. Roelfsema, J. P. Changeux, and S. Dehaene (2020), 'Conscious Processing and the Global Neuronal Workspace Hypothesis', *Neuron*, 105 (5): 776–98.

Mastropieri, D., and G. Turkewitz (1999), 'Prenatal Experience and Neonatal Responsiveness to Vocal Expressions of Emotion', *Developmental Psychobiology*, 35 (3): 204–14.

McAdams, D. P. (1985), *Power, Intimacy, and the Life Story: Personological Inquiries into Identity*, Homewood: Dorsey Press.

McAdams, D. P. (1996), 'Personality, Modernity, and the Storied Self: A Contemporary Framework for Studying Persons', *Psychological Inquiry*, 7 (4): 295–321.

McAdams, D. P. (1997), 'The Case for Unity in the (Post)Modern Self: A Modest Proposal', in R. D. Ashmore, and L. Jussim (eds), *Self and Identity: Fundamental Issues*, 46–78, Oxford: Oxford University Press.

McAdams, D. P. (2015), *The Art and Science of Personality Development*, New York and London: Guilford Press.

McAdams, D. P., and K. S. Cox (2010), 'Self and Identity across the Life Span', in R. M. Lerner (ed), *The Handbook of Life-Span Development, Vol. II*, 158–207, New York: Wiley.

McAdams, D. P., and B. D. Olson (2010), 'Personality Development: Continuity and Change over the Life Course', *Annual Review of Psychology*, 61: 517–42.

McLean, K. C., and M. Syed (2015), 'The Field of Identity Development Needs an Identity', in K. C. McLean, and M. Syed (eds), *The Oxford Handbook of Identity Development*, 1–10, Oxford: Oxford University Press.

McGranahan, L. (2017), *Darwinism and Pragmatism: William James on Evolution and Self-Transformation*, London: Routledge.

Mead, G. H. (1934), *Mind, Self, and Society*, Chicago: University of Chicago Press.

Mehler, J., and T. G. Bever (1967), 'Cognitive Capacity of Very Young Children', *Science*, 158 (3797): 141–2.

Meins, E. (2011), 'Social Relationships and Children's Understanding of Mind: Attachment, Internal States, and Mind-Mindedness', in M. Siegal, and L. Surian (eds), *Access to Language and Cognitive Development*, 23–43, Oxford: Oxford University Press.

Meins, E., C. Fernyhough, R. Wainwright, M. Das Gupta, E. Fradley, and M. Tuckey (2002), 'Maternal Mind-Mindedness and Attachment Security as Predictors of Theory of Mind Understanding', *Child Development*, 73 (6): 1715–26.

Meltzoff, A. N. (2013), 'Origins of Social Cognition', in M. R. Banaji, and S. A. Gelman (eds), *Navigating the Social World*, 139–44, Oxford: Oxford University Press.

Meltzoff, A. N., and A. Gopnik (1989), 'On Linking Nonverbal Imitation, Representation, and Language Learning in the First Two Years of Life', in G. E. Speidel, and K. E. Nelson (eds), *The Many Faces of Imitation in Language Learning*, 23–51, New York: Springer.

Meristo, M., K. Strid, and L. Surian (2016), 'Preverbal Infants' Ability to Encode the Outcome of Distributive Actions', *Infancy*, 21 (3): 353–72.

Merleau-Ponty, M. (1945), *Phénoménologie de la Perception*, Paris: Gallimard; Engl. transl. *Phenomenology of Perception*, London: Routledge, 2012.

Metzinger, T. (2003), *Being No One: The Self-Model Theory of Subjectivity*, Cambridge: MIT Press.

Michaelian, K. (2016), *Mental Time Travel*, Cambridge: MIT Press.

Millikan, R. G. (1984), *Language, Thought & Other Biological Categories*, Cambridge: MIT Press.

Millikan, R. G. (1989), 'Biosemantics', *Journal of Philosophy*, 86 (6): 281–97.

Mitchell, R. W. (1993), 'Mental Models of Mirror-Self-Recognition: Two Theories', *New Ideas in Psychology*, 11 (3): 295–325.

Mitchell, S. A. (1988), *Relational Concepts in Psychoanalysis*, Cambridge: Harvard University Press.

Moors, A., P. C. Ellsworth, K. R. Scherer, and N. H. Frijda (2013), 'Appraisal Theories of Emotion: State of the Art and Future Development', *Emotion Review*, 5 (2): 119–24.

Murray, L., and C. Trevarthen (1985), 'Emotional Regulation of Interactions between Two-Month-Olds and Their Mothers', in T. Field, and N. Fox (eds), *Social Perception in Infants*, 137–54, Norwood: Ablex.

Musholt, K. (2015), *Thinking about Oneself: From Nonconceptual Content to the Concept of a Self*, Cambridge: MIT Press.

Neisser, U. (1976), *Cognition and Reality*, San Francisco: Freeman.

Neisser, U. (1988), 'Five Kinds of Self-Knowledge', *Philosophical Psychology*, 1 (1): 35–59.

Neisser, U., ed. (1993), *The Perceived Self: Ecological and Interpersonal Sources of Self-Knowledge*, Cambridge: Cambridge University Press.

Neisser, U. (1995), 'Criteria for an Ecological Self', in P. Rochat (ed), *The Self in Infancy*, 17–34, Amsterdam: Elsevier.

Nelson, K. (1989), *Narratives from the Crib*, Cambridge: Harvard University Press.

Nelson, K., and R. Fivush (2020), 'The Development of Autobiographical Memory, Autobiographical Narratives, and Autobiographical Consciousness', *Psychological Reports*, 123 (1): 71–96.

Newen, A. (2018), 'The Embodied Self, the Pattern Theory of Self, and the Predictive Mind', *Frontiers in Psychology*, 9: 2270. https://doi.org/10.3389/fpsyg.2018.02270.

Nichols, S., and M. Bruno (2010), 'Intuitions about Personal Identity: An Empirical Study', *Philosophical Psychology*, 23 (3): 293–312.

Nichols, S., and S. P. Stich (2003), *Mindreading*, Oxford: Oxford University Press.

Nicholson, T., D. M. Williams, S. E. Lind, C. Grainger, and P. Carruthers (2021), 'Linking Metacognition and Mindreading: Evidence from Autism and Dual-Task Investigations', *Journal of Experimental Psychology. General*, 150 (2): 206–20.

Nielsen, M. K., and C. Dissanayake (2004), 'Pretend Play, Mirror Self-Recognition and Imitation: A Longitudinal Investigation through the Second Year', *Infant Behavior and Development*, 27 (3): 342–65.

Nielsen, M. K., T. Suddendorf, and V. Slaughter (2006), 'Mirror Self-Recognition beyond the Face', *Child Development*, 77 (1): 176–85.

Nielsen, M. K., L. Slade, J. P. Levy, and A. Holmes (2015), 'Inclined to See It Your Way: Do Altercentric Intrusion Effects in Visual Perspective Taking Reflect an Intrinsically Social Process?', *Quarterly Journal of Experimental Psychology*, 68 (10): 1931–51.

Nisbett, R. E., and N. Bellows (1977), 'Verbal Reports about Causal Influences on Social Judgments: Private Access versus Public Theories', *Journal of Personality and Social Psychology*, 35 (9): 613–24.

Nisbett, R. E., and L. E. Ross (1980), *Human Inference: Strategies and Shortcomings of Social Judgment*, Englewood Cliffs: Prentice Hall.

Nisbett, R. E., and T. D. Wilson (1977), 'Telling More than We Can Know: Verbal Reports on Mental Processes', *Psychological Review*, 84 (3): 231–59.

Norman, D. A., and T. Shallice (1986), 'Attention to Action: Willed and Automatic Control of Behavior', in R. J. Davidson, G. E. Schwartz, and D. Shapiro (eds), *Consciousness and Self-Regulation*, 1–18, New York: Plenum Press.

Nour, M. M., L. Evans, D. Nutt, and R. L. Carhart-Harris (2016), 'Ego-Dissolution and Psychedelics: Validation of the Ego-Dissolution Inventory (EDI) (2016)', *Frontiers in Human Neuroscience*, 10: 269. https://doi.org/10.3389/fnhum.2016.00269.

Norton, D. (1976), *Personal Destinies. A Philosophy of Ethical Individualism*, Princeton: Princeton University Press.

Nussbaum, M. (2001), *Upheavals of Thought: The Intelligence of Emotions*, Cambridge: Cambridge University Press.

Oesterdiekhoff, G. W. (2013), 'The Role of Piagetian Cross-Cultural Psychology to Humanities and Social Sciences', *American Journal of Psychology*, 126 (4): 477–92.

Ohman, A. (1986), 'Face the Beast and Fear the Face: Animal and Social Fears as Prototypes for Evolutionary Analyses of Emotion', *Psychophysiology*, 23 (2): 123–45.

Ohman, A., and J. J. F. Soares (1994), 'Unconscious Anxiety: Phobic Responses to Masked Stimuli', *Journal of Abnormal Psychology*, 102: 121–32.

Onishi, K., and R. Baillargeon (2005), '15-Month-Old Infants Detect Violations in Pretend Scenarios', *Science*, 308: 255–8.

Onishi, K., R. Baillargeon, and A. M. Leslie (2007), '15-Month-Old Infants Detect Violations in Pretend Scenarios', *Acta Psychologica*, 124 (1): 106–28.

Oyama, S. (2000), *The Ontogeny of Information*, Durham: Duke University Press (orig. ed. 1985).

Perner, J. (1991), *Understanding the Representational Mind*, Cambridge: MIT Press.

Perner, J. (2010), 'Who Took the Cog out of Cognitive Science? Mentalism in an Era of Anti-Cognitivism', in P. A. Frensch, and R. Schwarzer (eds), *Cognition and Neuropsychology: International Perspectives on Psychological Science, Vol. 1*, 241–61, Hove: Psychology Press.

Perner, J., and T. Ruffman (2005), 'Psychology. Infants' Insight into the Mind: How Deep?', *Science*, 308 (5719): 214–16.

Perovic, S., and L. Radenovic (2011), 'Fine-Tuning Nativism: The "Nurtured Nature" and Innate Cognitive Structures', *Phenomenology and the Cognitive Sciences*, 10 (3): 399–417.

Peterfreund, E. (1978), 'Some Critical Comments on Psychoanalytic Conceptualizations of Infancy', *The International Journal of Psychoanalysis*, 59: 427–41.

Peterson, C. C., and M. Siegal (2000), 'Insights into Theory of Mind from Deafness and Autism', *Mind and Language*, 15 (1): 123–45.

Peterson, C. C., J. L. Peterson, and J. Webb (2000), 'Factors Influencing the Development of a Theory of Mind in Blind Children', *British Journal of Developmental Psychology*, 18 (3): 431–47.

Piaget, J. (1952), *The Child's Conception of Number*, London: Routledge & Kegan Paul (orig. ed. 1941).

Piaget, J. (1959), *Language and Thought of the Child*, 3rd edn, London: Routledge & Kegan Paul (orig. ed. 1923).

Piaget, J. (1968a), 'Quantification, Conservation, and Nativism. Quantitative Evaluations of Children Aged Two to Three Years Are Examined', *Science*, 162 (3857): 976–81.

Piaget, J. (1968b), *The Moral Judgment of the Child*, London: Routledge & Kegan Paul (orig. ed. 1932).

Piaget, J. (1970), *Structuralism*, New York: Basic Books (orig. ed. 1968).

Piaget, J. (1974), 'Need and Significance of Cross-Cultural Studies in Genetic Psychology', in P. Dasen, and J. Berry (eds), *Culture and Cognition*, 299–310, London: Methuen.

Piaget, J. (1985), *The Equilibration of Cognitive Structures*, Chicago: University of Chicago Press (orig. ed. 1975).

Piaget, J. (1997), *Child's Conception of the World*, London: Routledge (orig. ed. 1929).

Piattelli-Palmarini, M. (1980), *Language and Learning: The Debate between Jean Piaget and Noam Chomsky*, Cambridge: Harvard University Press.

Piattelli-Palmarini, M. (2019), 'Reflections on Piaget. Chomsky, Fodor, Epigenetics and the Baldwin Effect', *Paradigmi*, 37 (1): 23–52.

Postle, B. R. (2006), 'Working Memory as an Emergent Property of the Mind and Brain', *Neuroscience*, 139 (1): 23–38.

Povinelli, D. J. (1995), 'The Unduplicated Self', in P. Rochat (ed), *The Self in Infancy: Theory and Research*, 161–92, Amsterdam: Elsevier.

Povinelli, D. J. (2001), 'The Self: Elevated in Consciousness and Extended in Time', in C. Moore, and K. Lemmon (eds), *The Self in Time: Developmental Perspectives*, 75–95, Mahwah: Erlbaum.

Povinelli, D. J., K. R. Landau, and H. K. Perilloux (1996), 'Self-Recognition in Young Children Using Delayed versus Live Feedback: Evidence of a Developmental Asynchrony', *Child Development*, 67 (4): 1540–54.

Povinelli, D. J., and B. B. Simon (1998), 'Young Children's Understanding of Briefly versus Extremely Delayed Images of the Self: Emergence of the Autobiographical Stance', *Developmental Psychology*, 34 (1): 188–94.

Powell, L. J., and E. S. Spelke (2013), 'Preverbal Infants Expect Members of Social Groups to Act Alike', *Proceedings of the National Academy of Sciences of the United States of America*, 110 (41): E3965–72.

Prebble, S. C., D. R. Addis, and L. J. Tippett (2013), 'Autobiographical Memory and Sense of Self', *Psychological Bulletin*, 139 (4): 815–40.

Premack, D. (2007), 'Foundations of Morality in the Infant', in O. Vilarroya, and F. Forn i Argimon (eds), *Social Brain Matters: Stances on the Neurobiology of Social Cognition*, 161–7, Amsterdams: Rodopi.

Premack, D., and G. Woodruff (1978), 'Does the Chimpanzee Have a "Theory of Mind"?', *Behavioral and Brain Sciences*, 4 (1): 515–26.

Prinz, J. (2002), *Furnishing the Mind: Concepts and Their Conceptual Basis*, Cambridge: MIT Press.

Rakoczy, H. (2022), 'Foundations of Theory of Mind and its Development in Early Childhood', *Nature Reviews Psychology*, 1 (4): 223–35.

Prinz, J. (2004), *Gut Reactions: A Perceptual Theory of Emotion*, Oxford: Oxford University Press.

Prinz, J., and S. Nichols (2016), 'Diachronic Identity and the Moral Self', in J. Kiverstein (ed), *The Routledge Handbook of Philosophy of the Social Mind*, 449–64, London: Routledge.

Quine, W. V. O. (1960), *Word and Object*, Cambridge: MIT Press.

Reisenzein, R., and P. Schmidt (2022), 'Emotional Feelings: Evaluative Perceptions or Position-Takings? Introduction to the Special Section', *Emotion Review*, 14 (4): 233–43.

Ricœur, P. (1965), *De l'Interprétation. Essai sur Freud*, Paris: Le Seuil.

Richerson, P. J., and R. Boyd(2005),*Not by Genes Alone: How culture Transformed Human Evolution*,Chicago:University of Chicago Press.

Ricœur, P. (1969), *La question du sujet: le défi de la sémiologie. In Id., Le conflit des interprétations*, Paris: Le Seuil.

Robbins, E., and P. Rochat (2011), 'Emerging Signs of Strong Reciprocity in Human Ontogeny', *Frontiers in Psychology*, 2: 353. https://doi.org/10.3389/fpsyg.2011.00353.

Rochat, M. J., V. Veroni, N. Bruschweiler-Stern, C. Pieraccini, F. Bonnet-Brilhault, C. Barthélémy, J. Malvy, C. Sinigaglia, D. N. Stern, and G. Rizzolatti (2013), 'Impaired Vitality Form Recognition in Autism', *Neuropsychologia*, 51 (10): 1918–24.

Rochat, P. (2010a), 'Emerging Self-Concept', in J. G. Bremner, and T. D. Wachs (eds), *Blackwell Handbook of Infant Development*, 2nd edn, 320–44, London: Blackwell.

Rochat, P. (2010b), 'The Innate Sense of the Body Develops to Become a Public Affair by 2–3 Years', *Neuropsychologia*, 48 (3): 738–45.

Rochat, P. (2012), 'Primordial Sense of Embodied Self-Unity', in V. Slaughter, and C. E. Browner (eds), *Early Development of Body Representations*, 3–18, Cambridge: Cambridge University Press.

Rochat, P. (2015), 'Layers of Awareness in Development', *Developmental Review*, 38: 122–45.

Rochat, P., and S. J. Hespos (1997), 'Differential Rooting Response by Neonates: Evidence for an Early Sense of Self', *Early Development and Parenting*, 6 (3–4): 105–12.

Rochat, P., and R. Morgan (1995), 'Spatial Determinants in the Perception of Self-Produced Leg Movements by 3–5 Month Old Infants', *Developmental Psychology*, 31 (4): 626–36.

Rochat, P., and T. Striano (1999), 'Emerging Self-Exploration by 2-Month-Old Infants', *Developmental Science*, 2 (2): 206–18.

Rochat, P., and T. Striano (2002), 'Who Is in the Mirror: Self-Other Discrimination in Specular Images by 4- and 9-Month-Old Infants', *Child Development*, 73 (1): 35–46.

Rossano, F., H. Rakoczy, and M. Tomasello (2011), 'Young Children's Understanding of Violations of Property Rights', *Cognition*, 121 (2): 219–27.

Rossano, F., L. Fiedler, and M. Tomasello (2015), 'Preschoolers' Understanding of the Role of Communication and Cooperation in Establishing Property Rights', *Developmental Psychology*, 51 (2): 176–84.

Ruba, A. L., and B. M. Repacholi (2020), 'Do Preverbal Infants Understand Discrete Facial Expressions of Emotion?', *Emotion Review*, 12 (4): 235–50.

Rubio-Fernández, P., and B. Geurts (2013), 'How to Pass the False-Belief Task before Your Fourth Birthday', *Psychological Science*, 24 (1): 27–33.

Ruffman, T., and J. Perner (2005), 'Do Infants Really Understand False Belief? Response to Leslie', *Trends in Cognitive Sciences*, 9 (10): 462–3.

Rupert, R. D. (2018), 'Representation and Mental Representation', *Philosophical Explorations*, 21 (2): 204–25.

Russell, J. A. (2003), 'Core Affect and the Psychological Construction of Emotion', *Psychological Review*, 110 (1): 145–72.

Russell, J. A. (2015), 'My Psychological Constructionist Perspective, with a Focus on Conscious Affective Experience', in Barrett, and Russell (eds), 183–208.

Ryan, R. M. (1995), 'Psychological needs and the facilitation of integrative processes', *Journal of Personality*, 63: 397–427.

Ryle, G. (2009), *The Concept of Mind*, London: Routledge (orig. ed. 1949).

Samet, J., and D. Zaitchik (2017), 'Innateness and Contemporary Theories of Cognition', in E. N. Zalta (ed), *The Stanford Encyclopedia of Philosophy*. https://plato.stanford.edu/archives/fall2017/entries/innateness-cognition/.

Samson, D., I. A. Apperly, J. J. Braithwaite, B. J. Andrews, and S. E. Bodley Scott (2010), 'Seeing It Their Way: Evidence for Rapid and Involuntary Computation of What Other People See', *Journal of Experimental Psychology: Human Perception and Performance*, 36: 1255–66.

Savage, C. (1955), 'Variations in Ego Feeling Induced by D-Lysergic Acid Diethylamide (LSD-25)', *Psychoanalytic Review*, 42 (1): 1–16.

Scarantino, A. (2015), 'Basic Emotions, Psychological Construction, and the Problem of Variability', in Barrett, and Russell (eds), 334–76.

Scarantino, A. (2016), 'The Philosophy of Emotions and Its Impact on Affective Science', in L. F. Barrett, M. Lewis, and J. M. Haviland-Jones (eds), *Handbook of Emotions*, 4th edn, 3–48, New York: Guilford.

Scarantino, A., and P. E. Griffiths (2011), 'Don't Give Up on Basic Emotions', *Emotion Review*, 3 (4): 444–54.

Schechtman, M. (1996), *The Constitution of Selves*, Ithaca: Cornell University Press.

Schechtman, M. (2007), 'Stories, Lives, and Basic Survival: A Refinement and Defense of the Narrative View', *Royal Institute of Philosophy Supplement*, 60: 155–78.

Schechtman, M. (2010), 'Personhood and the Practical', *Theoretical Medicine and Bioethics*, 31 (4): 271–83.
Schechtman, M. (2014), *Staying Alive: Personal Identity, Practical Concerns, and the Unity of a Life*, Oxford: Oxford University Press.
Scherer, K. R. (2009), 'The Dynamic Architecture of Emotion: Evidence for the Component Process Model', *Cognition and Emotion*, 23 (7): 1307–51.
Schroer, R. (2013), 'Reductionism in Personal Identity and the Phenomenological Sense of Being a Temporally Extended Self', *American Philosophical Quarterly*, 50 (4): 339–56.
Schroer, J. W., and R. Schroer (2014), 'Getting the Story Right: A Reductionist Narrative Account of Personal Identity', *Philosophical Studies*, 171 (3): 445–69.
Schopenhauer, A. (2010), *The World as Will and Representation, Vol. I*, Cambridge: Cambridge University Press (orig. ed. 1819).
Schwitzgebel, E. (2019), 'Introspection', in E. N. Zalta (ed), *The Stanford Encyclopedia of Philosophy*. https://plato.stanford.edu/archives/win2019/entries/introspection/.
Scott, R. M., and R. Baillargeon (2009), 'Which Penguin Is This? Attributing False Beliefs about Identity at 18 Months', *Child Development*, 80 (4): 1172–96.
Scott, R. M., R. Baillargeon, H. J. Song, and A. M. Leslie (2010), 'Attributing False Beliefs about Non-Obvious Properties at 18 Months', *Cognitive Psychology*, 61 (4): 366–95.
Scribner, S., and M. Cole (1981), *The Psychology of Literacy*, Cambridge: Harvard University Press.
Searle, J. R. (2010), *Making the Social World*, Oxford: Oxford University Press.
Senju, A., V. Southgate, C. Snape, M. Leonard, and G. Csibra (2011), 'Do 18-Months-Olds Really Attribute Mental States to Others? A Critical Test', *Psychological Science*, 22 (7): 878–80.
Seigel, J. (2005), *The Idea of the Self. Thought and Experience in Western Europe Since the Seventeenth Century*, Cambridge: Cambridge University Press.
Serrano, J. M., J. Iglesias, and A. Loeches (1992), 'Visual Discrimination and Recognition of Facial Expressions of Anger, Fear, and Surprise in 4- to 6-Month-Old Infants', *Developmental Psychobiology*, 25 (6): 411–25.
Serrano, J. M., J. Iglesias, and A. Loeches (1995), 'Infants' Responses to Adult Static Facial Expressions', *Infant Behavior and Development*, 18 (4): 477–82.
Shallice, T. (1988), *From Neuropsychology to Mental Structure*, Cambridge: Cambridge University Press.
Shea, N. (2018), *Representation in Cognitive Science*, Oxford: Oxford University Press.
Shirokogoroff, S. M. (1935), *The Psychomental Complex of the Tungus*, London: Kegan Paul, Trench, Trubner & Co.
Shoemaker, D. (2021), 'Personal Identity and Ethics', in E. N. Zalta (ed), *The Stanford Encyclopedia of Philosophy*. https://plato.stanford.edu/archives/fall2021/entries/identity-ethics/.
Shontz, F. C. (1994), 'The Ecological Self in Historical Context', in U. Neisser (ed), *The Perceived Self: Ecological and Interpersonal Sources of Self Knowledge*, 89–101, Cambridge: Cambridge University Press.

Shook, J. R. (2001), *The Chicago School of Functionalism*, Bristol: Thoemmes Press.
Siegal, M., and K. Beattie (1991), 'Where to Look First for Children's Knowledge of False Beliefs', *Cognition*, 38 (1): 1–12.
Siposova, B., S. Grueneisen, K. Helming, M. Tomasello, and M. Carpenter (2020), 'Common Knowledge That Help Is Needed Increases Helping Behavior in Children', *Cognition*, 196: 104144.
Smith, C. A., and R. S. Lazarus (1990), 'Emotion and Adaptation', in L. A. Pervin (ed), *Handbook of Personality: Theory and Research*, 609–37, New York: Guilford Press.
Song, H. J., and R. Baillargeon (2008), 'Infants' Reasoning about Others' False Perceptions', *Developmental Psychology*, 44 (6): 1789–95.
Sorabji, R. (2006), *Self: Ancient and Modern Insights about Individuality, Life, and Death*, Chicago: University of Chicago Press.
Southgate, V. (2020), 'Are Infants Altercentric? The Other and the Self in Early Social Cognition', *Psychological Review*, 127 (4): 505–23.
Southgate, V., C. Chevallier, and G. Csibra (2009), 'Sensitivity to Communicative Relevance Tells Young Children What to Imitate', *Developmental Science*, 12 (6): 1013–19.
Southgate V., C. Chevallier, and G. Csibra (2010), 'Seventeen-Month-Olds Appeal to False Beliefs to Interpret Others' Referential Communication', *Developmental Science*, 13 (6): 907–12.
Southgate, V., M. H. Johnson, and G. Csibra (2008), 'Infants Attribute Goals Even to Biomechanically Impossible Actions', *Cognition*, 107 (3): 1059–69.
Southgate, V., A. Senju, and G. Csibra (2007), 'Action Anticipation through Attribution of False Belief by 2-Year-Olds', *Psychological Science*, 18 (7): 587–92.
Spelke, E. S. (2022), *What Babies Know*, New York: Oxford University Press.
Sperber, D. (2001), 'In Defense of Massive Modularity', in E. Dupoux (ed), *Language, Brain and Cognitive Development: Essays in Honor of Jacques Mehler*, 47–57, Cambridge: MIT Press.
Sperber, D., F. Clément, C. Heintz, O. Mascaro, H. Mercier, G. Origgi, and D. Wilson (2010), 'Epistemic Vigilance', *Mind and Language*, 25 (4): 359–93.
Sroufe, L. A. (1996), *Emotional Development: The Organization of Emotional Life in the Early Years*, Cambridge: Cambridge University Press.
Stavans, M., and R. Baillargeon (2019), 'Infants Expect Leaders to Right Wrongs', *Proceedings of the National Academy of Sciences of the United States of America*, 116 (33): 16292–301.
Sterelny, K., and B. Fraser (2017), 'Evolution and Moral Realism', *British Journal for the Philosophy of Science*, 68 (4): 981–1006.
Stern, D. N. (1985), *Interpersonal World of the Infant*, New York: Basic Books.
Stern, D. N. (2009), 'Pre-Reflexive Experience and Its Passage to Reflexive Experience: A Developmental View', *Journal of Consciousness Studies*, 16 (10–12): 307–31.
Stern, D. N. (2010), *Forms of Vitality*, Oxford: Oxford University Press.

Sternberg, R. J. (1988), *The Triarchic Mind: A New Theory of Human Intelligence*, London: Penguin.

Strawson, G. (2004), 'Against Narrativity', *Ratio*, 17 (4): 428–52.

Strawson, G. (2020), 'On the Use of the Notion of Narrative in Ethics and Psychology', in E. Nahmias, T. W. Polger, and W. Zhao (eds), *The Natural Method: Essays on Mind, Ethics, and Self in Honor of Owen Flanagan*, 119–155, Cambridge: MIT Press.

Strohminger, N., and S. Nichols (2014), 'The Essential Moral Self', *Cognition*, 131 (1): 159–71.

Suddendorf, T., and M. C. Corballis (2007), 'The Evolution of Foresight: What Is Mental Time Travel and Is It Unique to Humans?', *Behavioral and Brain Sciences*, 30 (3): 299–313; discussion 313.

Sullivan, H. S. (1953), *The Interpersonal Theory of Psychiatry*, New York: Norton.

Surian, L., S. Caldi, and D. Sperber (2007), 'Attribution of Beliefs to 13-Month-Old Infants', *Psychological Science*, 18 (7): 580–86.

Taylor, C. (1989), *Sources of the Self*, Cambridge: Harvard University Press.

Tajfel, H. (1981), *Human Groups and Social Categories*, Cambridge: Cambridge University Press.

Teasdale, J. D. (1999), 'Multi-Level Theories of Cognition-Emotion Relations', in T. Dalgleish, and M. J. Power (eds), *Handbook of Cognition and Emotion*, 665–81, Chichester: Wiley.

Thelen, E., and L. B. Smith (1994), *A Dynamic Systems Approach to the Development of Cognition and Action*, Cambridge: MIT Press.

Thiel, U. (2011), *The Early Modern Subject: Self-Consciousness and Personal Identity from Descartes to Hume*, Oxford: Oxford University Press.

Ting, F., M. Buyukozer Dawkins, M. Stavans, and R. Baillargeon (2020), 'Principles and Concepts in Early Moral Cognition', in J. Decety (ed), *The Social Brain: A Developmental Perspective*, 41–65, Cambridge: MIT Press.

Tippett, L. J., S. C. Prebble, and D. R. Addis (2018), 'The Persistence of the Self over Time in Mild Cognitive Impairment and Alzheimer's Disease', *Frontiers in Psychology*, 9: 94. https://doi.org/10.3389/fpsyg.2018.00094.

Tomasello, M. (2016), *A Natural History of Human Morality*, Cambridge: Harvard University Press.

Tomasello, M. (2019), *Becoming Humans*, Cambridge: Harvard University Press.

Tomkins, S. S. (2008), *Affect Imagery Consciousness: The Complete Edition*, 4 vols, New York: Springer.

Tolman, E. C. (1948), 'Cognitive Maps in Rats and Men', *Psychological Review*, 55 (4): 189–208.

Tooby, J., and L. Cosmides (2008), 'The Evolutionary Psychology of the Emotions and Their Relationship to Internal Regulatory Variables', in M. Lewis, J. M. Haviland-Jones, and L. Feldman Barrett (eds), *Handbook of Emotions*, 3rd edn, 114–37, New York: Guilford Press.

Tooby, J., and L. Cosmides (1990), 'The Past Explains the Present: Emotional Adaptations and the Structure of Ancestral Environments', *Ethology and Sociobiology*, 11 (4–5): 375–424.

Trevarthen, C. (1979), 'Communication and Cooperation in Early Infancy. A Description of Primary Intersubjectivity', in M. Bullowa (ed), *Before Speech: The Beginning of Human Communication*, 321–47, Cambridge: Cambridge University Press.

Trevarthen, C. (1993), 'The Self Born in Intersubjectivity: An Infant Communicating', in U. Neisser (ed), *The Perceived Self*, 121–73, Cambridge: Cambridge University Press.

Tronick, E., H. Als, L. Adamson, S. Wise, and T. B. Brazelton (1978), 'The Infant's Response to Entrapment between Contradictory Messages in Face-to-Face Interaction', *Journal of the American Academy of Child Psychiatry*, 17 (1): 1–13.

Tsang, C. D. (2012), 'Habituation in Infant Cognition', in N. M. Seel (ed), *Encyclopedia of the Sciences of Learning*, 1415–16, Boston: Springer.

Tulving, E. (1972), 'Episodic and Semantic Memory', in E. Tulving, and W. Donaldson (eds), *Organisation of Memory*, 381–402, New York: Academic Press.

Tulving, E. (1983), *Elements of Episodic Memory*, Oxford: Clarendon Press.

Tulving, E. (1985), 'Memory and Consciousness', *Canadian Psychology/Psychologie Canadienne*, 26 (1): 1–12.

Tulving, E. (2002), 'Episodic Memory: from Mind to Brain', *Annual Review of Psychology*, 53: 1–25.

Tulving, E. (2005), 'Episodic Memory and Autonoesis: Uniquely Human?', in H. S. Terrace, and J. Metcalfe (eds), *The Missing Link in Cognition: Origins of Self-Reflective Consciousness*, 3–56, Oxford: Oxford University Press.

Turiel, E. (2006), 'The Development of Morality', in W. Damon, R. M. Lerner, and N. Eisenberg (eds), *Handbook of Child Psychology, 6th edn, Vol. 3. Social, Emotional, and Personality Development*, 789–857, New York: Wiley.

Tye, M. (1995), *Ten Problems of Consciousness*, Cambridge: MIT Press.

Uexküll, J. von (2010), *A Foray into the Worlds of Animals and Humans with a Theory of Meaning*, Minneapolis and London: University of Minneapolis Press (orig. ed. 1934).

Vaish, A., M. Missana, and M. Tomasello (2011), 'Three-Year-Old Children Intervene in Third-Party Moral Transgressions', *British Journal of Developmental Psychology*, 29 (1): 124–30.

Valsiner, J., and R. van der Veer (2000), *The Social Mind: Construction of the Idea*, Cambridge: Cambridge University Press.

Vandekerckhove, M. M., and J. Panksepp (2009), 'The Flow of Anoetic to Noetic and Autonoetic Consciousness: A Vision of Unknowing (Anoetic) and Knowing (Noetic) Consciousness in the Remembrance of Things past and Imagined Futures', *Consciousness and Cognition*, 18 (4): 1018–28.

Van den Broeck, K. (2014), *Specificity and Vantage Perspective of Autobiographical Memories in Borderline Pathology*, PhD dissertation. University of Leuven.

Van Gelder, T. J. (1995), 'What Might Cognition Be, If Not Computation?', *Journal of Philosophy*, 92 (7): 345–81.

Varga, S., and C. Guignon (2020), 'Authenticity', in E. N. Zalta (ed), *The Stanford Encyclopedia of Philosophy*. https://plato.stanford.edu/archives/spr2020/entries/authenticity/.

Vasil, J., and M. Tomasello (2022), 'Effects of "We"-Framing on Young Children's Commitment, Sharing, and Helping', *Journal of Experimental Child Psychology*, 214: 105278.

Vygotsky, L. S. (1997a), 'The History of the Development of Higher Mental Functions', in R. W. Rieber (ed), *The Collected Works of L. S. Vygotsky, Vol. IV*, 1–252, New York: Plenum Press (orig. ed. 1930).

Vygotsky, L. S. (1997b), 'Consciousness as a Problem for the Psychology of Behavior', in R. W. Rieber, and J. Wollock (eds), *The Collected Works of L. S. Vygotsky, Vol. III*, 63–79, New York: Plenum Press (orig. ed. 1925).

Vygotsky, L. S. (2012), *Thought and Language*, Cambridge: MIT Press (orig. ed. 1934).

Walker-Andrews, A. S. (2008), 'Intermodal Emotional Processes in Infancy', in M. Lewis, J. M. Haviland-Jones, and L. F. Barrett (eds), *Handbook of Emotions*, 364–75, New York: Guilford Press.

Wallon, H. (1959), 'Le Rôle de l'Autre dans la Conscience du Moi', *Enfance*, 12 (3): 277–86.

Wang, Y., and A. M. E. Henderson (2018), 'Just Rewards: 17-Month-Old Infants Expect Agents to Take Resources According to the Principles of Distributive Justice', *Journal of Experimental Child Psychology*, 172: 25–40.

Warneken, F., F. Chen, and M. Tomasello (2006), 'Cooperative Activities in Young Children and Chimpanzees', *Child Development*, 77 (3): 640–63.

Weary, G., and R. Arkin (1981), 'Attributional Self-Presentation', in J. H. Harvey, W. Ickes, and R. F. Kidd (eds), *New Directions in Attribution Research, Vol. 3*, 223–46, Hillsdale: Erlbaum.

Wegner, D. M. (2017), *The Illusion of Conscious Will*, Cambridge: MIT Press.

Wellman, H. M., D. Cross, and J. Watson (2001), 'Meta-Analysis of Theory-of-Mind Development: The Truth about False Belief', *Child Development*, 72 (3): 655–84.

Wellman, H. M., and D. Liu (2004), 'Scaling of Theory-of-Mind Tasks', *Child Development*, 75 (2): 523–41.

Westra, E. (2017), 'Spontaneous Mindreading: A Problem for the Two-Systems Account', *Synthese*, 194 (11): 4559–81.

Westra, E., and P. Carruthers (2017), 'Pragmatic Development Explains the Theory-of-Mind Scale', *Cognition*, 158: 165–76.

Wheeler, M. A., D. T. Stuss, and E. Tulving (1997), 'Toward a Theory of Episodic Memory: The Frontal Lobes and Autonoetic Consciousness', *Psychological Bulletin*, 121 (3): 331–54.

Whiten, A., and R. W. Byrne (eds.) (1997), *Machiavellian Intelligence II: Extensions and Evaluations*, Cambridge: Cambridge University Press.

Williams, D. M. (2010), 'Theory of Own Mind in Autism: Evidence of a Specific Deficit in Self-Awareness?', *Autism: The International Journal of Research and Practice*, 14 (5): 474–94.

Williams, D. M., and F. Happé (2010), 'Representing Intentions in Self and Others: Studies of Autism and Typical Development', *Developmental Science*, 13 (2): 307–19.

Wilson, T. (2002), *Strangers to Ourselves*, Cambridge: Harvard University Press.

Wimmer, H., and J. Perner (1983), 'Beliefs about Beliefs: Representation and Constraining Function of Wrong Beliefs in Young Children's Understanding of Deception', *Cognition*, 13 (1): 103–28.

Winkielman, P. (2010), 'Bob Zajonc and the Unconscious Emotion', *Emotion Review*, 2 (4): 353–62.

Winnicott, D. W. (2005), *Playing and Reality*, 2nd edn, London: Routledge.

Winsler, A., and J. Naglieri (2003), 'Overt and Covert Verbal Problem-Solving Strategies: Developmental Trends in Use, Awareness, and Relations with Task Performance in Children Aged 5 to 17', *Child Development*, 74 (3): 659–78.

Woodward, A. L. (1998), 'Infants Selectively Encode the Goal Object of an Actor's Reach', *Cognition*, 69 (1): 1–34.

Yeung, E., D. Askitis, V. Manea, and V. Southgate (2022), 'Emerging Self-Representation Presents a Challenge When Perspectives Conflict', *Open Mind: Discoveries in Cognitive Science*, 6: 232–49.

Zajonc, R. B. (1980), 'Feeling and Thinking: Preferences Need no Inferences', *American Psychologist*, 35 (2): 151–75.

Zimbardo, P. G. (2007), *The Lucifer Effect: Understanding How Good People Turn Evil*, New York: Random House.

Index

Addis, Donna Rose   40–2, 152–4
affect mirroring   60–5, 84, 91, 177
affect programs   58, 68–70, 72–5, 80, 82–3, 186 n.6
affective self-awareness   51
affective self-regulation   64, 177
attachment   13, 18–19, 32, 63, 65, 74, 92–3, 177, 183 n.7
  Adult Attachment Interview (AAI)   21
  and autonomization   21
  and the contextualistic and systemic approach   20–5
  figure of   21, 29, 52, 84
  internal working models   21, 154
  and mindreading   92–3, 187
  as motivational system   19–20
  and object relations theory   74, 174
  primary love   20
  psychopathology of   65, 173, 175–7
  secure base   21
  strange situation paradigm   21
  styles of   21, 66, 92
  theory of   16, 18, 20, 22, 25, 60, 136, 169, 174–5
autobiographical
  arguments   169
  memory   40, 149–54, 158, 168, 177, 179
  narrative   158–60, 172
  reasoning   149, 162, 164, 168, 179

Bahrick, Lorraine   32–3
Baillargeon, Renée   98–100, 102–4, 110–11, 115, 136–40, 144, 188 n.11
Balint, Alice   20
Balint, Michael   20, 174–5
Barrett, Lisa Feldman   54, 79–81, 83, 186
basic fault   175, *see also* ontological insecurity

Bermúdez, José Luis   35, 38, 47, 49–50, 184
Bever, Thomas G.   183
Bluck, Susan   164, 190
Bodei, Remo   3
Bowlby, John   16, 20–1, 154, 183 n.6
Brentano, Franz   11–12, 40
Bruner, John   29, 161

Carruthers, Peter   81, 110–13, 116, 119–20, 123, 125–31, 135, 161, 186 n.11, 188 n.11, 189 n.10
Chomsky, Noam   13, 25–8, 104
coherence (in life narratives)   5, 154, 158, 165, 173, 177
  causal   155–6, 164–5, 168
  temporal   155–6, 164, 168
  thematic   164–5, 168
confabulation   120–1, 130, 135, 180
consciousness
  autonoetic *vs.* noetic   41, 149–53 (*see also* autobiographical, memory; Tulving, Endel)
  as a first-order representational state   11–12, 38, 127
  and intentionality   11, 17, 40, 182 n.13
  object/primary   9–11, 15, 38, 40, 47
  phenomenal   11–12, 39–41, 53–4, 88, 182 n.14, 192 n.18
  as a second-order representational state/metarepresentation   65, 84, 91
  transitive *vs.* intransitive   11, 47
constructivism
  epigenetic   26
  individual-based/Piagetian   13, 25–8, 164
  and naive psychology   103, 110
  psychological/emotional   60, 77, 85, 91

sociocultural   28
sociolinguistic   22
contingency detection module
    (CDM)   32–5, 45, 60, 62–6, 68, 75–6, 78, 83, 91, 185
    necessity and sufficiency indexes   34
    proprioceptive   33, 42
    spatial   33
    temporal   32–3
Conway, Martin   153–4, 192 n.18
core affect   52, 68, 77–81, 83, 85
    phenomenology of   52, 79
core cognition/knowledge   27–8
crisis
    of identity (Erikson)   160, 163, 170–1
    of presence (De Martino)   4

Damasio, Antonio   54, 59, 78, 86–7, 186 n.15, 187 nn.16–18
Darwin, Charles   10, 14–16, 22, 69–71, 183 n.3
De Martino, Ernesto   x, 4–6, 168, 174, 182 n.8
defence
    apologetic defensiveness   135
    and autobiographical reasoning   168
    as characteristic adaptation   159
    defensive dimensions of introspection (or self-consciousness, or narrative identity)   4, 7, 16, 135, 150, 168–9
    defensive survival circuits   80, 82
    in Freud   174–6
    and identity   x, 15, 172–4
    and the intrinsic fragility of the ego   174, 176
    maladaptive   170
    narcissistic   172, 176
    and ontological insecurity   174–6
    psychodynamics of   74
    self-defensive use of causal attributions   135, 172
    and self-image   135, 170–2
    system of defences   xi, 150, 174
    teleology of self-defence   174
delayed video self-recognition test   155, 157
demystifying hermeneutics (Ricoeur)   161–2
Dennett, Daniel   3, 17, 41, 96, 161, 180

ecological theory of perception (Gibson)   36
ego
    development (Loevinger)   159
    evanescence of (James)   8
    Freudian (*das Ich*)   174, 192 n.20
    pure   7
    solidity of   x–xi, 7, 136, 171, 174, 176
    (*see also* fragility of the self; I)
Ekman, Paul   69–71, 78
embodied appraisal theory (Prinz)   54, 59–60, 78
emotion(s)
    and background feelings   85–7, 186
    basic   68–74, 78, 80, 82–5, 91, 179, 186
    basic emotion theory (BET)   60, 69–74, 78, 82–4, 91 (*see also* affect programs)
    James-Lange hypothesis   85
    formal *vs.* particular object   54–6, 59
    phenomenology associated to   65, 77–8, 80, 83–4, 91
Erikson, Erik   9, 158, 160, 163, 170, 177, 192 n.19
eudaimonia   56, 169, 172–3
evolutionary systems, theory of   22, 28

false belief task
    explicit version   95
    implicit version   97
Fernyhough, Charles   132–4, 190 n.12
Ferrara, Alessandro   172–3
Fonagy, Peter   11, 60, 177
forms of vitality (vitality forms)   46, 70, 77, 81, *see also* vitality affects
Freud, Sigmund   ix–x, 16–20, 162, 174–6, 183 n.4, 192 n.20
functionalism
    functionalistic school of Chicago   16, 22, 185
    in James' Darwinian psychology   14

Gallagher, Shaun   38–9, 47, 49–50, 184 n.7, 191 n.10
Gergely, Gyorgy   11, 29, 34, 45–6, 60–9, 76, 83, 92–4, 112, 141, 158, 185 n.3, 188 n.1

Giddens, Anthony   158, 167–8, 175, 191 n.16
Global Neural Workspace (GNW)   124–7
Goffman, Erving   ix–x, 172, 180, 192 n.22

Habermas, Tillman   ix, 165, 168–9, 191 n.8, 192 n.18
Hobbes–Freud scheme   17–18, *see also* narcissism, primary
Howe, Michael   152–4
Hume, David   viii, 3, 8, 9, 41, 182 n.10

I, *see also* ego; self (James)
  as a causal centre of gravity   xi, 180
  as a confabulatory by-product (Dennett)   180
  as a fiction   7
  I think (Kant)   9
identity, personal, *see also* ego; I; self; self-consciousness/self-awareness
  and consciousness (in Locke)   8
  description of   8–9, 42, 136, 155, 174 (*see also* self-description)
  diachronic   3, 41, 152, 160, 168, 179 (*see also* self, self-concept; sense of, self, over time; temporally extended self-representation)
  diffusion of   170
  essential link with self-consciousness   9, 42
  interpersonal validation of   136
  as a matter of work and conquest   3–4, 12
  moral   145–7
  narrative   10, 149–50, 158–9, 162, 168–9, 172, 179, 191 nn.7, 11 (*see also* self, autobiographical)
  objective (for others)   1 (*see also* self, objective-structural sense)
  physical/bodily   42, 166, 179 (*see also* self, bodily; self-consciousness, bodily)
  precariousness of   x, 7, 168
  as a reflexive project   168
  social   8, 166
  solidity of   180

subjective (for ourselves)   10, 13, 17, 25, 29, 31, 136, 147, 158, 163, 168–9, 179–80, 191 n.16 (*see also* self, subjective-experiential sense)
imitation
  and altercentric bias   114
  in ecopraxia   181 n.5
  in protoconversation   62
  synchronic *vs.* deferred   46–7
individualism
  Chomskian internalism   28
  in James   14
  methodological   28–30
  in Piaget   25, 28
infant research   6, 13, 39, 76, 92, 169, 180
infant subjectivity   39
  adultism   39
  psychic equivalence   11
  subjective world (*Umwelt*)   10
innate sociomoral principles   137–40
inner speech   124, 128, 131–4, 190 n.11
intentionality   11, 17, 40, 182 n.13
  collective   143–5
  detector (ID) 87–8, 94
  of emotions   54–60
  individual   140–1
  joint   141–3
intermodal bodily schema   35–6, *see also* self, bodily; self-consciousness, pre-reflective
introspection
  data on confabulation   120–1, 130, 135
  emotional   60, 63, 66, 77, 83–5, 91 (*see also* social biofeedback)
  inner sense, theories of   119, 123
  interiority   2, 8, 136
  Interpretive Sensory Access (ISA) theory   123–31
  introspective reflexivity   52
  just-like-me hypothesis   61
  Locke's definition   vii, 52, 92
  self-other parity thesis   92, 119–21, 128

Jervis, Giovanni   8–9, 12, 15, 19, 161, 174
Jung, Carl G.   159–60, 172

Kant, Immanuel   4–6, 9, 12, 14–15, 39, 174, 179, 181–2 n.8
Kenny, Anthony   54–5
Köber, Christin   164–5, 168–9, 192 n.18
Kohut, Heinz   ix–x, 1, 176–7, 184 n.4

Laing, Ronald   174–5
LeDoux, Joseph   71, 80, 82, 186 n.7
Lichtenberg, Joseph   19
Locke, John   viii, x, 1–4, 7, 12, 15, 36, 52, 59, 92, 106, 136, 145, 160–1, 163, 181 n.3, 191 n.5
Lyyra, Pessi   11

McAdams, Dan   8, 149, 158–60, 164, 170, 172, 192 n.20
Mead, George Herbert   ix, 29, 183–4 n.14, 185 n.2
Meltzoff, Andrew   46, 61
memory
  altercentric bias   115–17
  associationist-behaviorist theory of   103–5, 110
  and attachment   92–3, 187 n.1
  autobiographical   40, 149–54, 168, 179, 190 n.1
  episodic   41, 126, 150–4, 189 n.5
  and language   113–14
  Mental Time Travel (MTT)   133, 142, 151–2
  mindreading/mentalization/naïve psychology
  Minimal Theory of Mind (MinToM)   105–10
  semantic personal   126, 150–2
  shared attention   95, 187 n.18
  system of (Baron-Cohen) 87–8; (Carruthers)   119, 127, 131, 161
  teleological reasoning   94–5
  working   110, 123, 125, 131, 134, 153
Mirror Self-Recognition (MSR) test   44–6, 48, 152–4
  rich vs. poor interpretations of the MSR test   44–6
motivation   13, 19–20, 69, 83, 130, 153, 159, 164–5
  vs. motive   121, 188 n.2
  motivational systems   21, 189 n.9
Musholt, Kristina   35, 48–9, 184 n.6

narcissism
  narcissistic object relationship   176
  narcissistic personality disorder   170, 175, 177
  primary   18, 20
naturalism
  bottom up   15
  Darwinian   14–16
  de-centring of the subject   26
  vs. Kantian transcendentalism   15
  Quinean   14
  sociological antinaturalism   22, 25
  systemic–relational   16, 31, 179
Neisser, Ulrich   16, 36–8, 43, 184 n.5
Nelson, Katherine   149–58
Nichols, Shaun   43, 145

Onishi, Kristine   98–100, 103, 115
ontological insecurity   173–6, see also basic fault
orthogenetic principle (Werner)   159

Paternoster, Alfredo   xi, 23, 39, 184 n.7, 191 n.9
person
  in Locke's definition   2, 8
  as primarily non unitary   4, 15, 159
personality
  characteristic adaptations   149–50, 159
  layers of   149, 159–60, 172
  maturation of the   171–2 (see also self-realization)
  personological approach to narrative identity   149, 158, 172
  traits of   158–60, 164, 172
Piaget, Jean   13, 21, 25–8, 131–2, 137, 145, 153, 163–4, 166, 183 n.10, 191 n.11
  organizational tendencies   159
Piattelli Palmarini, Massimo   27–8, 183 n.11
Povinelli, Daniel   155–7
Prebble, Sally   40–2, 152–4
proprioception   38, 49
protoconversation   34, 62–4, 66, 68, 76–7, 84

Quine, Willard V. O.   14

representational nativism 28, 103
Rochat, Philippe 33–5, 37, 39, 43, 136, 143, 146
Russell, James 54, 78–81, 186 n.14

Schopenhauer, Arthur 8, 12
self, *see also* I; self-consciousness; self-identity; self-knowledge; selfing
   autobiographical/narrative 10, 158, 162, 177, 191 nn.6, 10 (*see also* identity, narrative)
   bodily 36, 49, 50, 153, 157, 184 n.1 (*see also* self-consciousness, bodily)
   cohesion of (Kohut) x, 176
   minimal 135, 184
   in the objective-structural sense 35–6, 48 (*see also* identity, objective)
   presentation of the (Goffman) ix–x, 172, 180
   psychology of 9
   self-concept 41, 45, 47, 155–6, 158, 169, 171, 177–8, 192 n.18
   self-description 9–10, 136, 169, 174, 179
   self-objects (Kohut) 176–7
   self-perspective 116
   self-specifying information 31, 35–8, 50–1
   sense of 36, 39–42, 63, 115, 145–6, 151, 178, 184 n.7
      over time/self-continuity 153–5, 169, 192 n.18
   in the subjective-experiential sense 35–6, 48 (*see also* identity, subjective)
   temporally extended self-representation 155
self (James)
   and Darwinian naturalism 14–16
   duplex 9, 40
   empirical 8
   I x–xi, 5, 7–9, 40–2, 149, 158–9 (*see also* selfing process)
   material 8, 42, 153, 155, 166, 170
   Me 8, 40–2, 152
   social 8, 166, 170

spiritual 8, 92, 166, 170 (*see also* introspection; self-consciousness, psychological/introspective)
self (Neisser)
   conceptual 36
   ecological 35–8, 43, 184 n.5
   interpersonal 36–7
self-knowledge/knowledge of the self 9, 15, 36–7, 65, 84, 119–23, 131, 135
self-consciousness/self-awareness
   as awareness of the existence 9, 39
   bodily/physical 12, 31–2, 37, 42, 44, 47, 49–52, 84, 91, 152, 179, 184 n.1 (*see also* self, bodily; identity, physical
   defensive nature of 4, 7, 16, 135, 150, 168–9
   degrees of 165–7
   diachronic dimension of 3, 42, 152, 156, 160, 18, 179, 184 and n.8 (*see also* identity, diachronic; self, sense of, over time; self, temporally extended self-representation)
   essential link with identity 9, 42
   and intentionality 11, 17, 40
   non-conceptual 38, 47–9, 184 n.6
   and object consciousness 9–11, 15, 40
   pre-reflective 31, 35, 38–42, 47–51, 152–3, 183 n.14, 184 n.7, 187 n.17 (*see also* ubiquity thesis)
   psychological/introspective 52, 64, 136, 149, 162, 167–9, 179 (*see also* identity, narrative; self-description; self, spiritual; identity, subjective; self, subjective-experiential sense)
   solidity of 136, 174 (*see also* identity, solidity of)
selfing process x, 7–9, 14–15, 87, 150, 159–60, 162, 172, 174, 179, 192 n.20
   and Freudian *das Ich* 174, 192 n.20
Self-Memory System (SMS) 153–4, 168
   autobiographical memory knowledge base 153–4, 168
   conceptual self 154

and Internal Working Models   154
working self   153–4, 184 n.4
self-realization   168, 170, 172, *see also* personality, maturation of the
  autonomy   19, 145, 168–71, 174
  individuation   159–60, 168–70, 172
social biofeedback
  and beliefs   89–90
  exteroception *vs.* interoception   62
  interiorization of basic emotions   60, 65–6, 83–5, 91
  as natural pedagogy   66–8, 89–90
  parental mirroring of basic emotions   60–1, 64, 91
  and simple desires   87–9
  vs. strong intersubjectivist position   61–2, 92
  theory/model of   60, 62, 67–8, 185 n.5
Spelke, Elizabeth   27, 139, 144
Stern, Daniel   62, 75–7, 85–7, 184 n.4, 186 n.15, 187 n.17
Sternberg, Robert   163

Still-face paradigm   35
Sullivan, Herbert Stack   ix, 1, 29

Tippett, Lynette   40–1, 153–5
Tomasello, Michael   136–7, 139–45, 188 n.6, 190 n.14
Trevarthen, Colwyn   35, 61
triarchic theory of intelligence (Sternberg)   163
Tulving, Endel   149–51, 192 n.18

ubiquity thesis   38–9, *see also* self-consciousness, pre-reflective
Unoka, Zsolt   60–2, 67–9, 92–3, 188 n.1, 185 n.3

vitality affects   76, 186
Vygotsky, Lev   25, 28–9, 131–4, 136, 166, 183–4 n.14, 189–90 n.10, 190 n.11

Watson, John   32–4, 60, 62–6, 122
Winnicott, Donald   20

Zahavi, Dan   38–9, 47, 49–50, 184 n.7

www.ingramcontent.com/pod-product-compliance
Lightning Source LLC
Chambersburg PA
CBHW071831300426
44116CB00009B/1505